Wilderness Survival Handbook

Wilderness Survival Handbook

Revised Edition

A Practical, All-Season Guide to Short Trip Preparation and Survival Techniques for Hikers, Skiers, Backpackers, Canoeists, Snowmobilers, Travellers in Light Aircraft —and Anyone Stranded in the Outdoors

Alan Fry

Macmillan Canada
Toronto

Canadian Cataloguing in Publication Data

Fry, Alan, 1931–
    Wilderness survival handbook

Rev. ed. of: Survival in the wilderness.
Includes index.
ISBN 0-7715-7340-5

1. Wilderness survival.   I. Title.
II. Title: Survival in the wilderness.

GV200.5.F79   1996   613.6'9   C96-931339-X

This book is available at special discounts for bulk purchases by your group or organization for sales promotions, premiums, fundraising and seminars. For details, contact: Macmillan Canada Special Sales Department, 29 Birch Avenue, Toronto, ON M4V 1E2. Tel: 416-963-8830.

1   2   3   4   5-00   99   98   97   96

CONTENTS

Acknowledgments

I have been assisted so much in writing this book that it is beyond me to acknowledge every helping hand, every source of some useful piece of information.

I do wish, however, to make specific acknowledgement to several particular sources of assistance.

My father, Julian Fry, chose to go bush-ranching in central British Columbia in the nineteen-twenties. He hardly had this book in mind, but without the opportunity to grow up in bush country, an advantage of my life which I rate over all but a very few others, it is not likely I would have written these pages.

Monty Alford of the Yukon Territory provided excellent criticism and nudges in the right direction on snow shelters and cold-weather clothing.

Wilf Taylor of the Yukon Territory checked out my deadfall and snare sketches and gave me advice on useful inclusions from his own collection, which is more extensive by far than my own. He also introduced to me a superior design of reflecting tent which I had not come on previously.

The staff of the Northern Outdoors clothing, backpacking, and ski equipment store in Whitehorse responded helpfully to a multitude of spur-of-the-moment questions on recent innovations in clothing and gear.

My dear friend Dr. William Mitchell-Banks reviewed my chapter on safety and first aid with useful comments for its improvement. George Howell, senior pilot with Trans North Turbo Air in Whitehorse, gave me valuable time and comments on the signalling chapter. Finally, a word of thanks to Jones Tent and Awning, manufacturers of outdoor clothing, tents, and sleeping bags under the Pioneer label in Vancouver, British Columbia. While I do not give unqualified endorsement to every item of gear produced by this firm, I have had good service from Pioneer-brand goods for the better part of fifty years so far, and I particularly appreciate several items supplied during the writing of this book.

Introduction

This book is written for everyone who, for recreation or in the course of employment, ventures into the woods of Canada and of the more northern of the United States.

Woodland travellers setting out for the day and expecting to be snug at home again by nightfall inevitably take the chance, whether consciously or not, that they might fail to be out of the woods before dark and, with no more than they wear and carry, might have to spend the night outdoors.

Depending on what such people do in fact wear and carry and on what use they contrive to make of material at hand in the woods, this mere fact of an unexpected night outdoors can have vastly differing results: at the one extreme, a pleasant and comfortable time with sound sleep and rest, at the other extreme, a miserable death.

People who go out for the day wish to go lightly and they *do* go lightly. The deer hunter, the forester out for a day's cruising, the young couple for an afternoon's stroll, the cross-country skier — these people are not going to carry a tent and a sleeping bag. The party taking off in the morning in a small aircraft from the local strip and expecting to land at a destination before day's end where food and shelter are available will not burden the aircraft with the line of gear that would go on board if a remote destination and a two-week campout were in mind.

It is these day travellers who are at risk because, in the absence of abundant gear should they unexpectedly have to camp out, they must turn to the material at hand around them, applying skills, ingenuity, and traditional woodlore to keep safe with which modern urban living has seldom equipped them. The predicament is often compounded by inadequate clothing and footwear.

I am not writing about what you do with abundant gear. There is a profusion of material already written on that subject. The market is saturated and the need is met. I am writing about what you do with no more gear than you'd have with you on an afternoon's walk in the woods. *That* is what there is neither sufficient nor accurate writing about and my hope in this book is to overcome the deficiency.

A day's excursion by small aircraft differs from a day's excursion on foot only in two respects: there is opportunity to have along rather more gear, and the time out if something goes amiss will probably be longer.

Let me give examples of some day trips by aircraft, on skis, and by vehicle which went wrong.

Two people went down in a small aircraft in the Yukon Territory, having taken off from Whitehorse in poor weather in early winter. They survived for over forty days and were then spotted and picked up. They had virtually no food on board. It is generally believed that they got through on body fat, both being overweight at the time of going down. *They were frustrated by the sight of varying hare all about their crude camp.* They did not know that in the electrical and control systems of an aircraft there is an abundance of suitable wire, nor how easily one can make snares with this wire to catch game, particularly varying hare.

A party of skiers set out from a warm chalet in the Rocky Mountains near Banff, Alberta. A slide that occurred during the day blocked their return route. They died during the night. They need not have died, but they did not know what to do to save themselves.

Three young men set off from a small prairie community in winter weather in a four-wheel-drive vehicle for a pleasure drive on a remote road. They were dressed in light town clothes and town shoes — the popular dress of the teenage and early-twenties set. Far from town a tire went flat and they couldn't change it. They ran the motor to keep heat in the cab until the fuel ran out. Then they tried to walk back to town. Two died and one survived, badly frostbitten. Adequate clothing and footgear would have made this no more than a forced walk — a small misadventure to laugh about the next day.

Now the backpacker is in a rather different category. Modern industry has produced a splendid range of extra-light but durable and superior gear for his or her use. The backpacker plans to be out for several or many days and takes everything in the pack which will be needed throughout the journey. On the face of it he needs no knowledge of making brush beds and brush shelters and of managing fire through the night in such a way that good periods of sleep can be had in its warmth.

But in fact the backpackers do need a good knowledge of the traditional woodlore, even though it appears to be made obsolete by their packful of superior gear and supplies. They need it as a back-up in the case of failure or loss of gear, particularly because, with their gear, they so often travel many days away from the nearest point of re-supply.

In addition, this book is about many aspects of outdoors travel which are common to all those venturing into woodland: the crucial role of clothing and footwear in outdoor safety; practical bush-country orientation; first aid, with emphasis on the prevention and management of injury in the outdoors; effective methods of signalling for outside help if it is needed; and a range of useful improvisations. Therefore, I offer this book to backpackers, confident of its usefulness to them even though the specialized gear which is pivotal to backpacking is outside the scope of the work.

I offer this book as well to anyone who travels across wooded country by light aircraft. It is a fact that light aircraft are sometimes forced down far from the beaten track and that people often survive the landing. Whether they then survive until they are picked up or until they walk out will depend on what they have with them and what use they make of material at hand in the vicinity of the forced landing. Traditional woodlore can be crucial to success, including the skills by which one may gain food — principally meat and fish — from the land.

This book came to be written in large part out of my dissatisfaction with the run-of-the-mill survival manuals, of which there are so many. These manuals focus altogether too much on what you do after the so-called survival situation has developed, and not nearly enough — often hardly at all — on the steps you should have taken much earlier to reduce the possibility of having to spend an unexpected night out and to ensure that, should it occur, it would not have life-or-death implications.

Most seriously, these manuals often fail altogether to explain the vital role of clothing and footwear in outdoor safety. I often observe to others interested in the subject that decisions made in a clothing store are more important for survival than any single thing that you will do in the survival situation itself, supposing it arises. Invariably the response is one of vigorous agreement.

I dislike, in fact, use of the word survival in application to an unexpected time out in the woods. A survival situation, it seems to me, is one in which life hangs in the balance. Death lurks at hand and must be fended off with exceptional skill and ingenuity. However, given reasonable preparedness on the part of the traveller, the boreal and sub-boreal forests of North America — those great stretches of wilderness which those of us who live near them refer to as the bush — are a safer place in which to spend an unexpected night out than are many of the cities of this same continent.

Now, this book is written specifically for those who venture into or over these vast stretches of boreal and sub-boreal forests of Canada and the northern reaches of the United States. Most of the forested mountain slopes of the West fall within this category, with the exception of the rainforests of the coastal region. The woodlore I offer must be supplemented by further study and experience by those who venture into rainforest, as the climate there puts special demands on the traveller which lie outside my present scope. That said, much of what is written here will be useful in rainforest country.

It is obvious, too, that woodlore has no application beyond the treeline. If you venture there, you need knowledge and skills peculiar to arctic terrain and to the limited mountain country that is south of the continental treeline but above the elevation at which useful forest growth can be found.

Another point I wish to discuss before we go into the subject chapters, so that you may keep it in mind as you read, is that you should not go into the bush on any venture, however short the trip and benign the weather at the time, without a few bits of gear in addition to your clothing and footwear. Just what these bits of gear should consist of will become clear to you as you make your own decisions about them in response to what I have written.

Also, it is agreed among outdoors people who have made a specialty of survival methodology that you should separate your gear into what you might wish to have with you for other purposes, and what you have with you specifically against the possibility of not returning when you expect and having to camp out. Your camera, binoculars, bird book, and lunch can float around in your day pack; your waterproof matches, emergency ration, and signalling mirror, along with whatever else in the same category you consider essential, belong in a different and well-secured kit from which you cannot be separated come hell or high water.

Almost universally this kit is called a survival kit, although I prefer to call it a kit of core items. Suit yourself, but keep it in mind, and as you read the subject chapters you will develop a concept of what you will want in your core, or survival, kit.

Next let me acknowledge that writing this book has kept me face to face with the very real limits of my own knowledge and experience. It is one matter to see in broad scope the range of subject material which is necessary in a comprehensive review; it is quite another matter — and far more exacting — to deliver sufficient detail in all subject areas that the information can be put to practical use. I need look no farther than my immediate friends and associates to be reminded of my shortcomings: Buster Hamilton of Lac la Hache in British Columbia hunts with such consistent skill that I wonder why I presume to know anything much at all; Monty Alford of Whitehorse in the Yukon Territory can build at a safe guess three good snow shelters to my one that will just do; Wilf Taylor, Safety and Training Officer with the Canadian Department of Indian and Northern Affairs, has brushed out under a tree more nights than I have cared to leave the comforts of my home camp; countless older Indian women everywhere in the North set snares for small game with a proficiency which I will never match.

Yet the several subject matters I attempt to cover here needed to be brought together for the benefit of the increasing numbers of people who venture, from mainly urban experience, into woodland. To the extent that I have in fact succeeded you will now benefit from my good fortune in having had good teaching, good counsel, good advice, and helpful criticism from so many others of greater knowledge and skill than I possess.

Lastly, a word about words: to many of us who live in or beside the boreal and sub-boreal forests of North America these forests and the land they grow on are known simply as the bush. We seldom say forest, wilderness, woods, wilds, north woods, and so on. We say bush.

When a man goes to his trapline, he goes into the bush. When he returns, he comes out of the bush. If the isolation has made him a little queer in his ways, we say he is bushed. A small aircraft used to travel between settlements and camps in the bush is a bush plane, and the man who flies it a bush pilot. Where does a prospector spend his lonely summers? In the bush.

I live in the bush and my home is a bush camp. When I write about the bush I may be regarded by editors and others in distant places as being rather bushed on account of my liberal use of the word bush. They may be right, but now you know what I mean when I say bush and that is what matters.

It is important when one travels to go well, not poorly. To go well is to journey in reasonable comfort without too great a burden of baggage, to be safe against the hazards of the way, and to find food, shelter, and a place to sleep at nightfall.

Never is it more critical to go well than when you travel far from the beaten track, either alone or with one or two others, and with only yourself to rely on. It is good to go well in the bush, hazardous to go poorly.

Prepare yourself and you will go well in the bush.

Wilderness Survival Handbook

ONE

Clothing

■ **PRINCIPLES OF HEAT LOSS AND RETENTION**

The bush country is in many ways a nurturing mother. It provides you with wood which will burn readily in your fire and with abundant brush for your shelter and your bed at night. It provides you with food in the form of small and large game and, at some seasons of the year, it supplies edible plants. It can, of course, be capricious about food, offering little or even nothing in some regions and an abundance in others.

Yet there is one way in which the bush is decidedly a severe mother. The climate of the bush country, year-round, produces weather against which you must protect yourself; moreover, in high summer, when you just might be able to survive both days and nights outdoors for a short period without adequate clothing, it will produce a constant horde of mosquitoes. The bush is no place to go scantily clad.

Your clothing is your first line of defence against this harsher side of the bush; if you are well clothed, what would otherwise be the cause of misery and suffering becomes a source of invigoration and joy.

When I go out from my camp in the crisp mornings of January as the returning sun first spills its golden splendour over the frozen landscape, my heart sings.

I travel on snowshoes along the edge of a meadow and past a beaver dam to see what may have happened there in the night. At one place a moose crossed, not two hundred yards from my camp. Here a weasel popped into the snow and burrowed through to pop out just there, do you see? Doubtless he was hunting the abundant shrew, the tracks of which are all about.

There are no words to capture the joy of such a morning. The air, fresh from the high arctic, is crisp and invigorating. By the thermometer which hangs in a tree in my camp it is chilled to exactly $-43°$ C ($-45°$ F), and in my delight at how life thrives in this forest through these winter months I am pleased with the thought that tomorrow morning it may be colder yet.

Now what joy could there possibly be in this winter morning if I were chilled to the bone, if my fingers were numb with the cold, or if my feet were in pain at the onset of frostbite? Yet, for want of a few pounds of just the right clothing and footwear, misery and even danger would have replaced pleasure and delight.

Were I clad in rubber boots in place of these moccasins, in last summer's favoured denims in place of these wool trousers over wool underwear, in cotton or leather gloves in place of these moosehide mitts with woollen inners, in a tight-fitting, fashionable short jacket in place of this loose-fitting parka with its great fur ruff and its generous length which protects me down to my knees—if I were so clad, I could not be out here for the morning, much less the day, without being miserable in the cold.

If by chance I had to spend the night outdoors in such an outfit, I would probably perish, and in my misery in the daytime and my perishing at night I would illustrate the two most important functions which clothing, in all seasons, must fulfil: first, it must give you protection with convenience in the daytime, and second, should the need arise, it must help substantially to conserve your body heat through the night.

That's important to remember, so let's state it again: *your clothing must give protection with convenience in the daytime and help substantially to conserve body heat through the night.*

Another cardinal fact about clothing is that, in order to fulfil the twofold function we have just identified, it must allow the continuous free escape of body moisture. Even when at rest and just warm enough to be comfortable, you are losing moisture through your skin. If moisture cannot escape through your clothing, it must then accumulate in your clothing. Your clothing then loses its ability to insulate, and in severe temperatures the result could be fatal.

The only time when there is an argument to be made for clothing which prevents the outward movement of body moisture is during heavy rain when there is much more moisture trying to get in than needs to find a way out. Nevertheless, many people of long experience in the bush (remember, I am not speaking of rainforest) find so little need of waterproof rain gear that they simply do not keep any in their outfit. More on that later.

For now, let's repeat this second cardinal fact about clothing: *it must allow the free escape of body moisture.*

Finally, functional clothing for the bush *must be adjustable to an increase or decrease in the body heat you generate and to changes in air temperature.*

A friend said to me recently that it is important in the bush not to keep comfortably warm but to keep comfortably cool. I thought about that for a while and decided that it hits the nail on the head very precisely indeed.

While I enjoy a good sweat, it is only a good idea in the hot days of summer, when it serves a good purpose, or, in other seasons, if you have fresh clothing on hand.

In all the seasons when it is extremely important to conserve body warmth it is distinctly counterproductive to overdo the job and get up a sweat. At best, in cool weather the result is discomfort, both from the prickly dampness of moist clothing against your skin and, after the period of overheating is over, from a sense of tiredness and chill.

In cold weather, the result of getting up a thorough sweat can be sheer disaster. When you stop feeling too warm, severe chill sets in and it is impossible to feel warm again unless you have the time and opportunity to light a fire and stay in the warmth beside it until your clothing is dry and once more can provide efficient insulation.

You cannot avoid the fact that your level of activity varies during the day and that, therefore, the amount of body heat you generate also varies. In easy going in the morning you are comfortably cool with everything on. Climbing steadily up a long gentle incline toward noon with your snowshoes sinking into the soft snow at every step, you can only be comfortably cool with your parka off and strapped to your pack and your shirt open all the way down. Occasionally you may even hold your undershirt out from your body to let cooling air come in to ventilate your skin. Coming down the slope in the afternoon on your broken trail, you may have your parka back on but open down the front. Perhaps on the last mile into camp, as the sun goes down and the temperature drops, you will be done up snugly, and very glad of it.

What you have done illustrates this third principle about functional clothing in the bush: that it must be adjustable to changes in the body heat you generate and to changes in the air temperature so that notwithstanding these changes you can remain comfortably cool.

Wear layers of clothing so that you can take layers off as you warm up, and then put layers back on as you cool down. This technique is known as layering, and it is the most practical way of adjusting your clothing to the changes in your body temperature which are inevitable in response to your activity level and to air temperatures.

So now we've identified three main criteria for clothing that is suitable in the bush: *first, it must give you protection with convenience in the daytime and help substantially to conserve body heat during the night, should that need arise; second, it must allow the continuous free escape of body moisture; third, it must be adjustable to changes in the amount of body heat generated and in air temperature.*

Then there is one further quality which we must look for in bush clothing, and we have had to worry about this mainly since the arrival of the synthetic fibres. Bush clothing must be resistant to fire, at least to the extent that it burns only by smouldering or, on going to flame, burns moderately. You cannot escape the fact that sometimes you must use fire to cook, to dry clothing, and to keep you warm while you are sleeping. You cannot avoid momentary contact of clothing with flame or the occasional landing of a burning ember. Cloth which bursts into flame on the first contact is lethal. We will discuss this in more detail later in this chapter.

We can now have a look at the sorts of material from which clothing is constructed, and the kinds of garments which are genuinely useful in the bush—a true first line of safety and protection.

■ CLOTHING MATERIALS AND THEIR PROPERTIES

There is such a profusion of materials now about for the manufacture of cloth of every kind that one hardly remembers the time,
brief years ago, when if you understood the uses of cotton and
wool and to a minor extent of leather and fur, you knew all there
was to know on the subject. Now with the addition (to name the
commonest) of rayon, nylon, and polyester, together with the variety of blends of these not only with each other but with wool and
cotton as well, you may be forgiven if it seems impossible for you
to make knowledgeable choices.

I have in front of me at this moment samples of material rang-
ing in weight from a light broadcloth to a heavy woollen type of
trouser cloth. The mix is various to say the least. There are four
different light cloths of pure nylon. There is an extra-light shell
cloth of polyester, cotton, and nylon in proportions of 55-25-20.
There are two cloths, each different from the other, of polyester
and cotton in a 65-35 and a 67-33 mix respectively. Then we have
a cloth in cotton and nylon in a proportion of 66-34 and, finally,
two weights of a wool-like cloth, one a mix of wool, rayon, and
nylon in proportions of 60-25-15 and the other of wool, nylon, and
polyester in proportions of 75-15-10.

What does a body make of all *that?*

Let's consider some of the clothing materials available to us
and the properties which they offer, starting with the basics.

WOOL

Wool must rank among the most useful materials which the white
man brought in trade days to the North American bush. While it
is undeniably true that clothing made from animal skins by the
Indian people was often the finest possible for the purpose, wool
proved to be immediately useful; and, as supplies of skins de-
creased because of changes imposed by European occupation,
wool became a vitally important material in both clothing and
bedding.

The Hudson's Bay Company blanket, bearing its point marks
to signify relative weight of cloth, was both a standard of quality
and a staple item in trade. Indians valued these blankets for daily
use and commonly used one as a burial shroud on the death of a
tribe member. I saw the remains of a three-point blanket come out

of a grave accidentally disturbed during road construction in the Skeena River country in the early sixties. The skeleton and the blanket, its point marks still in evidence, were carefully re-interred by the occupants of the present-day village located not far from the old burial site.

I have a pair of three-and-a-half-point blankets in my camp outfit, and they are in everyday use in the lounging area at the back of my lodge, where a visitor may throw one about his shoulders should the evening turn cold and I pay insufficient attention to the fire.

The Hudson's Bay Company also trades a product known as duffle cloth, available, in substantial width, by the yard. It is a thick wool blanket-cloth of exceptionally resilient quality. If you press it between thumb and forefinger it will compress somewhat under the pressure, but as you release it you feel it return to its full, durable thickness. It is used extensively in the northern bush as an inner liner in moosehide moccasins and—in combination with an outer shell of a tightly woven windbreaking cloth—in the construction of parkas.

Wool has excellent insulating qualities and has the enormous advantage of retaining much of its insulating quality while damp or wet. In this regard it is out in front of any other natural material by a country mile, and many people in bush conditions prefer a wool jacket to rain gear in wet weather. It is slow to let the water through. You may feel it growing heavier and heavier, but it's a rare rain that lasts long enough finally to wet you to the skin. Even then you aren't miserably chilled by the experience.

For the same reason, a leading quality of wool is that it resists becoming seriously wet from constant contact with wet snow. I have on occasion worked my way for hours through thickets of young conifers laden with wet snow, and have become a walking snowman from the wet snow constantly brushing onto my clothing. Yet, at the end of such a journey I have been fairly dry and certainly comfortable inside my clothing, the wet snow having for the most part not managed to wet the wool garments beneath the surface.

Many of the garments I once bought in pure wool I now buy in a wool-and-synthetic-fibre mix. The cloth performs nearly as well so far as I can discern, and undeniably wears far longer.

A disadvantage to wool in some applications is its weight. If you must carry your bedding on your back, you soon give up wool in favour of down or fibre fill.

COTTON

Cotton materials are widely used in the bush with versatility and good results, but please be aware of their limitations. In stout denim, cotton stands up to heavy use and provides good protection against insects. In a light but tightly woven cloth, it makes an excellent windbreaking outer shell for use in cold winter weather, usually in a mix with polyester. Many users believe the best shell cloth is found in sixty-five percent polyester to thirty-five percent cotton. In shell cloth, cotton and cotton mixes let body vapour move out effectively.

Though cotton is widely used in light underwear for spring, summer, and fall, veterans of the trail generally agree that it's dangerous stuff and best avoided. It has no place in underwear in any season—except perhaps in briefs.

Cotton takes up water like a blotter. Wear cotton trousers in wet snow and you will be soaked to the skin—and not only to the depth of the snow you are walking through. The damp will creep a good long way up your legs besides. The same seems true of cotton and synthetic mixes. Avoid cotton in keep-warm layers and in trousers and jackets in damp conditions. Denim jeans may be great around camp, but will accelerate heat loss if you are caught out overnight in a drizzle.

SYNTHETICS AND BLENDS

Early experience with using synthetics in bush clothing was not good. For example, nylon parka- and jacket-shells stiffened in cold weather and crinkled with a loud noise a moose could hear a mile away. Material which needed to breathe often didn't, while some garments were a fire hazard.

The response of many people in the bush to this initial experience was to avoid the synthetics and stick to garments of cotton and wool, according to the season and the weather. There has been, however, enormous progress in the development of synthetics, and now many not only are free of the early disadvantages but also offer positive qualities which, either independently or in combination with natural fibres, give us cloth which is arguably superior to anything we had before their arrival. This is particularly true of the blends.

When it comes to the primary qualities one looks for in a material—insulative ability, protection against brush, wind, and in-

sects, the free passage of body moisture, and resistance to moisture from wet snow—one usually finds that the mixed materials will
now perform as well as the natural material after which they are
designed and will outwear the natural material by a long shot.
Heavy pants of a wool, rayon, and nylon blend in proportions of
60-25-15 seem to function, so far as one can discern by wearing
them, at least as well as pure wool, and undeniably will outwear
pure wool by seasons. The shell on my fine cold-weather parka is
of cotton and polyester in proportions of 66-34, and is certainly as
effective as the best tightly woven cotton shell-material. It will outwear pure cotton by years.

As to fabrics of a straight synthetic composition—rather than
a mixed composition with natural fibre—experience seems varied.
Work socks of synthetic fibre do not give the comfort of wool and
few people care to use them. On the other hand, straight nylon
cloth, used to contain down or fibre fill or employed in some shell
materials, seems quite satisfactory. The lining of my parka is a
nylon fabric and I find no fault with it.

Light woven or knitted material in both polypropylene and
polyester is quite successful in light underwear for comfort next
to the skin. It has no absorbency and rapidly rids itself of unwanted moisture.

Striking in recent years have been the synthetic fleece fabrics.
The pilling and shedding associated with earlier versions have been
overcome, and very durable fabrics, easy to care for and successful in application, are now used in a variety of weights for underwear and outerwear of many sorts. More on this later (see p. 12).

One must, of course, adding that quality in a cloth is a question
not only of the natural or synthetic fibre used in its manufacture
but also of the diligence and craftsmanship of the maker. Shoddy
material can be made up from cotton and polyester at least as easily as the very finest, so you must search for quality at the same time
as you determine the components in the mix. Judging by the consistent serviceability of the garments I have used for years in bush
conditions, I am certain that the garment-makers whose products
I buy in turn buy top quality from the cloth-makers.

CLOTHING MATERIALS AND FIRE HAZARD

As we mentioned earlier, it is very important that bush clothing is
fire resistant.

Invariably, in camp, a fire starts in clothing and bedding in one of two ways: either an ember is thrown from the fire to land on cloth or, on the other hand, flame comes in direct contact with fabric. The latter will occur if someone stands too close to the fire or if a gust of wind lifts the flame to strike bedding or clothing that has been hung near by to dry.

In some measure when you consider your uses of clothing you must also consider your expected use of fire and, I suppose, your confidence in your own knowledge about basic fire safety. If you think you are the sort who might stand next to the fire to warm up, then absentmindedly forget what you are about until a gust of wind throws flame on your outer clothing, I suggest you either avoid the use of fire or wear nothing on the outside but wool.

On the other hand, if you feel confident that you can keep your clothing out of the flames, you can wear outer garments of synthetic materials as much as you like. They do not appear to ignite from thrown embers.

Remembering that the sources of ignition are the thrown ember and an exposure to flame, we can make some general statements to help you use fabric with safety around open fire.

First, it does not seem practical to use fire-retardant substances to treat everyday clothing. These are used in making safety clothing for firemen, for example, but in general use are not practical. Except perhaps in very costly and specialized products the retardant is removed by washing or dry cleaning and one must continually re-treat the garment.

Of all fabric materials, natural or synthetic, wool seems to be the single material that is stubbornly resistant to ignition from either embers or contact with flame. If you want to burn wool you must work at it.

Of all fabric materials, natural and synthetic, cotton seems unique in that if a hot coal lands on it, it will burn with a persistent smouldering, which will sometimes consume the entire piece in a progressively enlarging circle of glowing fabric edge. Cotton will, of course, ignite and blaze progressively from direct contact with flame, but not with the vigour of most synthetics.

All synthetic materials which I have tested, with the exception of those mixes in which natural wool predominates, are hazardous to some degree if exposed to flame, but are safe from thrown embers, and you must assess their usage accordingly. I would rather throw a polyester-cotton cover over my bedroll than a piece of canvas, because none of the polyester-cotton fabrics I have tested will start to smoulder from contact with a hot coal—even though polyester is very dangerous where there is any chance of exposure to flame. A mixed fabric of sixty-five percent polyester to thirty-five percent cotton is one of the best around these days for a shell cloth, but do be aware that because of the high content of polyester this fabric will burn with the vigour of good fire-starter.

Those mixed materials in which wool predominates appear resistant to ignition both from thrown embers and from contact with flame. Straight synthetic materials which appear and function as wool are also resistant to thrown embers, but will burn quite readily on exposure to flame.

The down in a filled garment is not at all a fire hazard, but the hole melted through the shell cloth by an ember, if not patched at once, will allow serious leakage of the down.

Fleece fabrics will melt and harden in a spot where an ember lands, but will not go to flame. The nap will melt and the fabric over the affected area will no longer insulate. These fabrics will burn with the vigour of good fire-starter on more than momentary exposure to flame.

Now, my testing has been rudimentary. On a November day in camp at the south end of Lake Laberge I spent part of an afternoon applying hot coals from the fire and the flame from large wooden matches to seven different pure and blended samples of cloth provided by a leading manufacturer of outdoor clothing. I included wool and cotton, both alone and in mixes with synthetics. I suggest that you do your own testing on any outer clothing, such as a shell garment that you expect you might wear around a campfire, by buying a small remnant of cloth of the same weight and mix as is in the garment and exposing it to flame and hot coals. You will then know the nature of what you wear.

My own conclusion is that, although fabrics of wool or mixes in which wool predominates are the safest around a campfire, with proper care on my part I can make much use of cotton, straight synthetic, and mixed fabrics. We will have more on this later.

FILL MATERIALS

There are further materials, not fabrics but fills, which are widely in use now in cold-weather clothing: waterfowl down and the synthetic fibres which are meant to serve the same purposes as down.

Waterfowl down has been used as the insulating fill in sleeping bags for many years, particularly in those intended for use in very cold weather. In recent years it has become widely popular as a fill material in parkas and jackets.

A very light amount of down fluffs up into a magnificent thickness, trapping air in countless tiny pockets. At the same time it allows the escape of body moisture. The good-quality synthetic fills, made up of special polyester fibre, will do the same job, but at a modest increase in the weight of fill required for equivalent insulating strength.

In the dry and extremely cold conditions of the northern bush in winter, the person who wears a well-constructed down- or fibre-filled parka in good condition will be well protected and will enjoy freedom from the weight associated with winter outerwear which uses wool as its basic insulator.

There are, however, limitations to the usefulness of fill as an insulator in garments for bush use, and there are differences between down and synthetic fill which must be understood. Down has become popular not only for its usefulness but also as a symbol of personal status because of its acknowledged excellence and its premium cost. People who must always be seen wearing only the best will often buy a down-filled garment for use in conditions in which they would be much better served by wool or synthetic fleece—at a fraction of the cost.

Filled garments are superior in cold, dry weather. Their lightness, affording freedom of movement and freedom from extra weight all day, is a great boost to one's well-being in the bush when arctic air prevails.

However, filled garments are not the best choice in damp or wet weather. Once down becomes wet it does nothing for you, and you would be better off by far in wool. Fibre fill, on the other hand, does continue to insulate to a useful extent when wet and will dry out much faster than down. Yet wool or fleece will be a better choice in this type of weather.

During light activity over moderate intervals you can use a filled garment under a waterproof shell, but this is a limited arrangement. Go with it for a day of steady activity, and body moisture will build up in the fill to the point at which wool alone, even though exposed to the damp or wet weather, will be more comfortable.

If you propose to use down and/or fibre fill there is more you should know about both than I can give you in full detail here, but I will summarize some basic facts to start you off.

Down, on a weight-to-insulative-strength ratio, is superior to fibre fill.

Down comes in widely varying quality, and it will be virtually impossible for you to tell the quality by inspecting the garment. The quality of workmanship of the garment in other respects and the reputation of the manufacturer are probably your best indicators.

Fibre fill made specifically for use in sleeping bags and garments is a specially processed polyester fibre. DuPont offers Hollofil and Celanese offers Polar Guard, and doubtless there are others. The important point is that polyester is better than other synthetics for this purpose—but only polyester prepared specifically for garment and for sleeping-bag fill should be accepted.

Down is useless when wet, but the fibre fills when wet will continue to insulate to a surprising extent. This is more significant in sleeping bags than in clothing because, when it comes to clothing, wool or fleece is a clear alternative to either of the fills when getting wet is a serious possibility.

Cleaning filled garments can be an arduous task and instructions have varied over the years—with down, I have been admonished both to wash but never dry-clean, and to dry-clean but never wash. You can now buy detergents specifically for washing down-filled garments and sleeping bags, but follow the makers' instructions carefully. Fibre-fill is certainly washable but avoid *hot* water and *hot* air in the drier! To further complicate the question, with filled garments of any sort, the shell material often calls for separate dry-cleaning. Check cleaning instructions before you buy.

Fibre fill is much easier to dry out than down, particularly under camp conditions.

Both down- and fibre-filled garments must be stored loosely in a fluffed-out condition. If they are stored in a compressed condition, they will deteriorate more rapidly than they would in use.

Finally, down is substantially more expensive than fibre fill.

SYNTHETIC FLEECE AND PILES

Synthetic fleeces and piles are neither broadcloth nor fill; they function much as do natural fleece or fur. Napped and/or dense standing fibres trap air in multitudes of tiny pockets, inhibiting the outward movement of your body heat to the colder air beyond.

Often the terms fleece and pile are used interchangeably. Here we will refer to the short-fibre, napped fabrics, which often resemble close-cropped natural fleece as fleece, and speak of the longer, but still very dense, standing-fibre material, which more closely resembles fur, as pile.

There are a number of brands of fleece-type fabrics and quality varies considerably. The Polartec fabric from Maldon Mills, polyester-based and available in several weights, is presently a market leader. These fabrics are light and insulating and can be layered to whatever degree of insulation you require; they pass moisture freely; if they get wet they dry quickly; and they continue to insulate to some degree even when wet. If you layer up with fleece you will find it useful to top off with a wind-resistant shell cloth, particularly on cold or windy days.

Pile has been used for many years as a liner in the body section of jackets and parkas and as a fur substitute in some headgear, including the trim on parka hoods. Good quality pile is functional in many applications but I doubt it's outstanding in any. It's a useful substitute for those who object to the use of fur.

PERFORATED FILM

Now we go to a most innovative material, a perforated film which purports to do what had never been done before it arrived: keep the rain out, yet still allow the free escape of body moisture.

It has always been a basic principle that material designed to keep water out must also prevent the free escape of body moisture. It is for this reason that many experienced people do not use waterproof rain gear in the bush but rely on wool and recently the synthetic fleeces, for the amount of rain which is usual in bush country. Remember, we are not talking about coastal rainforest.

This microporous, polymeric film is sold under the trade name Gore-Tex. It is a continuous film of waterproof material that has profuse numbers of tiny pore-like holes. They are too small to let water pass inward, but are large enough for water vapour to pass outward. The film is reinforced by laminating it on both sides to layers of conventional types of cloth.

Early reports showed that the material worked, but durability and the care required to keep it working raised some concern. Improvements followed and well-made garments incorporating the material now perform to the obvious satisfaction of a large market of outdoor enthusiasts of every kind. All leading retailers in the outdoor market now offer a wide range of clothing and footwear using Gore-Tex film. The products incorporating the film are generally good to excellent in both design and quality of material.

Still, as one major West coast vendor cautions, while Gore-Tex remains the best-performing waterproof/breathable material available, unrealistic expectations can still cause dissatisfaction. It is not air-conditioning. During vigorous activity, you will generate body moisture faster than the film can pass it outward and clamminess will develop. This vendor also stresses the importance of keeping your garments clean if they are to continue to function as intended; wash them frequently and heed the care instructions on the label.

Garments incorporating Gore-Tex are now in regular use on serious expeditions by highly experienced outdoors people in a wide range of climatic conditions. That is a strong endorsement.

SUMMARY

Perhaps by now you have begun to appreciate the extent to which modern innovation has increased the range of choice in materials from which clothing may be manufactured and, in doing so, has complicated for us all the task of choosing which garment in what material will be best for us in field use.

My own long reliance on wool, coupled with a firm scepticism about the claims of industry, has delayed my acceptance of many of the new materials.

Also, no sooner does one accept a new product than an even newer one lands in the marketplace, claiming to do an even better job than all its predecessors.

The best course perhaps is to have a yardstick and, when it comes to material used for insulation in garments of all kinds, I recommend earnestly that you gain a thorough understanding of what wool will do for you in a wide range of bush conditions. If you know what wool will do, you know the performance level which the alternatives must match or exceed.

Even in rainproof garments I tend to use wool as a measurement. Will I in fact be more comfortable inside this rainproof gear, with the attendant problem of body moisture building up in my clothing, than I would be simply with wool, in spite of the fact that the wool will pick up some rainwater?

In shell cloth I am persuaded of the superiority of a tight weave in sixty-five percent polyester to thirty-five percent cotton in all respects—except that it will burn with vigour if ignited. A widely used and successful alternative, which burns with much less vigour, is a tight weave of about sixty percent cotton to forty percent nylon.

Well, there we come to the end of a general discussion of clothing materials and their properties. With these materials put to use in the right sort of garments we can indeed go well and in all weather.

So there is the next question: what are the right sort of garments?

■ CLOTHING

The right clothing helps you to live. The wrong clothing may help you to perish. Decisions made long before in a clothing store are perhaps the most critical of any that will affect your chance of survival if you are caught out unexpectedly in the bush in harsh weather.

Clothing is not incidental to safe venturing and to survival but *cardinal* to them. Keep it ever in mind.

I have said that your clothing must help substantially to conserve your body heat through the night should the need arise, even though your intention may have been to be out for only the day. What exactly does this mean?

Briefly, the basic test of the effectiveness of your clothing is as follows: the clothing you wear and carry in the day pack, combined with any supplementary sheltering material you may carry, such as a piece of canvas, should permit you, during the night, to sit or lie on a brush mat (the proper construction of which we will discuss in a further chapter) in a spot sheltered from the wind and be tolerably comfortable for two or three hours. If you can do this, you know that you will be safe if you have to spend the night out and have no opportunity to do more than stay beneath a sheltering tree. It won't be paradise, but you will survive.

Then, with this basic level of dress and using material at hand in the bush to provide additional shelter (sheltering techniques are discussed in Chapter 5), you can achieve a degree of comfort which should permit sleep and which will significantly increase your margin of safety.

It is paramount that you maintain this level of dress in your ventures abroad and that you test your requirements beforehand: You *must* sit out for two or three hours in the clothing you believe will be adequate to the season. Remember, we are talking about *sitting* for two or three hours, not going for a walk. *Throughout this time you must remain tolerably comfortable.*

What do I mean by tolerably comfortable? I mean that you should feel *warm* throughout the main trunk and abdominal region, that cold spots should only occur on the legs and perhaps on the outside of the arms and at points of pressure on the brush mat, that these cold spots will not be so severe as to force you up to move around to regain warmth, that you will experience no discomfort with ears, hands, and feet, and that your level of comfort will not noticeably deteriorate during the test period.

You should be comfortable enough that your mind is free to wander about on subjects which interest you, rather than on why, at the behest of that chap Fry, you are out on a December night in the snow when you could be home in your cosy bed. If your mind is totally riveted on the cold spots about your body, you will know that you have too many of them and they are too severe and you'd better beef up your outfit and try again.

Please, don't skip the sitting-out test. It's a life-saving reality check.

Now, before we discuss garments in relation to the needs of the season I must caution you that we cannot come up with one best outfit for any particular season, nor can we say that one material, used in a particular construction, necessarily results in a garment that is superior to all others.

Your needs vary according to your activity and immediate field conditions. If you backpack, you will rate down ahead of wool for its high ratio of insulation strength to weight and its space-saving compressibility. If you are out for the day in early winter when there is wet snow on every branch, you will rate wool far ahead of down.

Then, too, your clothing on any occasion is an assemblage of garments, and out of the combinations you choose you hope to gain advantages which would not likely exist in any individual garment. A loosely knit wool sweater will not keep you warm in a chilling wind and neither will a shell garment, but the two in combination may be just what you need. In very few situations will you find any advantage in an all-in-one garment that you cannot improve on with layers of clothing, and most often a number of light layers are superior to a few heavy layers.

Now we can consider some specific possibilities.

SUMMER CLOTHING

In summer, the ever-popular denim will be at its most useful. Stout denim pants wear well and give excellent protection against brush and mosquitoes. They will be most comfortable, particularly in hot weather, if they are an easy fit. They need not be oversize, but worn too tight, they restrict circulation, prevent full freedom of movement, do not ventilate effectively, and wear out more quickly.

A useful alternative to denim pants is a work trouser in strong drill of a cotton-polyester blend. These generally outwear denim, and are altogether comfortable, for they ventilate as easily as cotton. But stop here and remember: When cotton is wet it is useless as an insulator and actually hastens the loss of body heat. On a hot summer day that is not a problem. On a summer night, caught out unexpectedly in a steady rain, you will be at high risk of hypothermia if you rely on cotton clothing such as denim to keep you warm.

If I can keep dry and if I have some light wool or synthetic underwear in my day pack to wear beneath the denim or cotton-polyester drill, I will get by. At the same time, I would be safer yet if I wore trousers of a light but tightly-woven, tough wool whipcord. These are not uncomfortable in the heat of the day and they will help considerably to conserve body heat at night, even to some extent when wet or damp.

Once you are off the roads and into the bush proper you are dependent on your feet for all your travel, and, therefore, for the success of your entire venture. Give the care of your feet the utmost priority by cushioning them well. I will discuss boots and moccasins in a further chapter, but here I recommend to you that thick, resilient wool socks, reinforced in the heel and toe with synthetic fibre for longer wear, are a wise choice. Always keep them clean and have a spare pair or two in the day pack.

As an alternative choice there are socks made from cotton and constructed with a cushioning depth in the sole. In general I doubt that these have any advantage over wool socks unless you have a special difficulty in wearing wool.

Most of us go without underwear, save for briefs, in high summer, but you might consider an undershirt of a fishnet design. This material, made of connected small loops of cord-like fabric, consists of more space than fabric and keeps your outer shirt away from your skin without itself adding another layer of solid fabric. Many people believe that these undershirts keep them much cooler in hot, sticky weather.

For your outer shirt, cotton is cooler than straight synthetic material, but a cotton-polyester mix seems as useful as cotton. I find denim shirts quite serviceable, but I am satisfied that any well-fitting, good-quality shirt of cotton or cotton and polyester will do. Just be sure that the material is heavy enough to protect you from mosquitoes and that you have adequate other clothing in your day pack. In wet conditions, this shirt will be of little help and possibly downright harmful.

Now, there is an alternative to a shirt or a shirt-and-undershirt combination for which I have a definite preference in summer weather, particularly the hotter spells of it. This alternative is a bush jacket. Until recently these have been devilish hard to come by but at this writing, Tilley Endurables, a Canadian retailer, and Cabela's, a mail order retailer in the U.S., now offer them.

The bush jacket was developed for use in bush country in hot climates where good ventilation, protection from brush, and protection from insects are of principal importance.

The jacket should be constructed from a medium-weight cotton or cotton-polyester mix, rather like denim in weight but perhaps a little softer and less dense in the weave. It will fit *loosely* and come down below the hips to the top of the thighs. It should be generously supplied with large pockets, two at breast level and two more just above the hem. It will have a belt held in place by a couple of loops, and the belt can be as loose or as snug as you wish for comfort, or not be used at all.

If you want to try one, the trick is to wear it in place of, rather than in addition to, any other top garment. You are well protected from brush and insects and the free movement of air between the jacket and your skin provides excellent ventilation. I am personally convinced of its superiority as a hot-weather top garment.

Once again, this cotton or cotton-polyester bush jacket will be little help in a rain unless you and the jacket can keep dry under shelter. Have other clothing in the pack for the possibility of the hot summer day turning wet and cool and of night finding you still in the bush.

I think a hat is a good idea for summer wear in the bush. I like a durable felt hat with a moderate brim, but a wide variety of hats and caps seem to do the job. The best hat I ever had was a fine, imported Australian bush-hat, but I now find these hard to come by. A hat should protect you from the sun, shield you from the brush when you choose to push through some dense undergrowth, and shed a moderate amount of rain. It is also, invariably, the handiest thing around to fan a fire if the wood is reluctant at first to get going. For all these purposes, I do find a felt hat with a moderate brim to be very serviceable.

Now let me add one item of wear. Please don't go into the bush in the summer months without a mosquito head-net or a square of mosquito netting large enough to come over your hat and protect your face and neck—even if you carry it tied to your day pack most of the time.

You may find as I do that, even in the worst of the season, you are not much bothered by mosquitoes as long as you can be walking through the bush at a good pace. But should you be pinned down with a turned ankle or be obliged to spend an unexpected night out, that piece of netting will be vital. I strongly recommend it even if you have found a brand of repellent which seems effective and to which your skin hasn't as yet developed any adverse reactions.

For the same reasons I recommend that, either on your hands or in your day pack, you have with you a pair of light leather work-gloves which will protect you up your wrists where the shirt or bush-jacket sleeves take over.

Given protection from the biting you can grow accustomed to the tedious whining hum of the mosquito. You cannot, on the other hand, have any peace or get any rest if you have no better defence against the onslaught of biting than frantic swatting.

Now, another important question: what sort of jacket should you carry in case it rains or you have to spend the night out?

This is one respect in which my bush jacket is at a disadvantage: It won't help in the rain, or add much on a cool night. A light but roomy wool or fleece jacket should go in the day pack and a light fleece top that will fit under either the bush jacket or the wool jacket will add a further margin of safety. If it rains, put the bush jacket in the day pack and rely on the wool and/or fleece layers. If you are caught out for a cool night, use both layers of wool or fleece, adding the bush jacket as a shell if conditions remain dry. *Do* remember that a hot summer's day in bush country may be followed by a night in which the air at ground level dips to, or just below, freezing. However hot the day, tuck your wool or fleece layers into the day pack. By themselves they won't be all you'd like if you must spend the night out unexpectedly, but along with other measures which we will discuss later they will make an essential contribution to your night's comfort.

Now let's not suppose that all the foregoing advice is cast in stone. For one thing, summer weather tends to come in spells—hot spells, wet spells, and unsettled cool spells. These spells of weather most often last for several days at a time. Luckily, we do have good forecasting services. You may or may not beef up your outfit to suit the weather at the time, but *never* go with less than what will be sufficient for safety. *Do* consider what the night may be like in case you have to spend it out, no matter how sure you are that you won't.

If you are travelling by light aircraft, remember that your un-expected night out might turn into many nights. In the pack which goes on the aircraft with you there should be, among other items, a more substantial jacket as well as long underwear suitable to the cooler seasons.

SPRING AND FALL CLOTHING

And what about these cooler, in-between seasons? I often think that the riskiest times of the year for the novice or careless person outdoors occur not in the dead of winter but in the spring and fall.

A warm October day with afternoon temperatures nudging 20°C (68°F), benignly reminiscent of the summer just gone by, may be followed by a night in which the mercury drops rapidly, reaching −8°C (17.6°F) in the last hours before dawn. Or the night might witness the arrival of the first of the winter storms from the distant ocean, with a cold, persistent wind driving a relentless and chilling rain.

An early spell of warm weather in April might clear the snow from your favourite stretch of bush, inviting you out in the last days of the month to recapture the happy mood of last summer's forays into the wooded hills. Suddenly, overnight, winter reappears for a last swift punch, taking everyone by surprise. Six inches of wet snow covers the landscape and clings to every limb and bush. The freezing level has slipped down the hillside to somewhere far below the place where, unexpectedly, you were obliged to spend the night.

I acknowledge the difficulty. On an afternoon that is almost summery, you want your day's hike in the bush to be a free, even spontaneous, adventure, unencumbered by winter clothing. Yet the basic imperative still holds: the clothing you wear and carry must be sufficient to contribute substantially to the conservation of your body heat in the event of an unexpected night out.

For your feet of course there is little problem. Wear stout wool socks and have a spare pair in the day pack.

Unless you find it too much altogether, try this: wear lightweight-wool or fleece long underwear in a two-piece outfit, then wool trousers which have lost their nap and worn a bit thin for winter use and a light wool or fleece shirt. Carry a light wool or fleece jacket in the day pack.

By stripping to your undershirt on top during the warm afternoon you will likely be cool enough that the heavier clothing from the belt down won't be too warm for comfort. If you're caught out you'll have two layers of wool or fleece on top, the wool trousers below, and underwear beneath everything. In combination, these items will provide pretty good protection against cold rain, wet snow, or a sudden drop in temperature to –6°C (21°F) to –8°C (17°F).

For spring and fall weather, I find that a down-filled vest, which adds little weight to the day pack, is useful as one of the layers. I may go out with light wool underwear, light wool shirt, down vest, and medium-weight wool jacket, in that order. The down vest and wool jacket might spend most of the day in the pack, and so might the underwear top, leaving me free to wear only the light wool shirt if the afternoon grows unexpectedly warm.

It is true that in the seasons when light clothing is most comfortable, yet something substantial must be carried against the possible sudden advent of harsh storms or sharp cold, it is tempting to rely on a down-filled jacket. Here, after all, is the finest in warmth without weight, and since the jacket is most likely to spend the whole hike in the pack, where we want the least weight possible, why not? In many cases this will be adequate; but you should remember that in a cold, driving rain it will give far less protection than a wool jacket. A wet, down-filled garment is of little use and is difficult to dry out afterwards. If you still choose down, perhaps you should carry as well the top half of a light rain-outfit; remember, however, that the longer you have to wear the rain outfit, the clammier you become inside it from trapped body moisture accumulating in your clothing. If you wear the more breathable rain gear incorporating Gore-Tex you will reduce this problem considerably.

Your summer hat, if it's a sturdy one which will shed some rain and protect you in the brush, will do in these in-between seasons, or you might prefer a wool cap with a piece to fold down over ears and neck against the chill.

You should also have gloves, either on your hands or in the pack. You won't need them in the daytime, but they will be vital if you are caught out overnight and winter returns.

Again, I do not suggest that the only way to go is the one I have outlined. You should certainly try out different combinations to find what is most comfortable yet at the same time most serviceable for you. Let me insist on only two points. The first is that to go well in the bush in these in-between seasons is to go prepared for the severe swings in weather and temperature which do occur. The second is that you should not shift from reliance on wool until you are certain that the alternative you prefer will truly do the job.

WINTER CLOTHING

We now turn to a consideration of winter. In the choice of clothing often rests the whole question of whether you will enjoy winter or thoroughly dislike it.

I enjoy winter. The storms of November and December bring the snow, and out of the high arctic come the successive surges of deep cold. The expanse of snow on a frozen lake sparkles in the moonlit night, and the forest, with the snow patched everywhere onto the branches of the evergreens, becomes a visible wonderland in which, by your great good fortune, you chance to live. Every wild creature that lives here, too, cannot move without leaving that plain fact evident in the snow, and each day of winter is filled with discovery. The moose, the deer, the wolf, the coyote, the fox, the hare, and the lynx, the beaver, the mink, the wolverine, the otter, the martin, and the weasel—all these and more make their living in this winter land, and they cannot keep their presence a secret from you now. At night in your camp, snug on your thick mattress of spruce boughs and soaking up the heat from your fire, you hear the wolf howl. In the morning you find the story in the snow: a small band of caribou crossed the river not two hundred yards from your camp, and the wolves made a kill there as a straggler reached the ice on the far shore. The caribou and the wolves are many miles gone now, and only the ravens stay by the kill to find the last scraps in the snow. The wolves and the ravens, after their nature, make their living too.

Who would trade this season off? Not I for one.

But I will clothe me well. And I will keep in mind as well that winter comes in two versions: a milder phase, usually at beginning and end, in which the air temperature hangs around the freezing point *and there is wet snow everywhere to be dealt with,* and then the colder phase, in which temperatures are well below freezing *and the snow is dry.* These are significantly different conditions and one must allow for the difference in one's selection of clothing.

Early and Late Winter

By the first snow I recommend most strongly that you are into your heavy wool socks—we'll discuss boots and moccasins later— and that you are also into long woollen underwear and wool trousers.

On underwear, I am adamant about avoiding cotton or any fabric incorporating cotton with other materials and I see no advantage in silk. Quilted down is offered along with a special soap for its washing, but I recommend you pass it by.

For those who can tolerate it next to their skin, wool has been a reliable choice for decades. I find comfort next to the skin in a softer-than-usual woollen underwear in a light, fine knit. I can then layer above that with heavy wool underwear of the sort that makes you itch just thinking about it.

Significant improvement in synthetic fabrics in recent years has led to a profusion of other functional choices in underwear. Next to the skin I also use polypropylene and polyester fabrics with much success. Currently a spun polyester combined with a stretch fabric is popular for its comfort on the skin combined with good insulating quality.

For warmer underwear, very good choices are available in

both polyester fleece and heavier weight polypropylene. Still, in early and late winter, we mainly want light underwear for a foundation over which we layer up to the degree we need with other garments.

I know of no material for trousers which defends you against wet snow in early winter as effectively as wool in a heavy weave with an abundant and sturdy nap. I also know of nothing which will take the joy out of an early winter's day more surely than being soaked to the knees. To reinforce my own experience I have noted that most of the people I have known who have lived and worked in the bush use some type of wool trousers throughout the winter. Interestingly, the frequency of such use increases with age!

On your upper body I suggest you layer above the underwear with shirt, sweater, and/or vest in wool or synthetic fleece. I favour a sturdy wool jacket on top, and I adjust for comfort by increasing or reducing the layers between the underwear and the jacket. This leaves the wool jacket always at work fending off the snow.

My preference for wool declared, if you have a fleece jacket by all means give it a try. It will work much as wool does. Try also if you wish a Gore-Tex shell though you may find that the constant loading of wet snow coupled with your exertion leads to moisture building up faster than the shell can move it out.

There are three main reasons for selecting your layers from this sort of mix: first, you can peel down as far as you need in order to keep comfortably cool and the spare layers won't be a burdensome weight while stowed in the day pack; second, you can always have wool, (or synthetic fleece, or Gore-Tex if you are satisfied with performance), on the outside layer for defence against the wet snow which lands on you from the bushes; third, you will have fit clothing with which to face the night if the need arises.

I am not in favour of a parka in this early stage of winter. If it is filled, it will get wet from the snow and be difficult to dry afterwards—in addition to being uncomfortable to wear while wet. Also, your parka should be a main investment for the truly cold weather later on and, as such, will be too effective to be comfortable in temperatures just below or around the freezing mark. Finally, if you put the hood up you'll be sacrificing side vision long before the weather is cold enough to make that necessary, and if you leave the hood down, you'll probably get it full of wet snow.

If you do wish to use a parka this early I would suggest one of duffle cloth without the tightly woven, windbreaking outer shell.

These parkas are not quite so efficient in insulating as are down- or fibre-filled parkas. In very cold weather you will want more layers beneath them than you would with a filled parka, but, by the same token, in warm, wet-snow weather, you may keep comfortably cool by wearing very little beneath them. I suggest removing the outer shell because the wool will resist snow moisture more effectively if it doesn't have to do its job under a wick-like layer of wet cloth. The windbreaking cloth is permeable to allow body moisture to escape, and it therefore cannot avoid soaking moisture up in quantity when it comes from the outside. In this application I believe wool has the best capacity to resist snow moisture from the outside, to let body moisture escape freely from the inside, and still to keep you warm if it does get wet.

My choice for this early stage of winter is a wool cruiser-jacket. This garment consists of two layers of a durable wool cloth (nowadays with some synthetic admixture), and has a substantial collar to turn up for protection of your neck and lower face and a good length which protects you well below your hip line. The particular cruiser jacket that I wear was made by one of the oldest garment outfits in Vancouver, Canada, now unfortunately out of business. Virtually the same jacket is still made by Filson of Seattle and is available through such catalogues as Cabelas of Sidney, Nebraska. It is a work coat that for several generations of ranch-workers and loggers outsold any other cold-weather work coat available.

Now a word about length. Any winter coat for the bush must have length. Jackets which come to or just below the belt line are fine about town if you wish, but they rob you of protection in the lower-back area and leave the lower abdominal area protected only by whatever you are wearing from the belt line down. Every time you bend over or sit down a short jacket lifts above your belt line to leave a gap which you feel at once in cool or cold weather. What you want against the weather is a thorough overlap of coat over trousers. Consider nothing which does not reach to at least halfway between your belt line and your knees. A good parka should reach to at least within four inches of the knees. Mine reaches to my knees.

What about your head? I still have a preference here for my felt hat with brim. It catches the snow which falls on my head, the brim at the back keeping it off my neck. Nonetheless, I need ear protection against the possibility of being caught out in a sharp drop in temperature. I therefore must have in the pack either a wool or a fur cap with a flap to turn down for neck-and-ear protection or an adequate cloth cap which can be worn under the felt hat. On balance, perhaps the simplest thing is to wear a cap which has optional ear protection and forget about the felt hat with its brim. Take your choice, but do have some form of ear protection to use should the need arise.

Finally, let us consider hand protection. It is certainly too warm in this early, mild stage of winter to wear the large moosehide mitts with woollen inners which are so useful at –40°C. Yet mitts must be in the pack, even if they are not being worn. Commercial leather gloves are not much use, as they don't insulate and they get wet from the snow. Indian tanned-buckskin gloves are delightfully supple and warm, but they, too, get wet and then are not much use. Once more I favour wool. Wool knit gloves will keep you warm and will hold out against the wetness of the snow as effectively as anything else. Also you should have a spare pair in the pack to put on dry when the day grows late and the temperature drops.

Consider this for your hands: wear one pair of knit wool gloves and have another pair in the pack, along with a pair of soft leather mitts. If the need arises, the leather mitts will back up the fresh pair of wool gloves against quite a cold night.

There are two choices in handwear which I recommend you avoid like the plague.

First, a waterproof glove or mitt, with or without a liner, is useless. The inside of the glove or mitt is soon wet with hand perspiration and you are miserable. In cold weather you are in danger of frostbite. This sort of gear is fine, if you like, for short intervals around town, but not for a day's hike into the bush.

Second, don't use a glove or mitt with a built-in liner. The liners must come out for drying in the event they get wet. It is too difficult to dry a non-removable liner. Again, this sort of gear is fine around town, but it has no place in serious use in the bush.

Another point which applies, of course, to all your clothing requirements, but particularly to hands, feet, and ears: some people just naturally keep warm more easily than others. Those with a robust metabolism and vigorous circulation will be going about bare-handed when others are already wearing mitts. You must discover for yourself where you fit between the extremes, but please remember these two admonitions: first, if you have cold hands, cold feet, or cold ears, you are putting the warmth vital to your entire body in jeopardy and you must do something about it, and, second, never be caught out without the protection which will be *necessary for you at night* for hands, feet, and head, irrespective of what may be comfortable in daytime temperatures.

In bush travel by aircraft in early winter you should be dressed for the prevailing conditions, but in the pack which goes on board the aircraft with you should be the clothing and gear you will want in the toughest of the weather ahead. Also, of course, you will see that your own best cold-weather sleeping bag goes in the aircraft as well. We will speak more about that in a later chapter.

Mid Winter

So let's go on to the depth of winter. The air is extremely cold, perhaps as low as −50°C (−58°F), depending on where on the continent your favourite stretch of bush is located. Also the snow is dry. When the air temperatures are consistently less than −5°C (−23°F), the snow will be dry—except for the slightly damp snow that you will sometimes have falling around that upper limit of the temperature range. Dry snow is useful snow and presents no difficulties in the way that wet snow does.

Once more, for your feet, use thick wool socks, and we will explain about moccasins in a chapter on outerwear for your feet throughout the seasons.

Now is the time to wear or have with you the best of long underwear and to remember that two light layers are superior to one heavy layer. You might wear light polypropylene underwear next to your skin and a medium wool next to that, or a soft wool next to the skin with a somewhat heavier and coarser wool as a second layer. Many users now favour synthetic fleece for heavier underwear. A variety of other synthetic fabrics, too numerous for exhaustive evaluation here, also have been incorporated into long underwear. All are better than cotton, which you should avoid at all cost.

Some people prefer a suit of fibre-filled underclothing in order to reduce weight without loss of insulation. I believe this underclothing can be successful, but do remember that, once damp, it provides less insulation than wool (although it is better than down) and it is somewhat difficult to dry out. Also, if you are caught out overnight, you might find the wool an advantage while lying down.

The fibre fill, compressed beneath you, may lose more of its insulating properties when compressed than does wool. At a very steep price you can buy down-filled underclothing. I don't dispute the potential for warmth without weight, but when I consider the cost, plus the fact that the instructions say dry-clean, don't wash, and then consider the disadvantage of down if it does get thoroughly damp or wet, I am inclined to leave it out of my kit. Also, when compressed beneath your sleeping body, down loses its insulating ability even more than fibre fill does.

For your upper body, wear several layers between the underwear next to you and the parka or jacket on the outside. Wool shirts and sweaters and a variety of synthetic fleece garments all offer excellent choices. A filled vest is useful, but again I suggest you do not rely entirely on down or fibre fill. If you use a fibre-filled undersuit and a down parka, have wool for the layers between.

If you like, by all means have a well-constructed parka with a hood and ruff and plenty of length. The hood should come straight up from your back, not constrict at the back of the neck, and it must *not* bear on the top of your head. The hood must fit loosely over your head. If it bears on top of your head you will be taking some of the weight of the garment there, and you will suffer heat loss from the compression of the garment in one of the last places where you want that to happen.

The hood, when fully up, should cause the full circle of the ruff to sit forward of your face. This will create a layer of pre-warmed air in front of your face, a factor which makes breathing easier and reduces the chance of frostbite to facial tissue.

Wolverine is the best fur for the ruff. Your breath will always condense on the ruff as frost, regardless of what fur or synthetic pile is used, but with wolverine fur there is much less problem with ice formation within the ruff. The collected condensation should always be brushed off regularly with the back of your mitt to reduce icing, but with wolverine fur the problem occurs to a lesser extent.

That said, one now must acknowledge that wolverine fur is terribly expensive and, second, there are moral arguments against the use of fur in clothing. The ruff is worth having, as it does serve an important purpose, but synthetic pile, though less effective, will do the job if fur is out of the question for you.

Should the parka have a zipper or other fastening down the front or should it be a pullover?

The original native garment was a pullover. It was also loosely fitted about the middle and provided with a drawstring. To ventilate and keep cool, one left the drawstring fully out. To reduce ventilation and retain more body warmth, one drew in on the drawstring. Also, the original pullover design fitted at the neck and chin in such a way that a slight flow of body-warmed air could escape to the face area.

So back to our question: pullover or zipper front? We don't have caribou skins and we do have zippers.

My own reckoning is that parkas of duffle cloth with a windbreak shell can be pullover *or* zippered, and that parkas of down or fibre fill *should* be zippered—provided that the zipper is of top quality and will not malfunction at *any* temperature; these do now exist. My reasons for this decision go back to the principle of layering and the need to keep comfortably cool.

Under a parka of duffle cloth and a windbreak shell you can have several layers, and as you warm up you can slip off the parka and tie it on the day pack (provided you have alternate ear protection) or you can take off one or more of the inner layers for stowage and put the parka back on. It doesn't much matter whether the parka is a pullover or is zippered.

With the filled parka, however, you have one garment with the insulative strength of several layers. You can't use many layers beneath it, and the difference between having it on or having it off is sometimes too great: with the parka on, you're sweltering; with the parka off, you're chilly. If it is zippered, you then have an intermediate stage between off or on: parka on, but open down the front.

For example, at –25°C (–13°F) I find I don't really need my best down-filled parka. I can be quite comfortable in my cruiser jacket with layers beneath. But if I go out some distance from camp on a January day at –20°C (–4°F), I want protection for the possibility of a night out at –30°C (–22°F) or even –35°C (–31°F), so I might wear my best parka over an undershirt and shirt. Breaking trail through the bush, I would have the parka tied to the pack, coming home toward evening on the same trail, now broken, I would have the parka on but open, and in the last mile along an open meadow walking into a light drift of wind I would have it done up—and all this in the same air temperature of –20°C (–4°F).

Now before we leave the parka question let's face an important issue head on—expense. More than any other garment choice, the parka raises the question of money. A high-quality, down-filled parka with a generous fur ruff is indeed a splendid garment and a pleasure to own and use. However, it also costs an arm and a leg to buy. If a ready-made parka is too much for your budget, you have perfectly functional alternatives. With a pattern, some duffle cloth, and some shell material, you can make your own parka for a third of the price. Or you can stick with the highly successful and time-tested choice of a large, loose-fitting wool jacket, under which you can wear as many layers as you need, using a good cold-weather cap or toque for head, neck, and ear protection. Excellent choices for all these layers are now available in synthetic fleece. A large shell garment slipped over everything will break the wind. I can say without equivocation that in order of vital priority, the right footwear and the wool trousers come ahead of the parka.

Being properly clothed for venturing in the bush in all weather does not require the most expensive and luxurious garments. It is true that you should buy quality, but buy it in wool or synthetic fleece, not down, if an eye must be kept on the budget. Many experienced people prefer wool or fleece in any case, irrespective of the savings in cost. These users argue that a super parka of down puts too much of your total insulation requirement into one garment. At even moderate activity levels you are too hot with it on, but have too little beneath it to be comfortable with it off. The concentration of insulating strength in a single garment deprives you of intermediate stages of insulation strength. These are valid arguments and I do agree with them, in spite of the fact that I also enjoy the considerable qualities of the down-filled parka.

Now, let's consider head and ear protection in conjunction with a parka. It is true that with the parka hood up, if it is well constructed and fits you properly, you are well protected. However, while you are active during the day you may want to remove your parka and stow it on the pack, and if you have no alternative ear protection, you have a problem. There are definitely times when body activity is generating enough heat that you will swelter with the parka on yet freeze your ears with it off.

The answer is a cap. You can use the quilted cloth cap with a fur or pile rim which turns down over your ears and the back of your neck, and simply stow it in the pack when it is cold enough to go back to the parka with the hood up. Or you might use a toque. Perhaps the most versatile solution is the woollen peak cap, with ear flaps that turn up inside the cap when not in use. This cap, because it is not bulky, can be worn with the parka hood over it. I first noticed this combination one day when I was standing about on the river bank in the arctic village of Old Crow in the Yukon Territory passing the time of day with a number of the men who live there, trappers and hunters every one. There was a stiff wind out of the northeast, and though it was not much below – 20°C (–4°F), we all wore parkas and all with the hoods up. We did our best to chat with each other and at the same time keep our backs to the prevailing wind, which makes for much talking to the side and a good deal of "Eh, what was that you said?" as the wind blows one's words away. It was then that I noticed that most of these men wore a woollen peak cap. The peak protruded from under the ruff of the parka hood, the fit of which seemed little affected by its presence.

Over the next few days I observed the versatility of this combination of cap and hood, and I saw a number of advantages to its use.

On the trail in the woods, travelling behind a dog team, a man could throw his parka on the sled and keep his cap on for ear protection.

In quite cold but not severe weather, a man might want his parka on, but prefer the hood down. Certainly a parka hood is a nuisance until you truly need it, since, as mentioned before, it severely restricts your vision to the side. To a hunter this is a vital consideration. A well-constructed parka hood will always form a protecting collar around the back of the head and neck and the lower sides of the face when worn in the down position but with the parka done up in front. This collar effect, along with the wool cap for the top of the head and ears, can keep you quite comfortable in fairly severe weather when you want better vision than you can obtain with the hood up.

Finally, the peak of the cap is useful when the hood is up, not only to shade your eyes when you look toward the sun but also to control, very precisely, the position of the hood and ruff. If you want the ruff up just enough to cover your ears, you push the cap well back. The peak, turning upward, holds the ruff where you want it. To bring the ruff forward to any stage, adjust the cap accordingly. A parka hood by itself is often quite contrary when you want it in an intermediate position short of fully forward, and this cap with the peak controls it admirably.

Now to handwear, and in the deep of winter, we need not just mitts, but the best of mitts. Without question, the best mitts are those made and worn by northern natives, Indians and Inuit. Mine were made by a Loucheaux Indian woman. Before I tell you about these splendid mitts, let's restate the vital principle: cold-weather clothing must allow the continuous escape of body moisture. This is never more true than with your hands, which is why Indian-tanned hide is perhaps the finest of all materials for the main outer mitt. It is soft, it is porous, and it is tough and long-wearing.

My mitts are of moosehide, large in the hand and with a large, wide cuff that reaches halfway from my wrist to my elbow. They are fully covered on the back with soft, tanned wolverine hide, cut to utilize the best of the fur. Inside, I wear a liner of either duffle cloth or wool knit.

I cannot stress enough the absolute importance of good handwear in very cold weather. Poorly clad, your hands will freeze. When your hands are gone, your life is very likely close behind.

The solution, though vital, is simple. Wear mitts of a soft and pliable yet thick and porous leather, inside which you have room for—and wear—a thick woollen liner. So clad, you will be safe, unless you have a disability in your circulation which puts your extremities, however well protected, at risk in cold weather.

I have spent many hours outdoors at –50°C (–58°F) and even on occasion at –55°C (more than –70°F) and have had no problem with cold hands when wearing such mitts.

Yes, there is a reason for those long, wide cuffs. They provide a generous overlap with the cuff of the parka sleeve, and if I should wish to belly-flop into the snow as one sometimes does when hunting, or should I do so accidentally, there is no risk of snow getting between mitt and parka sleeve. Also, when I walk against a stiff wind, I reduce the risk of freezing my face by holding my mitt-clad hands, backs to the wind, in front of my face. Finally, if I must spend an unexpected night out with little time to prepare a camp, I can keep safe by sitting on brush with my knees drawn up, my parka protecting my head and body, my moccasins protecting my feet and ankles, and my mitts protecting not only my hands but my leg fronts below the knees as well, a technique I will explain in detail later. I mention it now because these apparently oversize mitts play a part in it.

Finally, do as knowledgeable Indian trappers in the north do, use a mitt-string, a long, stout cord which ties the mitts together and which, when worn, goes up your arms and around the back of your neck. With the string at the right length, you can slip your hands out of your mitts for a quick task requiring your fingers without having to find a place to put your mitts down or to look for them afterwards. When you've done your task, your hands slip immediately back into the safety of your mitts, which were hanging there in position all the while.

Last, but not least, let us consider the question of fit. This is important in all seasons, but is of increasing significance as the weather grows colder. Clothing for functional use in the bush should be a loose fit—not so loose as to not be a fit, but a loose fit.

Tight clothing may be fashionable and neat and lend emphasis to the attractive contours of the body, but, with the possible exception of very specialized applications, it is not useful, and in very cold weather it is actually dangerous.

Tight clothing cannot insulate as well as the same clothing loosely fitted. Tight clothing can interfere with blood circulation by binding at critical points on the body. Tight clothing interferes with freedom and ease of movement, actually forcing more energy to be spent for any physical task.

Particularly when selecting winter clothing, make sure that a garment is large enough to fit over the layers which will be worn beneath it. Put these layers on before you go into the store to make a final decision to buy, and try the garment on over the layers. An outer jacket which just fits over a cotton shirt won't fit over a stout wool shirt and wool underwear.

Do not listen to store clerks on the question of fit. Invariably, when I buy a winter garment the clerk will protest that it is much too large for me. Convinced that he is right, he will go to great lengths to try to persuade me to buy a smaller size.

Please remember. Fit is vital. All that I have said up to this point will be useless if you get the fit wrong. Even the absolutely right clothes will still be wrong if they are too tight. Make sure your clothing for the bush is a loose and comfortable fit, providing absolute freedom of movement. If you feel restricted or encumbered or weighed down by your clothing, you are in serious difficulty.

When I go out from my camp on a very cold winter's night to walk in the moonlight along the shore of a frozen lake, I go dressed against the possibility of −50°C (−58°F) or more. And when I see the glint of moonlight caught by flakes of frost in endless sparkles over the perfect surface of snow that stretches nearly a mile away to the spruce forest bordering the distant shore, and when I look up and in the distance see a great mountain range gleaming in snowclad perfection by the light of this brilliant winter moon, when I have all this before me I all but burst with the joy of it.

Do you know what I sometimes do, notwithstanding that I am now long past my sixtieth winter? I dance. That's right, I dance. I cannot help it. It would be a funny sight if anyone were there to watch it, and when you consider that usually I'm out there in the moonlit night all by myself perhaps it's even a little dotty. But I do it just the same. If I'm walking along on snow which has been stirred enough by the wind that it is packed and may be walked on without snowshoes, just every once in a while I do a little dance out there in my moosehide moccasins.

Now, I want you to try this: put on your winter outfit—the whole outfit that you'd go out in on the sort of night I'm talking about—and do a little jig, just for the joy of it. Pick a cold night of course, in the snow and the moonlight. And if you have any difficulty doing that little dance on account of the fit of your clothes, you had better go back and start over, because something is definitely wrong.

But, you may say, what about specialized clothing sold for particular activities: ski wear for skiing, snowmobile suits for snowmobiling, hunting jackets for hunting, and so on?

I am not competent to comment on the suitability of this sort of clothing in relation to the activity for which it is designed, and I do not propose to do so. I will point out, however, that some of the clothing I have seen does not meet the basic requirements of the season in which it will be used. I have seen, for example, snowmobile suits which allowed neither for adjustment to changes in body heat generated nor for the free escape of body moisture. They are doubtless effective enough while you sit motionless on the machine which is doing all the work of travel for you, but how effective will the suit be for the long walk back to the truck if the machine breaks down? Or the preparation of an emergency camp? Will you sweat in the suit while you work, only to be chilled afterwards by the accumulation of body moisture which it won't allow to escape? It is probably advisable to buy the suit large enough to have layers underneath which will protect you when you remove the suit—which you must do if the machine stops and you have to exert yourself.

While writing this I have heard on the radio of skiers freezing to death in one of the national parks. They were not caught in a snowslide, but they were cut off by a slide from their return route to the ski lodge. I wonder how adequate their clothing was? I wonder if they had a small day-pack with a few bits of the sort of gear and small supplies which, though not heavy enough to burden their journey, would have enabled them to go well in the bush, not die there.

I wonder, too, if they knew that in selecting their clothing they should have asked themselves these questions:

1. Will it give me protection with convenience in the daytime, and also will it help substantially to conserve my body heat through the night if I am caught out?

2. Will it allow the continuous free escape of body moisture?

3. Will it be adjustable to the amount of body heat generated and to changes in air temperature? Do I have layers to take off while I am skiing with vigour, layers which I may put back on in the event that I must spend the night out?

4. Does it fit loosely enough that it can do the job on which my life may depend?

By all means buy specialized clothing for the sport which takes you into the bush but do ask these questions and do be sure you are satisfied with the answers.

Do so, just as we all must if we are to go well in the bush.

TWO

Footwear

Now we will look into footwear, and let's begin with the commitment never to shortchange our feet. Whether we journey on foot in the bush for a few hours, for a day, or for many days, we will go well for only as long as our feet will stand up to it.

■ LEATHER BOOTS

For most uses in the summer and in much of the spring and fall, well-constructed boots with leather or leather and 1000 denier nylon uppers, and tough, long-wearing soles of composition rubber are best.

Top-of-the-line hikers for the most serious applications—long-stay backpacking expeditions, for example—are still built in all-leather uppers. At the same time, recent developments in boot construction, utilizing 1000 denier nylon fabric and other innovations, offer us boots that are significantly lighter than the traditional all-leather hiker, yet are perfectly serviceable for day hiking and short stay backpacking in moderate terrain.

If you propose any serious time afoot in the bush, buy a boot which has been constructed for extensive hiking. There are many good-quality leather work boots available, and they are often less expensive than first-class hikers, but few if any of these will provide the comfort and serviceability of the true hiking boot—just as, in fact, few work situations, even outdoors, will demand as much from your feet during the day as will steady walking.

Hikers are ankle high, with uppers of thick, full leather which may be stiff in the toe cap but supple throughout the remainder of the boot. Particular protection is provided to the sides and the back of the heel and ankle by a layer of cushioning material between the outer leather of the upper and the soft but durable leather inner lining. There is, as well, a built-in stiffener of tough, rigid leather around the sides and back of the heel.

The boots will open all the way to the toe to permit adjustment of the lacing tension to the whole foot, with, of course, a durable tongue for full protection beneath the lacing. The boots will lace with a combination of metal half-rings secured to the leather by riveted brackets over the toe and instep and lacing clips up the front of the ankle. The clips prevent the lace from slipping, and therefore you may lace with light tension over the foot and instep, but increase the tension around the ankle, and this difference in tension will remain.

The back of the boot above the heel should be so constructed as to provide extra flexibility. This is the point where the back of your foot hinges at every step, and a good hiking boot must accommodate that flexing. There are different methods of accomplishing this, but be sure the boot you buy provides for it.

The soles will be thick and durable with a long-wearing composition rubber grip-surface on the bottom side. There will usually be cushioning in the insole, covered by a soft leather lining to take the wear from your foot. This feature, however, is not as critical as you might think, as you can always cushion your soles with removable insoles of foam or felt.

Hikers by most manufacturers are of a definite style and pattern and, in the quality lines, will all do the job. Your main concern is to check for signs of quality in the materials and thoroughness of construction, and these become evident as you make comparisons from boot to boot. Unfortunately, as is usually the case, quality costs money, and before you have been shopping from store to store for long you soon discover that some boots are not only clearly better built than others, but also more expensive.

If you are a novice, try to find an experienced hiker to help you choose and fit your boot. If this isn't possible, then look at all the boots offered by every store within reach, and keep looking until the differences in quality begin to be evident to you. When you are choosing the fit wear a heavy wool sock and be sure that the boot is neither tight nor loose anywhere about your foot. In boots, above all, the fit must be exactly right. You must have room in which to wriggle your toes, but not that extra room which means abrasion from shifting about in the boot.

One way to approach fit is to buy the boot which feels best over two medium-weight socks. Then you can go down one sock if, in use, you find the boot slightly snug. Some experienced hikers wear two pair of medium-weight socks at all times, buying their boots with this in mind.

A caution: some boots intended specifically for rock climbing—rather than merely hiking around the mountainsides—may closely resemble the hiker you are looking for. The difference is critical, however: the hiker has a flexible sole and the rock-climber has an extremely rigid sole. It is a specialty boot, and unless you are going rock climbing you do not want it. It is a horror for general hiking.

Now we come to the everlasting debate about the care, preservation, and waterproofing of leather boots.

First let's discuss waterproofing. Gore-Tex, as well as other fabrics intended to achieve the same waterproofing with breathability, is now available in a waterproof sewn-in sock liner or in another form of integral layer, in the construction of many good boots.

Also, a Gore-Tex sock is now offered. You wear this over your regular socks in your boots with the expectation that you will keep water out yet disperse foot moisture as vapour at the same time. A major Canadian vendor in mountain equipment is so certain you will be happy with these that they offer them with a money back guarantee.

At this writing, most top-of-the-line leather hikers do not feature a breathable-but-waterproof fabric in construction but depend on traditional boot care techniques. Whether or not you try the Gore-Tex option, I suggest you learn about these.

Some people claim that you can waterproof the leather of your boots and they will still ventilate, that is to say they will still allow the free escape of perspiration moisture. Others claim this is a contradiction; if the water can't get in, it can't get out either.

I do not propose to attempt the definitive statement on preserving and waterproofing leather boots. I will, however, offer you what seems to me from my experience to be the case.

I believe a thick leather of good quality can be made proof against short-term dampness, such as the dew on the grass of a summer's morning or a cloudburst in the afternoon or a brief passage through swampy ground. On the other hand, a boot which is flexing all day in wet grass, in my experience, is a wet boot by the end of it.

If I am going out on a day which starts with rain and promises to keep it up, I will wear a medium-high rubber boot, as I find the accumulation of a day's foot moisture more tolerable than the wet leather boots—and the wet feet inside them—that I suspect I'll have by day's end if I wear my leather boots.

I use a boot grease regularly. I use it to keep the leather soft and pliable and to extend its life. Also, I use the grease to get such waterproofing as I can. I'm a little dubious about these claims that you can waterproof the leather and still have it ventilate with much effectiveness. I'm quite sure that the more waterproof I manage to make the boot by constant dressing, the more dampness I have inside the boot by day's end. At the same time, however, there is absolutely no doubt that, as long as a leather boot does keep the water out, it is far more comfortable than a rubber boot, especially in hot weather.

I find some foot moisture in my leather boots by the end of the day in any case. Since I am often out in the bush for many days in succession, usually returning to my home camp each evening, I keep two pairs of hikers in service, wearing each pair on alternate days. Each pair then has a day between uses to dry out thoroughly and, if necessary, to receive a dressing of boot grease. In the bargain I have the advantage of boots fully free of foot moisture in which to start out every morning. At the price of good hikers this is a whopping investment in boots, but since I live a large part of my life on my feet in the bush it is, for me, altogether worth it.

Before we leave the open-season boot, the boot traditionally suitable from late spring through to early fall, we must consider an option now offered which can extend the useful season of this style of boot: the incorporation of an insulating layer in the boot frame. At this writing, material under the trade name Thinsulate is the most common.

I have a pair of mid-priced hikers incorporating this insulation. In outward appearance these are open-season boots, but I never wear them in summer. I use them considerably in late fall, and in winter for limited excursions where snow depth is not a factor. I have found these boots comfortable at much colder temperatures than I thought likely at first, and if you live where winters are moderate, you may find they will see you through the season. In my view, the incorporation of Thinsulate or other equivalent material does not convert a summer boot into a winter boot for serious use in a hard winter. It will, however, offer you considerable comfort in late fall and early winter, delaying the day when you must inevitably go to felt packs or moccasins.

■ RUBBER BOOTS

Rubber boots are useful over a surprising range of conditions, but what you wear inside the boot is crucial.

There is a nine-inch-high, lace-up rubber boot of the ordinary work variety which has been around in the same basic version for generations. It can be bought in most places for less than twenty dollars, and many people use it whenever conditions underfoot are sloppy. Some users also find it useful as a cold-weather boot. I use it extensively in spring and fall weather, and on very wet days in summer.

This boot is not to be confused with the oversized rubber boot with a leather upper in which you install a full, felt removable liner. This traditional rubber work boot is sized in width and length as is any other work boot, but is provided with greater depth so that you have room for one or two insoles, depending on their thickness, beneath your foot.

The significant fact about rubber boots is that they are totally waterproof. They keep out the slop and they keep in the foot moisture, and you will have no success with these boots if you do not deal properly with this foot moisture that is retained and accumulating.

Many users find that if they buy the boot large enough to wear two pair of medium-weight wool socks and at the same time keep one or two felt insoles in the boot, they will have good results in much of spring and fall weather and on thoroughly wet days in summer. The wool socks offer their usual comfort because the felt insoles will absorb and store enough of the excess moisture.

It is crucial to realize that this is a one-day-at-a-time arrangement, and you must, without fail, thoroughly dry out the socks and the insoles at day's end, either in camp by the fire or at home in the furnace room.

Now this is not at all a wise arrangement in truly cold weather. It will work for a few hours in the morning perhaps, but as the insoles become thoroughly damp they simply freeze up—and you will too if you persist with this nonsense. I have tried it, and it is instructive, to say the least, when you find the insole frozen fast to the bottom of the boot.

The secret to converting this inexpensive rubber work boot into serviceable cold-weather footgear is a mesh insole. You can make your own with built-up layers of screen-door mesh, or you can buy a tough insole of nylon mesh in most stores where first-class cold-weather footwear is sold.

First, buy the boot large enough that you have a good fit with two medium-weight socks on for basic insulation—three if you tend to need extra insulation about your feet. Then buy or make the mesh insole. If you make it, simply build up the layers of screen until the insole is almost a quarter-inch in thickness, which is a little over half a centimetre.

Place the mesh insole in the bottom of the boot, and, if there is enough space left in the boot when you try it on your well-socked foot, add a felt insole on top of the mesh.

Now, improbable though it may sound, this trick with a mesh insole is widely used in very cold weather in the north. The mesh insole creates a storage space for foot moisture. The moisture moves down to the mesh so effectively that your socks remain substantially dry and fully effective throughout the day. At day's end you must take the insoles out of the boot and let the accumulated moisture dry out.

■ FELT PACKS

Great improvements have been achieved in recent years in the category of boot variously called felt packs (or pacs), pac boots, or just plain packs. They descend from the first attempt to improve a rubber boot for cold weather use by giving it a leather upper and making it large enough to install a full liner of wool felt.

Boots in this category, and there are many versions to choose from, have a rubber lower structure which encloses the foot, a leather or densely woven nylon upper extending up the leg, and at minimum a full liner of felt. The boots for coldest weather have a combination of removable mesh and felt insoles and one or more removable liners of felt or duffle cloth.

Good felt packs offer excellent protection for your feet in cold weather. Do remember that if the boot is to work as intended, you must remove the liners and insoles immediately after use then set them to dry. If you fail here, the boots will fail you tomorrow. As your boots go, so will go your feet.

Some makers are providing a comfort rating for their boots, expressed as the degree of cold in Fahrenheit or centigrade to which the boot, they claim, will keep you comfortable. While this rating system is a helpful guide to the relative insulating strength of different boots by the same maker, I caution you not to take these ratings at face value. One maker offers a boot "comfort rated to –100°F." Few people alive have experienced –73°C (–100°F), but those of us familiar with –57°C (–70°F) will tell you that only in actual use will you discover to what extremes a particular boot will give you comfort. If ever you have the heady opportunity to go afield at –100°F, do so with extreme caution and take nothing for granted about *any* of your gear.

■ MOCCASINS

Now very popular for cold-weather footwear in the north is the high-topped moccasin, made of Indian-tanned moosehide with a canvas upper. I have used it with such success that I am tempted to claim for it more than perhaps in all circumstances it can offer.

The moccasin is exclusively for use in weather that is so cold that the snow is consistently dry. It is true that you can get by in wet snow during a spell of soft weather to some extent by wearing a rubber overshoe outside the moccasin, but this is not as practical at such times as a rubber boot.

The moccasin, unlike a boot, allows foot moisture to escape constantly into the atmosphere, and you do not have the problem of retained moisture to deal with. Although seasoned moccasin-users do always put socks, and felt liners if they use them, where they can dry out from any trace of moisture at day's end, the socks remain essentially dry through long periods of continuous use.

I will tell you how I secured the best pair of moccasins I have ever owned.

You could obtain—and still can, I hope, but for years I have seen none—moulded boot-socks of hard felt. A soft felt abounds these days in the boot liners which we discussed earlier, but, although useful, this soft felt is inferior to the old hard felt. This soft felt compresses underfoot and wears but a short while. The hard felt held its thickness and would wear for many seasons.

The socks made of this hard felt were seamless. The entire foot and the leg, which would reach halfway to your knee, were made all of one piece of felt, manufactured in that shape. They were without a heel. They were not a boot but a true sock, in spite of the fact that they held their shape much as a boot does.

Now, I went to the trader in the Yukon Territory who stocked these splendid felt socks, and with two pair of good wool socks in a medium weight already on my feet, I tried on felt boot-socks until I had the pair which fitted easily with plenty of toe-wriggling room.

Then I made haste to my friend the Loucheaux woman, who built a moccasin around the boot sock. The foot, to a little better than slipper height, she made of fine, soft, long-wearing Indian-tanned moosehide. Then for the legs, extending from the moosehide foot to a few inches above the top of the felt, she used a heavy but untreated canvas. At the top of the leg she inserted a drawstring so that once I had the moccasin on I could draw the string just enough to ensure a snow-tight fit around my leg.

That particular pair of moccasins, on account of the close fit of the felt on the leg, did not come outside my trouser leg. However, the overlap of trouser leg with moccasin top was sufficient that, even if I were to tramp through deep snow without snowshoes, I would have no difficulty with snow getting up the inside of my trouser leg.

I spent a good deal of time outdoors in Yukon winters in those moccasins at a range of temperatures going down to an extreme, twice, of −60°C (in excess of 70°F below zero), and not only did I never have frostbitten feet, I never had feet even mildly cold.

Ah, you say, that's all very well, but where these days do you find the felt boot-socks and the Indian-tanned moosehide and an experienced Indian craftswoman, unless you are fortunate enough to live near where all three are available?

And I say, never mind. If we lack the initiative to find alternative material which will do basically the same job and then to put together a pair of cold-weather moccasins for ourselves, we'd better stay out of the bush altogether.

First, try to find a pair of moulded, hard-felt boot-socks. Go to every possible source of supply. I doubt you'll succeed, but if we don't all try, how will anyone know what we really want? No luck? I guessed as much. Well, off to the boot shop with two pair of wool socks, medium- to heavy-weight. Try on and then buy the soft-felt boot-liners which we spoke about earlier, a pair which fits over your two socks on each foot. Put two felt insoles in each liner, as this soft felt crushes and you will need this extra material under your feet.

Now you need soft, porous leather, and in the absence of Indian-tanned moosehide, I think the best is the heaviest you can find in suede. Hobby shops which cater to the leather-craft enthusiasts are the likeliest source. You want supple leather which will let moisture pass through freely. Don't worry if you must buy a leather much lighter than you would expect to need in footwear. Snow is not hard on moccasins, and a little later on you will see that the rules forbid you to wear your best cold-weather moccasins anywhere but in snow or on camp brush, particularly since you are going to all this trouble to make them.

You'll need a piece of leather about 18"× 18" for each moccasin, so buy a piece 18" × 36". If you're new at this sort of thing, these dimensions will allow you a little room for waste. Also, you must find a store which sells a fairly stout canvas, untreated of course, and buy two-thirds of a yard of 36" material, that is to say a piece 2′ × 3′.

You will sew these moccasins by hand, unless you have a machine which will handle leather and canvas and some experience in using it. I won't discuss it in detail now, but in a later chapter you will read all about an excellent lock-stitch sewing awl which anyone who goes seriously in the bush will find invaluable. You can use this awl to sew your moccasins.

Figure 2:1 shows how to cut out your leather; I do not prescribe the dimensions, as these depend on the size of your liners. Perhaps the best method is to make a pattern out of some old canvas or denim. Begin a little on the large side and trim down until you have a fit. Only then should you cut into your precious leather, working from the pattern. Figures 2:2 through 2:7 show the subsequent steps in construction.

The final thing you'll want to do is put a couple of stitches through both the liner and the legging at the back just above the top of the leather, making sure as you do so that the liner is firmly

How to Make a Moccasin

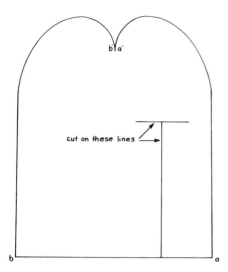

cut on these lines

b   a

Figure 2:1

All seams can be inside the moccasin.
Keep work inside out while sewing. Seams on
leather can be close to the edge. Canvas should
have 1" margin if edges are
left raw.

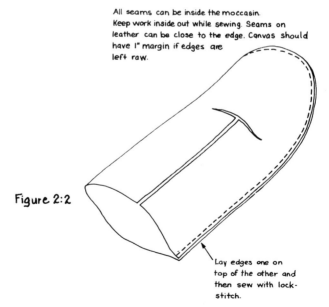

Figure 2:2

Lay edges one on
top of the other and
then sew with lock-
stitch.

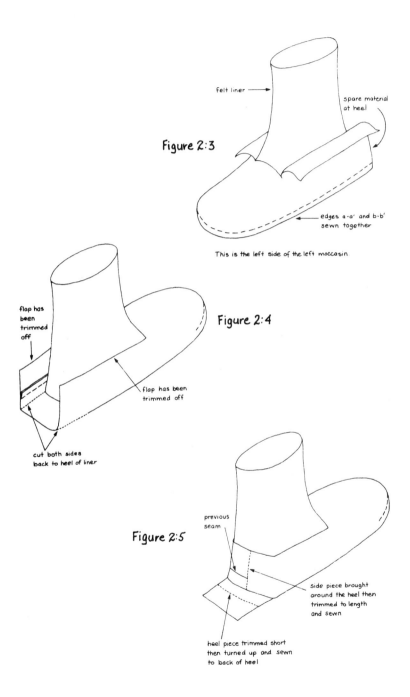

felt liner

spare material at heel

Figure 2:3

edges a-a' and b-b' sewn together

This is the left side of the left moccasin.

flap has been trimmed off

Figure 2:4

flap has been trimmed off

cut both sides back to heel of liner

Figure 2:5

previous seam

side piece brought around the heel then trimmed to length and sewn

heel piece trimmed short then turned up and sewn to back of heel

Cut canvas into two pieces 24"x18", then lay out
leg piece thus:

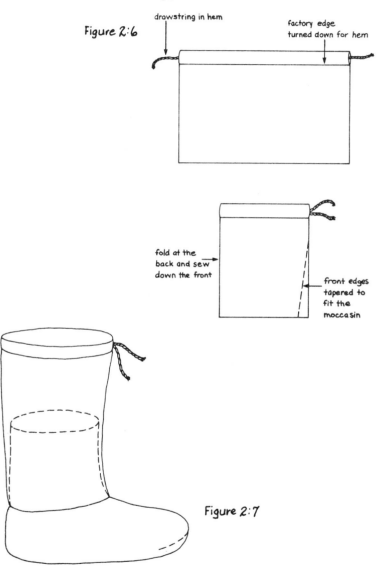

drawstring in hem

Figure 2:6

factory edge
turned down for hem

fold at the
back and sew
down the front

front edges
tapered to
fit the
moccasin

Figure 2:7

Legging made to fit and sewn to moccasin.
Drawstring placed in hem at the top to ensure
snug, not tight, fit around trouser leg.

down all the way to the bottom of the moccasin. Without this, the moccasin will have an annoying tendency to creep down the heel at the back and create a fold just at the bottom where the heel turns. This fold fills with snow which turns to ice, and though perhaps it does no great harm, you'd rather be without it. The stitches through both legging and liner will prevent this, and don't worry that you now cannot remove the liner from the moccasin. If by chance it does get wet, it will dry through this sort of leather quite readily.

Having this finest of cold-weather footwear is no use, however, if you don't understand the importance and the methods of keeping it in first-class condition.

First of all, this is a dry-snow moccasin. If the snow is wet, wear your rubbers. Generally speaking, the snow will be reliably dry from –10°C (14°F) on down. However, you will sometimes have snow falling at this temperature which is mainly dry but will turn wet quickly under the pressure of your foot, and thus you can end up with wet moccasins. (You will also end up with wet mitts if you are doing work which brings your mitts frequently into contact with the snow.) The guideline of –10°C is a good one, but keep an eye on what is happening near that upper limit.

Second, and this is *vitally* important, these moccasins are your cold-weather snow moccasins, *not* your house slippers. Never wear them indoors or in town on sidewalks. They can be used if you are driving a poorly heated vehicle in severely cold weather, provided you put a blanket or some spruce or fir brush on the vehicle floor to ensure that they pick up no dirt from that source.

I once watched with interest how some hunters who lived in cabins in an arctic village kept their best outdoor moccasins clean. They kept an old pair of moccasins hanging on the *outside* wall beside the door and would change to these *before* stepping through the door, thus preserving their outdoor pair.

Why all this scrupulous care? Indian-tanned hide, and the soft, porous leather, which will do the job if Indian-tanned hide is not available, helps keep you warm by constantly passing the perspiration moisture from your feet outward. The main job of insulating is done by the wool socks and the felt liner. Often in the north the liner is of duffle cloth, and this is excellent. Another alternative is just plenty of socks, several pairs. But whatever your main insulation, the hide in the moccasins allows the release of moisture. You stay both *warm* and *dry*. Anything which inhibits this free passage of foot moisture through to the outside reduces the effectiveness of the process. Clean moccasins work splendidly. Dirty moccasins work poorly. Keep your moccasins clean.

If, in the course of the day or when camping at night, you spend time standing or sitting beside a campfire, put brush down to put your feet on. This way, the warmth of the fire making the snow wet doesn't indirectly make your moccasins wet at the same time.

Finally, if you make camp, by whatever method is available to you to meet your particular need, put lots of brush on the ground in your camp. Walking from clean snow onto clean brush keeps your moccasins clean.

■ THE POLAR BOOT

Now, having talked all this time about the importance of getting foot moisture out of the way in order to keep warm, I will present you with an apparent contradiction: footwear in which all your foot moisture stays right in your sock but which keeps you warm nonetheless.

There is a boot developed for and used by the United States military called the polar boot. It consists of two rubber walls with a tough felt insulation between the walls. This layered construction includes the sole area and comes well up the ankle.

The insulation is completely sealed between the inner and outer wall, and you will only see it if, after you have worn out a pair of these boots, your curiosity sends you into the walls of the boot with a knife.

In this boot the foot moisture you generate is all retained, and at day's end your foot and sock are wet. Still, you have kept warm because the sealed-in felt insulation has kept dry—and thus effective. Your sock plays no part in the insulating function.

In all other boots and moccasins it is vital to keep the socks dry because they are the insulation; in the polar boot the sock serves only to protect your foot from abrasion against the boot.

■ SUMMARY

Now, for serious use in the bush I advise against any kind of conventional footwear which has a non-removable liner of fleece or

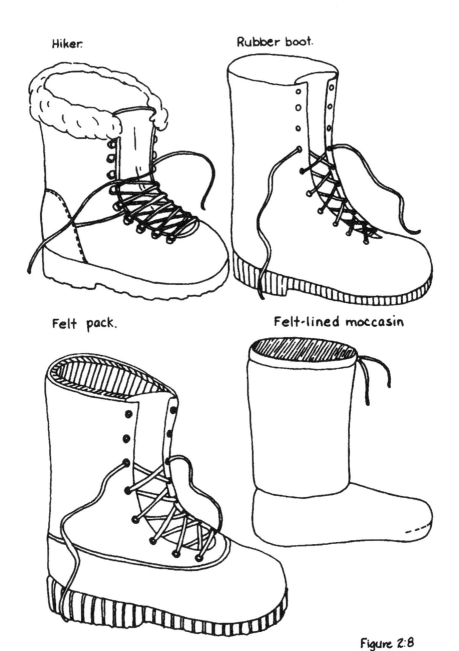

Hiker.

Rubber boot.

Felt pack.

Felt-lined moccasin

Figure 2:8

pile secured into the boot. It is just too difficult to dry the liners when you cannot remove them, and when the liners wear out you do not have the simple option of installing new ones.

I know that some lined leather boots can be comfortable for many hours if the leather allows good passage of foot moisture and if the boot opens well down to the toe to facilitate overnight drying. I also know that sheepskin- or pile-lined boots feel seductively cozy when you try them on in the shoe store, but they are a poor choice for serious use in the bush.

So there we have five basic kinds of footwear for general use throughout the seasons: leather hikers, rubber boots, felt packs, moccasins, and polar boots. In rubber boots and felt packs, the mesh insole is important for use in very cold weather.

But, you say, you cannot ski in moccasins or polar boots. Well, of course you cannot, but then you must have something along in the pack to turn to if the temperature drops and coincidentally you do not come out of the woods by nightfall.

Moccasins take up little space in the pack and will keep your feet safe after you stop to camp in far tougher temperatures than will ski boots.

Another choice is the down- or fibre-filled bootie with a composite sole. These would be a poor choice for the trail, but once you have the emergency camp together, they will see your feet through a very cold night, something you cannot say for a ski boot once the skiing activity is over.

If you ski in thoroughly crisp temperatures, you may well have insufficient protection in the boot, notwithstanding the vigour of your activity. Ski boots are not cold-weather boots. But you can buy a slip-over filled boot which will provide some essential insulation to the outside of the ski boot.

Now these latter products, the bootie and the slip-over ski boot, do not have general application to bush travel and are somewhat outside my scope, but they do represent the sort of useful innovation now available within specialized gear for a particular activity. If you know what cold-weather footwear has to have about it to do the job, then you know when you look at a special-purpose boot, such as a ski boot, whether it will do the job or whether you must beef it up when the temperature drops.

As your feet go, so usually goes the rest of you. If you would go well in the bush you must take care of your feet.

THREE

Miscellaneous Equipment

In the course of the chapters to come we will discuss many items of equipment and their uses. In passing we will make reference to uses without stopping to consider in detail the gear itself. We will, for example, say much of the need to have some essential gear and supplies along on a day hike, but nothing of the sort of pack in which we might carry it all. We will talk of the sorts of things we can do with an axe, but not much of the axe itself.

So, before we proceed, let us tidy up a few loose ends of that sort.

The enormous growth in popular interest in backpacking has brought great advances in useful, light gear and packs to carry it in. There is, in fact, a wider choice than there needs to be, with much opportunity for satisfying personal preference, apart from meeting specific needs.

■ PACKS

Which kind of pack should I have? is a primary question, and the answer is dictated largely by what you will be using it for. What suits for a day hike may not be the best for an aircraft journey.

CORE EMERGENCY KITS

Before we deal with that, however, we must deal with an even more primary concern: the separation of gear between the general pack and the much smaller collection of emergency items. There is widespread consensus that, since mishap may separate you from the larger volume of general gear, prudence demands that you have somewhere strapped to your person a compact package of core items with which you can manage after the loss of everything else. Travel by canoe perhaps best illustrates the need for this precaution: if you are dumped in fast water, you will have with you on reaching shore only as much gear as is inseparably fixed to your person. The rest will have gone down river with the overturned canoe.

It is harder to argue the necessity of this separation of core items on a day hike. If I carry a tear-drop pack with a waistband and a cross-tie between the shoulder straps at chest level, what likelihood is there that mishap will deprive me of the pack? It is arguably more securely fixed to my body than a kit carried by a single crossed-over shoulder strap.

Perhaps the clinching argument for the need for this separation between the general pack and the core emergency kit for the day-hiker is this: when you once have decided on the core items and have assembled them in a separate compact container, you need only pick up the container to know you have with you everything it is intended to have inside it. The day pack is loaded and unloaded frequently, and often something is forgotten. The emergency kit is never opened, except in the emergency for which it is carried; therefore there is no chance of items being forgotten.

If you believe that your day pack is as secure as you require for your core emergency items, you might wish to assemble these items in one package, which then remains permanently in the day pack with no chance of being disturbed by the sort of packing and unpacking of general gear which you will go through on an outing.

When you travel by any conveyance that calls for your general pack to be stowed during transit, the argument for separation of the core emergency items is unassailable, and these core items should be securely fixed to your body.

Now I do not intend to prescribe what should be in your general pack and what in your compact kit. Out of the ideas you will gain from this book, and from the practice you will undertake in the field, you will develop your own set of core items. If your experience is similar to mine, you will hope dearly never to be removed from your general pack, for a great deal of comfort and convenience will be lost if it goes. You will, at the same time, develop complete confidence in your ability to manage if you should be reduced to whatever is left about your person after mishap robs you of the general pack.

I do suggest you avoid the already-assembled personal survival kits which you can buy. These invariably contain items you will never use, and are often little more than a gimmick to separate people from their money.

Some items that should be included are obvious: the means of making fire, some strong line, a little snare wire. Others will be unique to the individual: a supply of an essential prescription medicine, a tension bandage for a bad knee, spare eyeglasses. Some items may be carried separately: if I have a stout knife securely fixed to my belt, I do not need another one in the separate kit of core items.

Do some thinking and do some practice in the field. If you have the concern and the intelligence to apply yourself to safety in the bush, you have what it takes to work out what should be in your personal emergency kit apart from what should be in your general pack.

TYPES OF PACK

Compact Packs

Now what about packs? First, consider the compact pack for the core items. Of increasing popularity is the fanny pack. It is secured by a wide strap around the waist and, as the name suggests, rides on your hips at your behind. It fits so that you can wear different sorts of packs above it without interference.

Another recommended pack for the core items is the metal container, of a size which can be fixed to your belt. You can, in fact, have two such containers on your belt at the same time, and the containers can be used in an emergency for carrying water and for cooking. They may be sealed watertight for your travel with strong plastic tape, and if you are dumped, they offer the advantage that they will have a slight net buoyancy. Used in a canoe, however, they must not interfere with your life jacket.

I have not seen them, but I have heard that there are now gear pouches of different sizes for canoe travel. They are sealed and inflated after being packed with gear, and a small version of such a pouch would be ideal so long as it functions as intended.

Some people prefer to use a stout canvas pouch about the size of a binocular or camera case. It is worn with a shoulder strap, but for security the strap must be passed over the head to the far shoulder.

I have seen it recommended that one can sew the components of an emergency kit into convenient locations on a favoured outdoor garment. The idea does not much appeal to me, but it might have value in some applications.

It is not vital that the container be waterproofed, provided any contents needing waterproofing, such as your matches, are individually protected. It *is* important that, even if the pack is waterproofed, such items as matches are waterproofed as well. Do not rely solely on the waterproofing of the container.

General Packs

Now what about the general pack? There is a profusion of packs on the market, and many of them are splendidly constructed and highly suitable to their purposes. The serious makers and suppliers have informative catalogues which you can read in addition to inspecting the packs at the retail store. Also, the outdoor stores often have backpacking magazines in which articles about packs are abundant and well worth reading.

I will not attempt to cover every choice but will review some main considerations to have in mind.

For light loads a frame is not required, and because it tends to restrict freedom of shoulder movement, it is usually avoided in a day pack. For heavy loads the traditional popular choice has been the external frame with hip belt. The frame ensures even pressure across the back, and the load weight can be divided between the shoulder straps and the hip belt. Between these extremes there exists an innovative variety of packs that have either internal frames or no frames at all, but are constructed to offer comfort between the load and your back. This, of course, is a principal reason for having the frame in the first place.

My own choice for a day hike is the tear-drop-shaped soft pack with two compartments. A fanny pack may be worn beneath it for the core items which one has assembled against an emergency and which one does not open unless the emergency occurs.

For heavy loads I favour an external frame with hip belt. If I am out for the day in hunting season and expect to bring in a first load of meat, I will wear the frame pack. On the other hand, if I am not so optimistic I might wear the light soft pack for its comfort, but carry enough line to hang the meat should I make the kill. I would then return the next day with the frame pack to begin carrying meat to camp. The frame pack interferes with a shoulder-slung rifle, whereas the soft tear-drop pack does not.

If I should travel by bush aircraft, I would take as luggage my frame pack with my general gear strapped to it, and, believe me, if the craft were forced down I would hope to have access to the contents of that pack. I would, in addition, have a small package of core items secured in some way to my person. A good part of the reason for the frame pack in this instance is that a frame pack designed for heavy loads can be very useful around a downed aircraft camp and, in addition, people have been known to have travelled out on foot from such camps. I also prefer a heavy-duty frame pack with hip belt when carrying gear for many days of travel.

■ SLEEPING BAGS

A sleeping bag is not, of course, a day-pack item, but if you are travelling by bush aircraft you are well advised to have your own, notwithstanding that regulations call for the aircraft to have one on board for each passenger. The fact is they often do not.

Once more, there is a profusion of sleeping bags about. The backpacking buffs are the people now who know most about sleeping bags, and very useful articles on the subject appear in backpacking magazines. Also, as with packs, the best of the manufacturers put out catalogues with much useful information about the fill, the type, the construction, and the seasonal suitability of different bags. Read all that you can lay your hands on and track down some enthusiastic backpackers in order to benefit from their experience.

Backpackers go for the lightest bag that will do the job in the season, and usually prefer down fill, except where the possibility of getting the bag wet is an overriding consideration, in which case fibre fill is preferred. However, remember from the discussion of fibre fill in Chapter 1 that a synthetic fill prepared specifically for garment and sleeping-bag fill should be chosen.

For your bush aircraft outfit you do want a light, compact bag so that you take the least possible weight and bulk on board. The difference in weight between down and fibre fill is slight enough that, for the advantage of a fill which will still be of some use when wet and can be easily dried, I recommend fibre fill.

As to style, the mummy bag is the lightest for equivalent insulation strength and makes into the most compact package in a stuff bag. Some people find the mummy bag too constricting and must go to a semi-rectangular bag, but for small-aircraft travel you will be appreciated more by the pilot if you do not take on board a bulky and heavy style of roomy bag suitable to a camping trailer or bunkhouse.

A good down bag will have the down in compartments separated by baffles and sewn in such a way that the down cannot shift and no seam is sewn through both inner and outer fabrics. Fibre fill will also be so anchored and sewn-through seams will be avoided. A draft-tube system will prevent drafts at the closure, and a hood with drawstrings will be provided for head protection. A collar with drawstrings, in addition to the hood, is a feature of the best coldweather bags.

Store your bag between uses and clean it when necessary, both according to the manufacturer's instructions. Particularly, do not store a sleeping bag in the stuff bag, but loosely in a fluffed-out condition.

Now, please, do much reading, looking, and listening before you buy a bag. Do talk with people in the local backpacking fraternity. Do be cautious of ill-informed salespeople intent only on a sale. Do not be persuaded that you *must* have a down bag at much greater cost than fibre fill. Do buy a bag adequate to the season of expected use—but not more than adequate. There is no point in a winter-weight bag in high summer. Do remember, finally, that a sleeping bag needs bottom-side insulation. Brush is good if correctly prepared, but self-inflating and closed-cell pads, both widely used by backpackers, are useful alternatives.

■ AXES

In bush country there is so much useful material at hand in the form of trees and saplings that to go afield without an axe is simply to deprive oneself of convenient access to an abundant resource.

Even in bush country where there is some restriction on cutting green material, considerable use can be made of dry. In an emergency one uses green wood and brush as much as necessary in any case.

But what sort of axe should you carry? In the milder seasons one hardly needs more than a belt axe, but it should be a good-quality belt axe, and quality is usually evident. A well-made head securely fixed to a straight-grained hardwood handle with an overall length of twelve to fourteen inches will serve you well.

Those who carry a belt axe frequently on a day-in-and-day-out basis often spend rather more money to have an axe in which the head and the handle are of one piece of steel and the handgrip is built up with leather. There is a little more weight to this axe, and the balance in the hand is better.

Keep a good edge on your belt axe, then use it with care, and you will find that you can manage wood of a surprising dimension with much success.

All aircraft flying in bush country should have on board a full-sized camp axe as part of the emergency gear in any season.

What about the foot traveller in winter weather? What sort of axe should he carry?

If you have made *and tried* some snow shelters and have decided that this is your way to go, then the belt axe will still serve your needs.

If, on the other hand, you have decided to rely on a lean-to and fire, then there is much to be said for carrying a camp axe of about twenty-four inches overall length. Enclose the head in a leather sheath and you will be able to sling the axe from the day pack with little inconvenience. You will also know that, should circumstance call for it, you will be able to produce a huge pile of firewood in a very few minutes. You will manage a dry-standing snag of up to eight inches or more in diameter, and with fire logs of this dimension you can look forward to long sleeping-intervals between additions of fresh fuel.

■ KNIVES

Next, what sort of knife should one carry in bush country?

For many years I always carried a folding pocket-knife of a standard two- or three-blade variety, and then during those seasons when I might be hunting, I would carry as well a fixed-blade knife of about ten inches overall length. This was carried on my belt and was the sort known as a hunting knife.

Now, this meant carrying two knives much of the time, and in recent years I have begun to use instead a larger folding knife with two blades. The knife is about five and a half inches closed, and is carried in a secure pouch on the belt. It may be secured further with a thong. I keep both blades well sharpened and therefore I always have one sharp blade in use and another in reserve.

Some people feel that a folding knife is unsafe, for you may inadvertently close the blade on your fingers while using it. If this concerns you, it is possible now to buy a good folding knife with a locking device to secure the open blade in position.

This larger, belt-carried folding knife replaces both the pocket-knife and the rigid belt-knife I once used, and I have found it the best alternative in most respects. I spend time in camp year round, and use my knife countless times every day for a variety of purposes. The pouch and knife go on with my belt and trousers in the morning and off with them at night.

Now knives of all sorts are manufactured and sold to satisfy a status yearning connected with knives from which large numbers of men suffer badly, even men who have little need for a knife at all. The material and workmanship in these knives are excellent, and they are often perfectly functional knives into the bargain. They are also terribly expensive, and your object should be to find a knife of first-class, functional quality without expensive embellishments. Such knives do exist.

■ SEWING MATERIALS

Now the maintenance of clothing and footwear is important to safe venturing in the bush. The sewing skills of Indian women were central to aboriginal life, and no serious outdoors person overlooks the importance of needle and thread. Waxed linen has long been favoured as a tough, all-purpose thread for outdoor clothing repairs, and now you can buy a superb thread of polyester and cotton. It is much lighter than waxed linen but remarkably strong. The brand I have is seventy-eight percent polyester to twenty-two percent cotton, and I use it for everything from sewing on shirt buttons to building tipis.

I believe the day-hiker's kit of core items should contain a couple of strong needles and a few yards of polyester-cotton thread, or alternately some waxed linen. Two or three strands of waxed-linen thread wound together will make a stout string, and if you have plenty of this thread you have both thread and strong string in the one item.

For any kit that I am going to take for a longer time out, I favour a sewing awl to a needle, though one must accept the greater bulk and weight. I have had in my outfit for years, and constantly use in camp, an awl with which I can repair not only clothing and canvas but leather as well. The handle is hollow and contains a supply of needles, while in front of the handle and just back of the working needle is a reel which holds ten to twelve yards of waxed thread.

The sketch (Figure 3:1) shows you what to look for, and I expect

Figure 3:1

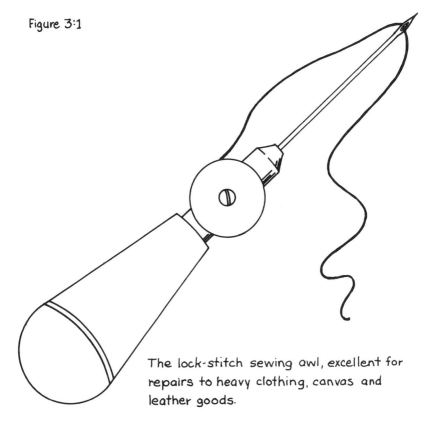

The lock-stitch sewing awl, excellent for repairs to heavy clothing, canvas and leather goods.

your best source would be a leathercraft and hobby-supply shop. If you have no luck locally, you can write to the C. A. Myers Co., 7007 N. Glenwood Avenue, Chicago, Illinois, who have made and supplied an awl of this type for many years. Even if you never find need to put this awl into your field kit, you will be delighted with its usefulness at home in maintenance and repair of your outdoor gear.

■ LINE AND ITS USES

Line of many dimensions and strengths is enormously useful in the bush and about camp. I go through so much line in the course of the seasons that I suspect my dogs of eating it in wholesale lots.

Certainly some line, from fishing line on up through stout cord to light rope, should be among the core items that are fixed to your person and will stay with you through whatever mishap. You will want to think this requirement through carefully, and then refine it by actual use when you put together practice camps.

You can buy line of twisted or braided strands. Braided line has the advantage that, apart from tufting out a short length at the end, it will not unravel. However, the tendency of twisted strands to unravel is easily prevented (Figure 3:2a and b).

Synthetic line of nylon or polypropylene is much stronger in a

Knots That Prevent an End from Unravelling

Snug this knot down and the rope end will not unravel. You can improve on this by splicing each end back into the rope, passing it under the first strand behind the one over which it has passed on its way out of this knot.

Figure 3:2a

Tighten this knot and you have a quick way to prevent an end from unravelling.

Figure 3:2b

given weight and diameter than any line of natural fibre. Polypropylene has largely replaced manila in most practical applications. Some synthetic lines are a little difficult to knot securely in some applications. Experience with a variety of knots so that one has alternatives will usually overcome this problem.

For many years I have used braided cotton line in what we call sash cord as a general-purpose line about camp. However, it is not as strong as synthetic line and is nowadays outrageously expensive. I like its handling qualities, but I am using more light synthetic line now in its stead.

In half-inch line I have been using polypropylene for many years. It deteriorates eventually, but not without warning, so it may be replaced in time.

Parachute shroud-line is often recommended for emergency kits. It consists of seven twisted threads, each of which consists of three smaller threads. You can use some of the line whole, some unravelled into the seven threads, and some unravelled still further to the smallest component threads.

Most twisted line consists of three strands, and will unravel successfully to these individual strands. These three strands of the original dimension will sometimes come down successfully to three or more still-smaller strands, and only trial will show what a particular line will offer in this respect.

Although one should expect to extract the lesser strands from any piece of twisted line if necessary, I think it preferable to start out with a variety.

In addition to some fishing line I would consider a hundred feet or more of very small-diameter nylon cord, suitable for lashing pieces of wood into a variety of structures. A hundred feet of this unbelievably strong cord will sit in the palm of your hand with room to spare, yet help you to make everything from shelters to snowshoes.

As an alternative to this thin-yet-strong nylon cord, I like an abundance of heavy waxed-linen thread. It does a fine job as thread, but serves as strong string as well and can be doubled for greater strength.

I would want a generous length — at least thirty feet — of soft, braided nylon line of $3/16''$ diameter in the core items against emergency, but I would have as well some medium-weight cord and perhaps more line of a slightly heavier weight in the general pack. The need will vary according to how you travel and therefore to how long you are out. Also, each person will develop individual techniques which need more or less line than others.

If you have fish net in your larger aircraft pack, have sufficient line with it for both the cork and the lead line that we will discuss later. This will save you having to use all your other line on the net, leaving none for general use in camp.

Now you must have a few knots well lodged in your head, as the usefulness of line depends on sound fastenings. Also it is of primary importance that the correct knot properly set in a particular use *can always be untied with ease even following full stress.*

The sketches which follow (Figures 3:3 to 3:12) will illustrate all this. In addition to the knots, you will find a few practical applications of lines and hitches.

64

Bowlines

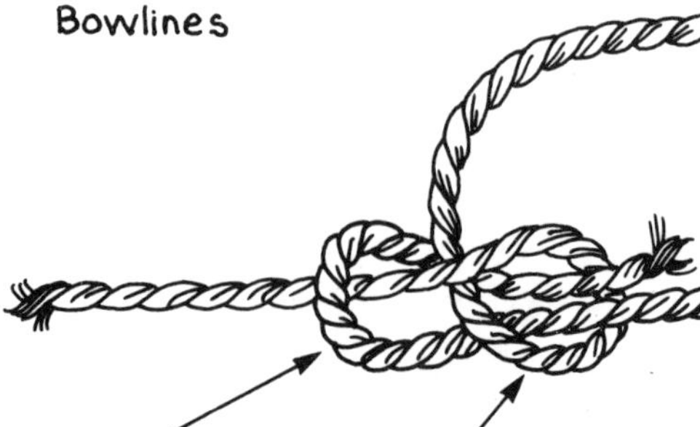

Leave this loop a little open as you snug the knot down and it will not bind.

Snug this loop down tightly.

Here is the basic bowline used to make a loop in the end of a line. You can place this around a crossbar or a tree to hold a load subsequently applied. With a little practice you will find how to set the knot so it will never bind, even under breaking strain.

The bowline used to put a running loop in the end of a line.

Figure 3:3

The double sheet bend for joining two lines of
unequal size.

The single sheet bend for joining lines
of equal size.

The square or reef knot for joining two
lines of equal size when no great strain
is expected.

Figure 3:4

Figure 3:5

Since both the sheet bend and the reef knot
will bind under heavy stress, you can join
two lines of any size with two bowline loops.
Once you get the knack of it you can set the
bowline so that it will _never_ bind.

Figure 3:6

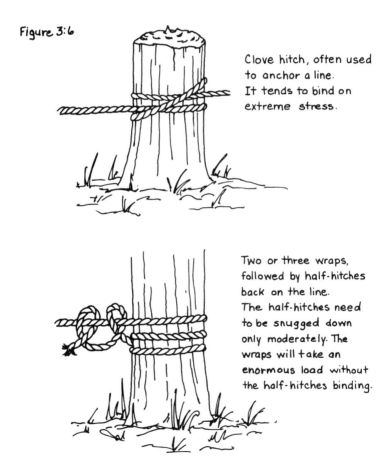

Clove hitch, often used
to anchor a line.
It tends to bind on
extreme stress.

Two or three wraps,
followed by half-hitches
back on the line.
The half-hitches need
to be snugged down
only moderately. The
wraps will take an
enormous load without
the half-hitches binding.

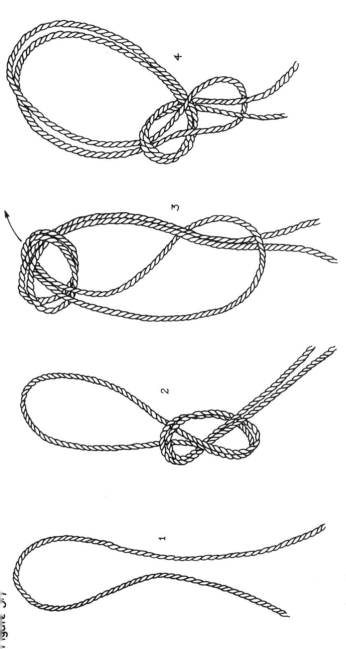

67

Figure 51

Sometimes you want a loop in the mid part of a line. Gather some line as in step1, then make a simple overhand knot as in step2. You now have a loop but the knot will bind hopelessly under stress. You must go on to the next stages of the knot.

In step3 you turn the large loop back over the knot from step2. Then you grasp the doubled line in that part of the knot indicated by the arrow and draw it out in the direction shown. You then arrive at step4 with a double loop. We call this a bowline in a bight.

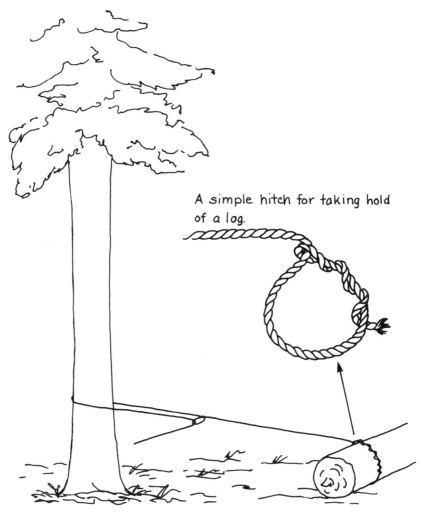

A simple hitch for taking hold of a log.

Bowline in a bight being used to gain a first stage of mechanical advantage on a draw. Once you get on to this knot you find it useful in many applications.

Figure 3:8

Figure 3:9

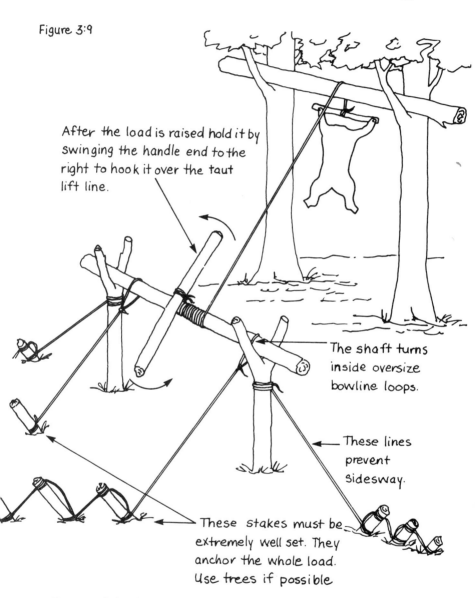

After the load is raised hold it by swinging the handle end to the right to hook it over the taut lift line.

The shaft turns inside oversize bowline loops.

These lines prevent sidesway.

These stakes must be extremely well set. They anchor the whole load. Use trees if possible

Be careful when using this windlass! If you lose control of the handle it can strike and injure you seriously.

Figure 3:10

Back-up Stakes

If you use a clove hitch at each
location you can do the whole
job with one line.

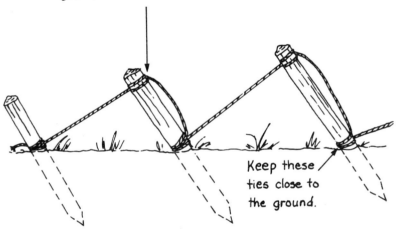

Keep these
ties close to
the ground.

When setting a stake as an anchor for a very heavy
draw, back the stake with two or more further stakes.

Sometimes, however careful you are, a dry snag you are felling for firewood hangs up against another tree. Get hold of your snag with a stout stick and a few wraps of rope as shown, and you can roll it out of the branches of the other tree.

Figure 3·11

72

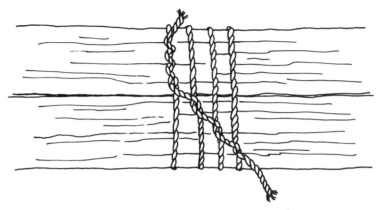

When you wish to bind two pieces of wood together
you can start your binding with half-hitches as
shown. Lay them tightly side by side and tightly
on the wood. Continue the wraps until you
have enough, covering two or more inches of
wood in a crutch stem for example, then finish
with four or more half-hitches at the end.

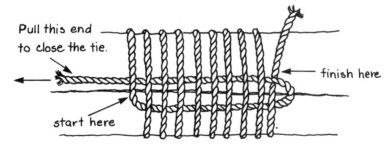

Pull this end
to close the tie.

finish here

start here

This makes a neat bind but requires very strong
cord for a long bind as the loop can be hard to
draw. Keep the individual wraps tightly side by side.

Figure 3:12

FOUR

Finding Your Way

By now you are probably growing impatient with me. After all, I've gone on for all these pages and we've only just got dressed, pulled our boots or moccasins on, and lined up some equipment. When do we get to the interesting bits about emergency shelters and setting snares and sending up smoke signals?

Well, I'm impatient, too. But remember, what we want to do is go well in the bush, preferably without getting lost in it. True, we propose to continue to go well in the bush if we *do* get lost in it — or are delayed in it by weather or injury or are simply unable to get out before dark because we ventured too far in — but first, let's spend some time on how to keep track, always, of where we are.

To go well in the bush, in the fullest sense. surely includes knowing at all times where we are.

Simply stated, if you know at all times which way you have come and where you are in relation to where you started, you know the way back. That sounds easy, especially if you say it quickly. Yet it is not easy in all terrain and is quite difficult in some. Let's do a proper job of it.

■ GETTING THE LAY OF THE LAND

First, get the lay of the land in your mind before you go into the bush. There are reliable maps available now for almost all the bush country in North America and with little trouble and a bit of forethought you can have one with you for any piece of bush which interests you.

Study the map. Where are the main roads and the side roads and the old logging tracks? Where are the watercourses, and which way do they flow, and to what main streams and rivers do they lead? Where are the main ridges, and which way do they lie?

But do more than this to get the lay of the whole ground in your mind. You will go to the point where you start your foot travel by some conveyance, usually motor vehicle. As you go along the road, stop at vantage points from which you can see parts of the high ground. Get your map out and determine your location, and then identify, on the map, the high ground which you can see. If in doubt, verify by compass-bearing.

Be concerned also with what you cannot see. You have identified a visible piece of high ground as part of this particular ridge here on the map. Well, what lies beyond it? Ah yes, it's a branch of the same stream we see beside the road here, but notice that the road swings away a mile or so before the confluence. So if we did get behind that hill we could work our way down that stream, then down this main portion below the confluence, and we'd be back to this road, hitting it upstream of where we are now.

If there is a piece of high ground above the road which might give you an overview of a significant piece of the ground in which you are interested, take the time to climb part or all the way up. Half an hour of uphill hiking will often give you an astonishing view of the whole ground, and with ease you can identify on the map everything that you see in the landscape.

Now it very often happens that, though you have the largest scale map available (*always* get the largest scale you can), the relief of the ground is not extreme enough to be picked up in detail by the contour interval on the map. The most significant feature of a stretch of bush, the one feature to which everything else can be related, may be a long ridge which doesn't show on the map at all. What does show is the far broader fact that this whole piece of upland is generally triangular and all lies at about forty-five hundred feet above sea level, and if you went twenty miles *that* way, you'd come to the Bear River. Not much help.

In such a case you may have to get the main lay of the ground by building it carefully in your mind through your own travelling. You usually have the road in as a starter. However, if the road, with lots of grass between the wheel tracks, is not on the map, you can put it there. Starting where it leaves a road that is on the map, plot its course. Bush roads often follow stream courses, which makes the task easier. Use your compass, and also record the distance between main changes in direction. Where the road passes any distinct feature such as a lake, a stream confluence, or a swamp meadow (often identified quite accurately on maps of bush country), stop to confirm the location and correct your plotting if necessary.

When you come to the point where you propose to leave the vehicle and go into the bush on foot, determine on the map the maximum perimeters of the ground you may cover. You are here now, at this point. You are going into the bush on the north side of the road; therefore you will be bounded on the south by the road. Does the road continue generally east and west? Yes, at least for as far beyond this point as you would walk in a day (this being evident from the map or because you have gone far enough ahead and come back to fix the fact).

You crossed a stream of substance three miles back. It rises from the northwest, and to reach the headwaters is much farther than you can walk in a day.

To the east and beyond in a continued northerly direction there isn't much on the map which is going to show clearly on the ground. It's all gently undulating ground with no distinct watercourses, just an intermittent small stream here and there.

You know now what you need to know. If at any time during your travels you wish to come out, you need only travel in any direction from due south to due east and you will hit either the road or the stream.

You have taken the most critical preventive step against becoming lost. You have established, before you go into the bush, what directions you must travel in to come to clearly definable features which lead back to your starting point, and these directions will serve you no matter how far or in what direction you travel before you decide to come out. You know you can't walk far enough in the day to go around either the end of the road or the headwaters of the stream course. The worst that is likely to happen is that you travel too far in before you start to come out. In that case you make an emergency camp and finish the journey back in the morning.

There is plenty of bush country in which every little swale, every little draw, every little gravel esker, every little spruce swamp, and even every little depression which might carry water in the freshet but is now dry (so that you can't tell the direction of the flow) all look remarkably alike. Even the most experienced bush traveller often cannot say with precision where he is in such country at every moment. Yet he always knows *which direction to travel in to come out* — and you will, too, if you do your bit of thorough preparation. There is much bush country you can define on the map and know in broad scope, but which defies definition in close detail. Know where you are in relation to the definable, broad features and you won't have to worry if, from time to time, you can't make head or tail of the detail. If you always know, before you go in, which directions will bring you out, these directions will remain valid even if all the while you are on that piece of ground you spend your time walking in circles.

Need I add that you will carry and know how to use a compass for establishing a direction and maintaining it while you walk through the bush? We'll have much on the use of a compass a little later on.

In bush country of sharp relief, country where the ground rises quickly and steeply from the river and creek bottoms to the ridge tops, it is much easier to keep track of where you are at all times than it is in the flatter, gently rolling country. For one thing, the road leading in will lie in a valley and will usually run close to the stream course. For another, because of the sharp relief, the contour interval on the map will pick up the features of the ground in excellent detail. Finally, you have a constant indicator of direction — the slope of the ground. The stream course is down the slope, the ridge top is up the slope. If you go into the bush on the right-hand side of the stream course as you face upstream, you will be going upstream when the high ground remains to the right, downstream when it lies on your left.

It is still possible to run into problems. If you are travelling in heavy bush on the contour, you may make a gradual turn into a tributary valley without realizing, immediately, that this has happened. In time you will suspect that something isn't quite what you have supposed, but the way out is still easily found. You can either turn about and keep the high side of the ground on the opposite hand to what it has been, or turn downward to pick up the stream course. The tributary will take you back to the main course.

A hazard with graver consequences can occur when the objective of your day's hike is the top of the ridge. Ridge tops are often of varying width and quite irregular, with broken ground between the main slopes downward on either side. On an overcast day in heavy bush or in a low-hanging mist in the open ground on the ridge top, it is incredibly easy to mistake one main downward slope for the other. Unless something tips you off early in the game, you may not realize anything is wrong until you are down to the stream course in the valley bottom, not in the one where your car is parked but in the next one over. Into the bargain, there may be no road and you can be sure the stream will be running in the wrong direction!

Please remember to be extra careful on ridge tops in heavy bush or in low-lying weather. Twice in all my years in the bush I have actually resorted to my compass. Both times I was on an irregular ridge top and about to start down the wrong slope. The sense of certainty I had about my directions on each of those occasions is very humbling to recall.

The rule, in fact, remains the same as it does for ground of low relief and indistinct features: know, before you set off into the bush, which direction will bring you back out. If the valley and its stream course run north and south, and you go in heading east, you will, of necessity, travel westward to come out.

A serious hazard in mountain ground, particularly in poor weather, is that, though you identify and follow the correct direction to bring you out, you may run into an impassable obstruction on the way, such as a sheer drop-off. In poor weather conditions with little visibility, you may be well advised to make camp and wait for the weather to improve. When you do begin to work your way out, rely on your compass. You know you must go west to reach the low ground in which lie the stream course and the road. If you were keeping track up to this point you will know whether you came in to the north or the south of where you are now. If you don't know that, begin a lateral exploration either north or south and, when the terrain allows it, begin making in a westward direction once more. Usually it is best to retreat from the obstruction some distance before making the lateral exploration for a new route. Keep track of your movements with your compass and your watch, so you know in which direction you have travelled and for how long. This will help you to ensure that you keep moving through fresh ground until you find a way out, rather than struggling about fruitlessly over the same piece of ground and finding no way out.

Now, what about those countless people who go in the bush for all or the better part of their lives and never so much as own a compass — much less carry one — and who never consult a map? It is said of these people that they have a compass built into their heads and they never get lost.

I have known many such people, and I know that they do have methods, of which often they are barely conscious, of keeping track of where they are in relation to where they've come from. Also, all of them, at times, lose track of where they are in precise detail. They never, however, lose track in broad scope.

When you are a long time in the bush, you develop the habit of having one part of your mind constantly on the question of which way you've come, of what lies to your left and what to your right, and on which way to bear to ensure that you strike some distinct feature that is a prime reference point in that particular area. Neither is this habit of mind successful only in your home bush. I am nomadic, and not a season passes in which I do not go extensively into bush in which I have never gone before, yet this habit of mind serves me successfully, day after day, season in and season out.

Let me oversimplify to make a point. Suppose that you turn off a defined road to your left, and you pick up a trail or two which takes you generally at right angles away from the road. As time passes, you bear somewhat to the right, in exploration of a series of small sloughs where you search for sign of game. You are aware of the fact — and when the time comes you will use it — that if you bear hard right you will cut back to the road. Moreover, if you bear too hard to the right, you will cut through the ground you crossed on your way in and you can go back out the same way. Hence you will bear a little harder to the right than you reckon you might need, simply because that will be better than not bearing hard enough. Into the bargain, whenever the sun is visible, even if it can only be seen as a brighter patch in the cloud cover, you keep track of your travel in relation to it, at all times. You will then know what course, according to the sun, you must follow when it is time to come out.

In this continuing orientation you never stop specifically to consider where you are. However, you leave a practised piece of your mind constantly attending to it; you pay attention. You pay attention to whether you climb a little or descend, to whether the wind is constant or shifting and how it strikes your line of travel, to how long you travelled in one direction and thence how long in another, to what lay earlier on your left and on your right and what

lies now on your left and on your right, to whether this game trail
you have used for the past hour is, in fact, still leading in the
direction you wish to go, or whether it has shifted enough to the left
that you must now cut away to the right.

You pay attention, and you develop the skill, and you find, by
and large, that your compass stays mainly in the day pack, not in
your hand.

Yet do, please, let it continue to reside in the day pack. If you
should need it in earnest only once in all your days in the bush, it
will have been worth every mile that you have carried it.

Then, what about the winter months when snow is on the
ground? Is the need for map and compass and paying attention not
made unnecessary by the simple fact that the way out is identified
by the trail in? Turn about when the time comes and track yourself
back out.

Well, I don't dispute the usefulness of that at times. Yet I should
hate to think that, for want of a compass, at three o'clock of a
winter's afternoon you had to resign yourself to retracing all your
wanderings since nine o'clock that morning in order to resolve a
confusion about direction when a compass bearing might have you
out within the hour. Also, though it is not a usual problem in the
bush, wind-driven snow can obliterate a trail quite quickly if you
happened to travel along the edges of open spaces. The unexpected
storm complicates the task of back-tracking just as surely as it
makes it even more important to get out quickly.

In all seasons, use your map and use your compass.

Now, finally, if you travel by bush aircraft do not leave it up to
the pilot to know where you are at all times. Secure maps of the
routes you travel and have your maps with you. Bush aircraft
usually must fly in visual contact with the ground, and you soon
learn how to keep yourself oriented from what you can see from the
window on your side of the aircraft. Continuously relate the features on the ground to the features on your map. Compass bearings
won't be necessary for this, although, if you wish, you can usually
see the flight compass from any seat in a small aircraft. Because
you are well above the landscape and looking down, it is very easy
to tie the ground and the map together. In addition, you learn more
about the land and make your journey more interesting.

Then, should bad luck prevail and the aircraft be forced down,
you will know where you are even if the pilot is killed in a rough
landing. You might, for example, be only a few days' walk from

a settlement, but how would you know that, or know how to get there, if you haven't your maps and your knowledge of where you are? Furthermore, please do not suppose that in such a circumstance it will merely be a matter of looking for the pilot's maps and figuring out where you are. Pilots often do not have the largest scale of maps on board, and if you have no idea where, on those maps, you are now camped, you may waste several days in the attempt to relate the landscape around you to identifiable features shown on the maps.

Keep track on your own maps. You may save your life and the lives of others by such a simple precaution.

You may also, as I have just occasionally done, pick up the fact that the pilot has made an error and gone off course. In fairness to bush pilots, they seldom do this and, if they do, in my experience, they are not only prompt to pick it up but suitably embarrassed as well.

■ USING A MAP AND COMPASS

Having now argued the necessity of using a map and compass to keep track of where you are we should review the basic techniques, which really are quite easy, by which you use both pieces of equipment. For many this is old ground, and may be skipped over lightly; but those not certain about the use of map and compass in the field should learn these essential skills before going into the bush.

The first purpose which your map serves is to show the ground you are going into to someone who stays behind. For this purpose it's a good idea to have a second copy of any map. The first, of course, goes with you; the second stays behind with details of your planned excursion.

You say to your spouse, or a friend, or, if this is a work journey, to a colleague at the office: "Now here, on the map, is where I expect to leave the vehicle, just by the confluence of these creeks. I plan to go into the high ground to the west. The farthest I could go would be to this tributary on the north and, at the outside, to the foot of the talus below the bluffs on the west. I don't expect to be south of the place where I'm leaving the vehicle at any time."

For confirmation, on another piece of paper, you should write down the map reference of the place where the vehicle will be parked. Then you should state your expected time of return and also give some guidance as to how long your friend should wait before sounding the alarm should you not return at that specified time.

It is true that, if you are thorough enough about your preparations to be leaving this information with someone, you are probably so well prepared anyway that no alarm will ever be required. However, there are few predicaments so difficult as that of the person left with this information, who has to decide, should you not show up, how soon to press the button for a search.

So add some guidance on this as well: "Now, I don't expect any problems, but of course anything could happen. If I'm not out tonight, don't be alarmed. I've got a good outfit in my day pack and I'm well dressed, and even if I'm injured I can keep safe. Give me until noon tomorrow before you ask for help to find me."

The map reference expresses any location by giving its latitude and longitude, in that order, as degrees, minutes, and seconds north (or south) of the equator, and degrees, minutes, and seconds west (or east) of the zero meridian, thus: 49° 43' 15" N by 119° 54' 30" W. The degrees and minutes will be found on the borders of the map sheet and the seconds must be estimated. By writing the map reference on a separate note you avoid messing up the map itself with X marks or arrows, and you eliminate the confusion which can arise if you use the names of streams or of estimated mileages on bush roads.

A map is simply a picture to scale on paper of what actually exists on the ground. Watercourses, lakes, roads, swamps, power lines, and structures are represented by lines and symbols which will be defined, along with the scale, at the foot of the sheet. Vertical relief, that is to say up-and-down terrain of valleys and ridges, is defined by contour lines.

All that is required to develop adequate skill in the interpretation of these symbols, and most particularly of the contour lines, is practice in the field. Get hold of a map of any stretch of country — preferably semi-open and with fairly prominent hills and draws — handy to where you live, and spend an afternoon outdoors relating the map to the landscape and the landscape to the map. For this initial exercise it is best not to use a compass, so that you will be obliged to develop the nimble imagination which, darting back and forth between map and landscape, orients the whole in a matter of moments. You will learn more about map reading in that one afternoon than you might by reading my instructions on the subject, even if I should devote the rest of this book to nothing else.

I can offer some pointers, however. First, when you lay the map out before you so that your eye may move easily back and forth between map and landscape, orient the map, that is to say place the map in such a way that directions on the map coincide with directions on the ground. You rarely need a compass for this. There will be a road or lake or stream so readily identifiable that you need simply turn the map so that the feature lies in the same attitude on the map as on the ground. Then you stand on whichever side of the map lets you look out over the map to the features of the landscape you wish to identify on the map. *Having done this you will find that a line between where you are on the map to a feature on the map, when projected to the landscape, will lead to the same feature in the landscape.*

This small piece of technique is as useful as it is simple, and I recommend it strongly. If you do this the first few times that you set about the job of relating map and landscape to each other — which is what map reading is all about — you will never set about the task in any other way. I find, by using this technique, that I seldom need my compass to identify every feature in view as far as the map or my eye will reach.

Also, do keep the scale in mind. If a feature is clearly many miles away in the landscape, then it's going to be some distance away on the map. Make the best estimate you can, and then search in the right direction at that distance on the map, according to the scale. Once more, this is simply a question of practice; but I have found it useful, particularly when I have had to switch to a scale different from the one I have been using, to be deliberately conscious of scale.

In the same way, pay attention to the elevations of various points of high ground. The highest ground in view will be the highest ground at a like distance away on the map, and with a little practice you soon learn how to allow for the perspective which makes a hill in the foreground appear as high as a mountain in the distance.

Now go out to do your practising in some nearby spot and stay at it until you are fully confident. You will find, after a bit, that not only do you tie map and landscape together quite quickly, but that you verify features by more than one reference, thus cross-checking your conclusions. That stream mouth is this one here on the map, because it leads from that draw which comes down the mountain beyond the higher of the two humps on the ridge. And there is the

island that lies midstream in the river just beyond, do you see? It all
ties together perfectly.

Now that you have learned the basics in semi-open country of
well-defined relief, you can set yourself some tougher assignments
by going to ground of greater cover and less relief.

Next, the compass.

In its simplest form this instrument need consist of no more
than a needle, magnetized at one end, which is balanced and free
to turn on a spike. If set in any location, free of other magnetic
influences, the magnetized end of the needle will point toward
magnetic north. In a more useful model, a dial, marked off in
degrees, will lie beneath the needle, and if we know the difference at
our location between true north on the map and magnetic north as
identified by the needle, we can determine any true direction which
will serve our purpose.

Let's go through the fundamentals of this method, as this will
remove the confusion which often occurs when people attempt to
use a compass in conjunction with a map.

The planet on which we live is, for practical purposes, a round
ball. It spins in a highly consistent way, and so you can think of an
imaginary shaft that runs through the ball and on which it turns.
The points at which this imaginary shaft comes out of the ball on
opposite ends we call the poles, north and south.

Wherever you may stand on the earth at any time, a straight
line between you and the north pole represents the true north
direction. Imaginary lines representing true north, from all con-
ceivable points on the earth, will converge at the north pole.

A map is a picture of a section of the surface of the earth, and
the maps that you will use in the bush are placed on the paper in
such a way that the true north direction goes straight up the sheet.
This means that the east and west directions lie horizontally on the
sheet.

We can tell the direction from one point to another quite easily
on the map. We can estimate it closely just by looking, and we can
measure it precisely with a simple protractor. If our task is to get
out of the bush when we know where we are (even if only approxi-
mately), and we know where we need to go *but cannot see that place
from where we are*, then we have to determine on the ground the
direction that is evident to us already on the map.

For this we use the compass — but there is just one small hitch.

This magnetic north to which the compass needle points is not in precisely the same direction as the true north. We must therefore know the relationship between magnetic north and true north. This is called the *magnetic declination*, and it is given on the map, usually at the bottom.

Magnetic declination will be expressed in degrees and minutes east or west. This is illustrated in Figure 4:1.

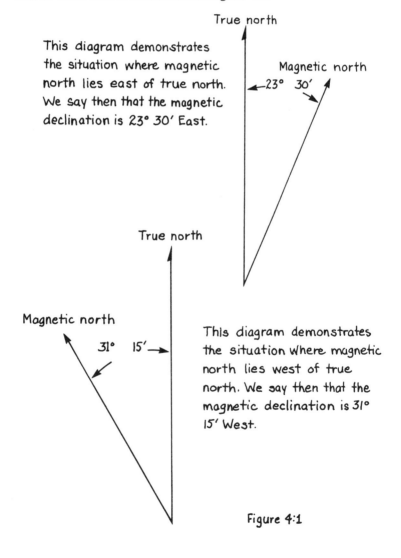

True north

This diagram demonstrates the situation where magnetic north lies east of true north. We say then that the magnetic declination is 23° 30′ East.

Magnetic north

23° 30′

True north

Magnetic north

31° 15′

This diagram demonstrates the situation where magnetic north lies west of true north. We say then that the magnetic declination is 31° 15′ West.

Figure 4:1

Suppose that the magnetic declination in an area is 25° 30' East, and you have determined from the map that you must travel in the direction of 140° in order to be certain to strike a water course which will lead you out. How do you determine the direction on the ground? Figure 4:2 illustrates the use of the compass to find the true bearing of 140°. You should bear in mind that in this diagram I am following the convention, which is now the most usual and which I

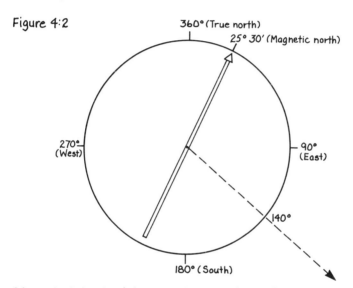

Figure 4:2

360° (True north)
25° 30' (Magnetic north)
270° (West)
90° (East)
140°
180° (South)

Steps to take to determine the direction of 140° on the ground:

1.– Turn the compass until 25° 30' on the dial lies under the needle. The needle is compelled by magnetic north and knowing that this is 25° 30' east of true north we cause the dial to indicate all directions correctly by coinciding the reading for magnetic north with the needle.

2.– We now find 140° on the dial and project the direction with our eye from the dial into the bush. We know that there is the way we now must travel in order to walk out.

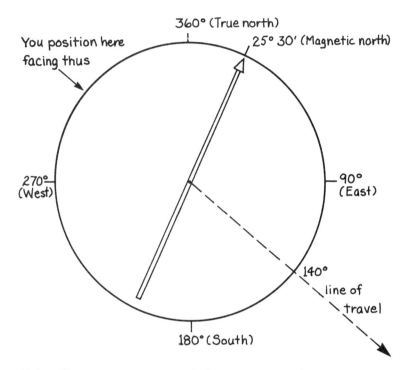

You position here
facing thus

360° (True north)

25° 30' (Magnetic north)

270° (West)

90° (East)

140°
line of
travel

180° (South)

Using the compass to maintain direction while walking.
Steps:

1.- As before, turn the dial so that the needle and
25° 30' coincide.

2.- Position yourself on the opposite side of the compass
to the line of travel, as shown, and adjust the compass
once more to the illustrated position, i.e. the needle
and 25° 30' coinciding.

3.- Start walking with the compass still held in your hand
before you and maintain the coincidence of the
needle with 25° 30' as you walk in the direction
indicated by 140° on the dial.

Figure 4:3

believe to be the least confusing, of using a compass dial marked off in a full 360 degrees, proceeding clockwise.

If the magnetic declination had been on a bearing west (say, for example, a declination of 31° 15′ West), you would convert this to the correct bearing on a full scale of 360° by subtracting from 360°, that is to say by going to the westward 31° 15′ to find magnetic north. Thus: 360° − 31° 15′ = 328° 45′.

Second, once you have determined from the map the direction that will take you from your present location to your eventual destination, you will know which way to walk so as to travel on that bearing. The next problem, of course, is how to *maintain* that direction. You set off with confidence, but not long after you have passed the specific spruce tree which the projected bearing of 140° indicated, you grow uneasy. Are you still walking on a bearing of 140°? Or have you, as is more than likely, drifted off course?

There is a simple way to use the compass to maintain direction while walking. Figure 4:3 illustrates this.

Now it's quite true, particularly if you are to walk along briskly, that the needle will be swinging to and fro, and you will also have to go to left or right of the bearing to avoid obstructions. It is difficult to be sure that you are following the course with much precision. You can help the situation by stopping a moment every so often to get the bearing accurately, simply following it as best you can between stops. You centre 25° 30′ between the swings of the needle as closely as possible as you glance down, every few steps, to the compass.

Some people can maintain a given direction in the bush with absolute ease, never having to give the matter a thought. Others, when left to their own devices, will be walking in circles in no time. This technique for maintaining direction with the compass is invaluable in such a case.

The remaining use of the compass is that of determining the direction from where you are standing to a feature or object in the landscape. Figure 4:4 shows how to proceed.

It is also important to know what sort of compass to purchase.

The simpler compasses consist of a circular box, covered by glass, in which the magnetized needle is balanced on a pin. The bottom of the box has bearings marked on it and comprises the dial. To turn the dial you turn the entire box. Some very simple compasses have no more marked on the dial than the four primary directions.

Figure 4:4

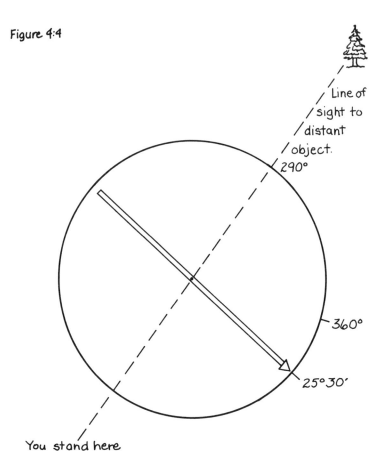

Line of sight to distant object.

290°

360°

25° 30'

You stand here

Determining direction from your position to another object.
Steps:

1.- Hold the compass between yourself and the distant object.

2.- Let the compass needle settle and then turn the dial so that the bearing for magnetic north, in our case 25° 30', lies beneath the needle.

3.- Sight across the compass to the distant object and the bearing which lies beneath your line of sight reflects the true direction from yourself to the object.

A simple compass of this type, particularly in the hands of someone familiar with bush travel, can be quite useful and save many an unexpected night under the stars. It is most often used simply as a check on the direction one takes when going into the bush, so that the direction necessary for coming out is roughly established.

If I go into the bush in a northwesterly direction, I can come out of it on a southeasterly direction and, particularly if the road runs roughly northeast and southwest, there is not much else I need to know.

On the other hand there are now available some excellent compasses of more complex design, which simplify the use of the instrument and enable you to achieve much greater accuracy. I'd give them some thought if I were you.

The prismatic compass has no needle, the dial itself being magnetized. This is a disc, marked off in degrees around the perimeter, which is free to turn on its centre. It is placed within a cylindrical box with a glass top which comprises the body of the instrument. Usually this type of compass is filled with a light, clear oil, in order to steady the spinning of the disc and cause it to settle quickly for reading a bearing. By means of a small prism, the dial can be read while the compass is held at eye level, enabling you to hold a line of sight and read a bearing with great accuracy at the same time. I have used a prismatic compass of this type to search for obscured survey monuments and have been nothing short of astonished at the results.

Because the dial and needle are not separate components in this type of compass, all bearings as read will be in relation to magnetic north and must be corrected. To convert a magnetic bearing to a true, or grid, bearing, the rule is to add the declination if it is east and subtract if it is west. Hence, with a declination of 25° 30′ East, a magnetic bearing of 95° becomes a true bearing of (95° + 25° 30′) = 120° 30′.

To convert a true bearing derived from the map to a magnetic bearing, reverse the process. If you determine from the map that you must walk on a bearing of 140° to get out to the road, then you will walk on a compass bearing of (140° − 25° 30′) = 114° 30′.

My own reckoning leads me to believe that the best compass for use in the bush is one which combines features from both the simple compass, consisting of a needle free to spin over a dial printed on the bottom of the box, and the prismatic compass, in

Three Main Types of Compass

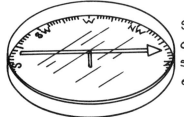

Simple compass. Dial printed on bottom of box, needle swings on a pin, glass top encloses.

Prismatic compass. Dial is in the form of a disc which floats in oil and settles in relation to magnetic north. Prismatic eye piece permits accurate reading at eye level while sighting into the landscape.

Versatile compass with declination setting which permits all bearings to be read true, not magnetic. Mirror makes possible simultaneous sighting across landscape with reading of bearing.

Figure 4:5

which the dial itself in the form of a disc spins and settles in relation
to magnetic north.

There are different styles of this sort of compass but the main
features remain the same. Once more the needle is independent of
the dial, and incorporated in the dial is a means of presetting the
magnetic declination so that all bearings as you read them are true
or grid bearings, not magnetic bearings. In the better models the
needle turns in an oil-filled capsule which steadies it so effectively
that you can walk with the compass held before you with minimal
swinging of the needle. A mirror in the hinged lid enables you to
hold a line of sight very accurately while you set the dial in relation
to the needle and thus obtain your reading. This compass also can
be used to read bearings from the map with great accuracy. The
dial turns in a transparent plate, and with the plate set in a north-
south direction on the map, the angle between that direction and
the desired direction can be read by turning the dial. Figure 4:5
shows the three main types of compass.

It is not my intention to endorse a particular product by one
manufacturer. Most products for use in the bush are available in
excellent style and quality from different makers. For purposes of
absolute clarity in this question of compasses, however, I do refer
you to a particular compass made by Silva of Stockholm which is
called The Ranger and is their Type 15T. You might want to look at
this compass, or its successor, before you invest in any compass.
Bear in mind that compasses by other makers that incorporate the
features of this particular instrument should definitely be com-
pared and considered as well. I name that specific product only to
make clear the type of compass I am talking about.

Finally, when you purchase a compass of the more complex sort
you will receive with it a very helpful book of instructions on all its
uses and applications. A compass is a long-term and important
investment for the outdoors person. Go for the best you can afford.

FIVE

Sheltering

With all the precautions you now can take against it, the possibility of becoming lost has been so reduced that it will likely never happen. Yet nothing has reduced the need to know how to keep safe through one or more unexpected nights out, for there are other reasons than being lost which can make this necessary. A severe storm, an injury, an unexpected obstruction in the terrain, or the simple business of going farther in than you had planned can all bring about the need to make camp.

Bush-line aircraft are forced down for reasons which you never expect and do not foresee. Motor-vehicle breakdown in severe weather confronts someone, somewhere, every winter, and it is damnable to hear, as I have in the winter of this writing, about lives lost for want of adequate clothing and a little basic gear that could have been loaded into the vehicle before departure. There are better ways to die than to freeze to death in a dead vehicle in the town shoes and light clothing that seemed so adequate before the engine quit, when the heater was running full tilt.

There are endless reasons for having to make an unexpected camp, and the variations of weather in each season present different problems. The nature of the bush at hand differs widely from one site to another, and the equipment in a day pack will be much less than you should find stowed in the emergency pack on an aircraft. Sheltering without a sleeping bag is altogether a different problem from sheltering when you have a fine winter-weight robe at your disposal.

■ BASIC CONSIDERATIONS

Still, to be able to cope with an unexpected night out the vital principles remain much the same: first, you should never be out without clothing adequate to the season, *with the nights of that season in mind*, as well as the days; second, you must be ready to apply yourself, with imagination and industry, to use the materials at hand, along with whatever you have in your kit, to keep safe and get as much rest as you can; finally, while you work on getting out, you must also reinforce your comfort and safety, improving your shelter and securing food according to the requirements of the particular situation.

I propose no one technique that is applicable in all situations. I will go through a variety of choices in the hope that whatever situation might confront you there will be an inventory of ideas in your head out of which you can pull some way of working with what lies at hand.

Keeping warm, and therefore safe, is not a question of keeping cold out, but rather *of conserving body heat by reducing the rate of heat loss to the point at least of safety, if not of total comfort.*

A major determinant in the difficulty of sheltering lies in whether or not you have a sleeping bag. If you are with a downed aircraft, you certainly should have, for it is your responsibility to take it on the aircraft with you; if you are out on a day's hike and are pinned down by unforeseen events, you almost certainly won't, for who really is about to turn a light day-pack into a bulky, long-stay backpack? I certainly never do and, although I will have enough gear to get by, the task of sheltering will be more difficult in the absence of a bag.

I must make another general point about the sheltering methods I will offer which, in the main, make abundant use of fire and brush and which require cutting both green and dry material from the bush around you. I am not suggesting that anyone, save in an emergency, should hack about with axe and knife. Liberal brush camping by any number of people would be an ecological travesty in much-used areas of woodland. The backpacker of good conscience takes all that will be necessary in on the pack and brings back out all the resulting waste wrappers and empty packages. He or she carries a sleeping pad, so that no brush need be cut for a mattress at night, and a light tent, so no brush lean-to need be built. Yet, with that said, the need still remains for the backpacker, as well as the day-hiker or skier or bush-plane traveller, to know what to do if an unforeseen circumstance forces him to shelter out with a minimum of gear and to fall back on forest materials for essential comfort and safety.

Now, in making shelter of any sort, it is generally true that two people together will shelter more easily than one person alone. The co-operation that is possible more than doubles the result of a given amount of work. A two-person snow shelter will be completed by two people in easily half the time that it would take one person to build a snow shelter for single accommodation. The fuel supply necessary to see one person through the night will see two through just as well. This will help you if it is your custom to go afield with one or more companions, but you must still know how to shelter alone, and your kit must be assembled for personal self-sufficiency. Much of what I present here is written for the person who is alone, yet it is adaptable to co-operative sheltering.

So, we are well clothed and we are delayed and must shelter out as best we can.

■ THE USE OF FIRE

A main problem lies in the use of fire. If you depend on fire to keep warm, you must accept that your sleep will be interrupted; to what degree depends on the firewood available and on your skill in fire-tending. If you can shelter adequately without keeping a fire burning through the night, you will sleep free of the task of fire-tending. Not all wood is the same. Sleep by a fire of lodgepole pine, started with dry and maintained thereafter with green wood, and you may sleep easily; sleep by a fire of spruce, and you run a risk of thrown embers starting a slow fire on your clothing.

I live, these years, in the lodge or tipi of the Plains Indian culture. It is, I believe, the finest of the shelters which permit an inside fire, and it has much to teach about firewood and fire management.

There are some basic rules to be learnt about ember throwing and safety: spruce is bad; pine is not bad; usually any deciduous wood is safer than any coniferous wood, but not absolutely safe. Some lots of aspen almost never throw an ember, others will throw an occasional ember and it will be hot and enduring — enough to start a slow, smouldering clothing fire. Trial of the wood is perhaps the safest course.

You should know, too, that the volume of wood necessary to keep warm increases at an astounding rate as the temperature drops. A pile of wood which will last for a month around the freezing point will go in a few nights at $-20°C$ ($-4°F$).

There is no comparison, in cold weather, between wood consumption in an open fire and in a light, sheet-metal camp heater. In winter cold, I close the smoke vent of my lodge with a strip of canvas, and then I use a camp heater, passing the stovepipe through the strip of canvas by means of a metal safety device. Wood that would last a week by open fire will last a month or more in the heater. However, so far as stoves go, in virtually all emergency camps we are in the same situation as the Indians were in aboriginal times. We have none.

Smoke is another difficulty presented by an open fire inside a shelter, whether that shelter is a canvas-covered tipi, an enclosed brush shelter on a conical frame, or a double brush lean-to. Clearing smoke from the shelter requires a flow of fresh air into the shelter, which then flows through and out with the smoke in a continuous process. In mild weather — anything down to the freezing point — this presents no difficulty, but as the temperature drops to severe levels, a dilemma confronts you: you are obliged to reduce the flow of fresh air in order to keep warm, stopping up all the inlets to make the shelter as tight as possible, so that the interior grows intolerably smoky.

Somewhere you find your compromise, trading off some heat for the essential fresh air. I'm sure that, at $-40°C$ ($-40°F$) or worse, the Plains Indians spent a good deal of their time inside their lodges wrapped in their buffalo robes. The Indians of the northern bush often wintered in brush shelters of the double-lean-to type, and an old Indian from the coast, who had married into an Interior trib in the last days of these aboriginal shelters, told, in the ninetee fifties, how as a young man he had suffered through his first winters in the interior. His eyes were constantly stinging from the smoke and his unaccustomed body cooked on the side toward the fire, yet froze on the side away from it.

A good general rule is that if you can arrange sufficient comfort to sleep without a fire, do so. If you need fire for essential warmth then get on with it at once and make the safest use of it that your circumstance will permit.

In respect of safety and other factors we will discuss fire management in detail in the next chapter but I would like to remind you of one point which we dealt with earlier: some cloth is safer near a fire than some other cloth.

Review what I told you in Chapter 1 about fabrics and fire hazard and do your own testing to your own satisfaction, but think about the clothing you wear in relation to any use of fire you reckon you might make in an emergency camp. For my part, I will sleep by a fire with more peace of mind in wool than in virtually anything else.

■ LATE SPRING, SUMMER, AND EARLY FALL SHELTERING

Let us begin in the seasons without snow, that is to say in late spring, in summer, and in early fall. Do have the mosquito net handy in summer for, if a shower does not get you, the mighty insect will.

SHELTERING WITHOUT A SLEEPING BAG

upplementary Gear

simplest camp is probably a large, spreading coniferous tree,
 you can stay close to the trunk under the shelter of the
 es. Put brush on the ground to sit or lie on and unless
 'ely heavy rain occurs, you will keep dry and therefore
 igh for safety. A good tree of this type often lets virtually
 iugh from one season to the next, and the ground
 round the trunk is almost always dry.
 supplementary gear might you have so that you
 ir your sheltering tree without having to light a
 ise a fire hazard?

Widely recommended for inclusion in emergency kits these days is the so-called space blanket, an aluminized plastic sheet which functions by reflecting body heat back to the user. You can buy them in a very light single-sheet version and in a somewhat heavier laminated style made up of several sheets. The very light ones tend to be a one-shot throw-away product, whereas careful handling will keep the heavier version in service over a number of occasions. The heavier style weighs only twelve ounces.

My trials with these reflecting plastic blankets suggest that they can be helpful in conserving body heat, and, *if used in conjunction with fully adequate clothing*, may be sufficient to see you through the night without the use of fire.

These reflecting blankets, however, will not make up for a deficiency of clothing, and you must try them out in the season in which you think you would use them to be sure you understand their limitations. *Reliance on the manufacturers' claims, particularly in cold weather, could easily lead to disaster. These are not a miracle product, and the claims made for them are seriously out of proportion to their actual usefulness.*

That said, how might you use them? Under a sheltering tree in the milder seasons you could lie down on a brush mattress and then pull one of these blankets over and tuck it in around you. You will be safe, though not altogether comfortable. The success of the venture will depend far more on the adequacy of your clothing than on the reflecting blanket.

Also, you will find condensation gathering on your side of the blanket. If you are well clothed, this may not create a problem; if you are poorly clothed, it will reduce the already limited effectiveness of your garments.

I much prefer, even to the sturdier version of the plastic reflecting blanket, a generous sheet of fairly stout and tightly woven cloth. A good sail cloth or a stout shell cloth will do; one does not want canvas because of its bulk and weight. This cloth will serve in many ways: you can tear it in strips for back-up bandages or for binding a splint; you can make a stretcher with it; you can have it in a bright colour to use for ground-to-air signalling; you can make a quick shelter with it for use before a fire; you can use it over a frame of sticks to make a fast roof on a snow shelter. You may find, as I have, that your piece of cloth becomes central to your emergency procedures, and you would not be caught without it.

What size and shape should it be? For a long while, I used

whatever came handy in a rectangular shape, since I could make a fast lean-to with it or, if it were not far off the square, a quick tent with one supporting pole under the diagonal of the piece. I found that I needed the sheet to be at least nine by seven feet to be useful, and even then one had not quite enough for the ends of the lean-to. More recently, I have become convinced of the greater usefulness of a triangular piece with all sides equal in length. These sides should be at least eleven feet long, but preferably twelve feet. Even at twelve feet to the side, the cloth need weigh no more than three pounds, and considering its versatility, it is well worth having in the emergency kit. At any given square footage of cloth, an equilateral triangle will do more for you than a rectangle. As we go through our sheltering choices you will see the uses for this cloth and the reasons why the triangular shape seems best.

Now, back to our simple shelter beneath the rain-shedding tree.

If you are adequately clothed you might just be warm enough if you lie down on your brush mattress and draw your emergency sheet over and around you. There is not much insulating strength in the fabric, but it may add enough in the mild seasons to get you safely through the night.

The Brush Mattress

I have already spoken of making a brush mattress, even in this most elementary of shelters. Insulation to prevent loss of body heat downward to the ground is crucial, during the resting hours, to any successful outdoor sheltering. When you lie down, you compress your clothing between your body and the ground and thus reduce its ability to insulate. You must provide additional insulation to compensate for this loss.

Let us talk for a moment about using brush for a mattress. Coniferous trees, particularly the spruces, the Douglas fir, and the alpine fir that grows at higher elevations and some northern latitudes, all provide brush which is essential to several elements of a bush camp — your mattress among them.

Not all trees provide good brush. Look for a tree, often to be found growing along the edge of an open clearing, which is heavily branched all the way down and on which the needles are thick on the twigs and the twigs are thick on the branches. You will soon see what a difference exists from one tree to another and which brush will pile up quickly into a soft, insulating mattress.

You do not need your axe or knife to gather the brush because you want only the branch ends and no farther up the branch stem than the place at which you can break it off with one hand. Still, do take a generous piece, as the job will take you forever if you gather only the extreme tips. Besides, the method of laying the branches in the bed effectively puts the coarse broken ends on the ground and the soft tips on top where you will lie on them.

The following sketch (Figure 5:1) will help you grasp the trick of laying the mattress.

Making a Brush Mattress

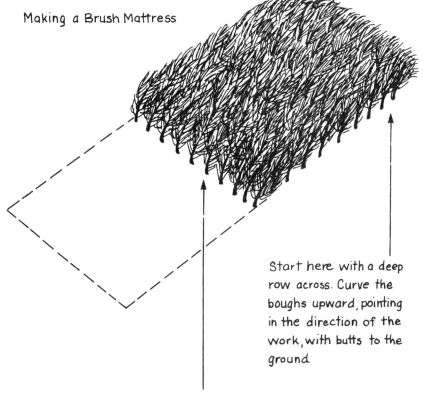

Start here with a deep row across. Curve the boughs upward, pointing in the direction of the work, with butts to the ground

Build in even rows across, butts to the ground and branches almost upright, leaning against the completed work.

Figure 5:1

You can see that once you have the first thick row across, pillow-like, at the starting end, the branches are laid almost upright. Keep them tightly together as you go, and keep the whole width (about three feet) even until the mattress is six and a half or seven feet long. By this method you get a much more insulating, even, and smooth mattress than if you merely pile the branches on the ground, all flat and one on top of the other. Should you stay in a camp several nights, you can reinforce the depth and quality of your mattress by adding another layer on top of the first one.

No ground sheet is necessary when you use brush, since ground moisture will not come up through the pile.

The Tree Shelter

Now, let's return to the main business of sheltering. You might decide that you will not be warm enough without fire, and yet you have no time to do much else but cut the night's supply of fuel. Building a shelter is out of the question.

In such a case, pick the type of sheltering tree we mentioned earlier, but make sure you can make the ground beneath it safe for a fire by scraping away all the organic debris from a large area. The fire will have to be small and will need frequent feedings. You can sit beneath the tree and tend a fire through the night, keeping in mind as you cut fuel that even a small fire will use up a great deal of wood before morning.

Once more you will want some brush to sit on, and this rudimentary camp will be much improved if you have either a plastic reflecting blanket or a generous fabric sheet to draw around your back and over your head to help contain some warmth from the fire.

I regard this as a very rudimentary way to make shelter, but it certainly can work. Some people are able to sleep reasonably well in a sitting position and catch a good nap between times of tending their small fire. Still, I would always wish to do rather better than that.

The Brush Lean-to

Often the sort of camp you put together for one night out, or the first of several nights, depends on how soon in the waning day you acknowledge the fact that you are not going to be out of the woods by nightfall. Make that acknowledgement a couple of hours before dark, and you'll have time to make a good camp; make it as darkness actually falls, and the best you'll do is sit under a tree for the night. You'll have only such fire as you can scrounge fuel for in the dark, or no fire at all.

Now the following sketches (Figure 5:2) show you an improvement on that tree shelter. This is perhaps the best known of the improvised shelters, the brush lean-to.

As to size, you want only a sleeping shelter, no more. As long as you make the lean-to long enough that you do not bump into the ends as you shift about and the roof high enough at the front for head clearance in a sitting position it will be enough. A primary purpose of any shelter intended to be used in conjunction with a fire is to trap and hold some warmth from the fire around you while you rest. In an emergency shelter, when you have no sleeping bag, the more compact the shelter the more surely it will hold sufficient warmth to let you catch good intervals of sleep.

Lay the brush on the roof frame the way you would shingle a roof on a house. Start at the ground and lay a thick row across with the butts upward and the bow of the bough outward. Then lay the next row with a generous overlap on the first row. If you have sufficient sticks in the frame you won't have a problem with the boughs falling through, and you'll find that they don't slide downward either. Brush in the ends as well. Finish up with a thick mattress under the shelter of the roof and you are ready to light your fire and be surprised at the comfort you have now made possible.

The Sheet Lean-to

However, that is still a lot of work and you would probably like an easier and faster way to make shelter. As I mentioned earlier, if you carry a rectangular sheet, you soon see that you can make a lean-to more quickly with the sheet than you can with brush. Yet in an even shorter time if your sheet is an equal-sided triangle you can make a different sort of heat-catching shelter.

The next sketch (Figure 5:3) shows you how to set up the shelter made with the triangular sheet. This shelter goes up in a few minutes, leaving most of your time for gathering mattress brush and fuel for the night.

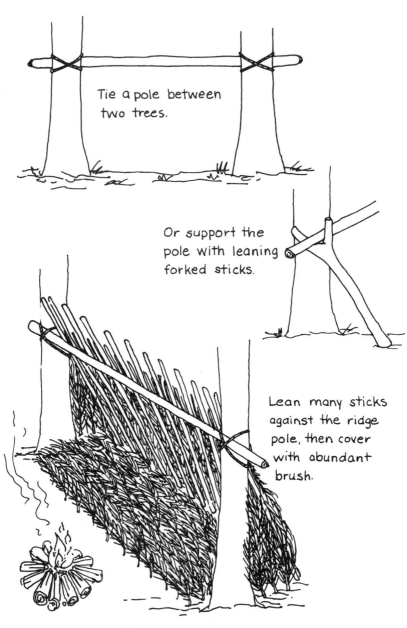

Tie a pole between two trees.

Or support the pole with leaning forked sticks.

Lean many sticks against the ridge pole, then cover with abundant brush.

Figure 5:2   The Brush Lean-to

Figure 5:3

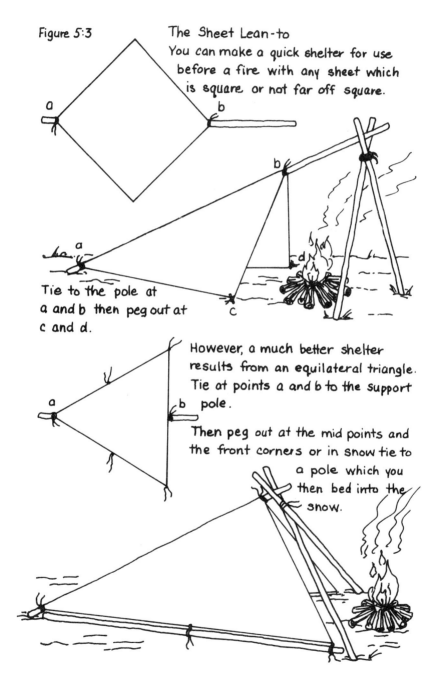

The Sheet Lean-to
You can make a quick shelter for use before a fire with any sheet which is square or not far off square.

Tie to the pole at a and b then peg out at c and d.

However, a much better shelter results from an equilateral triangle. Tie at points a and b to the support pole.

Then peg out at the mid points and the front corners or in snow tie to a pole which you then bed into the snow.

104

Insulating with Natural Materials

If you are going to be out for several nights you might look for insulating material to keep warm with while you sleep so you can avoid having to maintain a fire.

Very commonly in the summer and fall in bush country you will find sedge growing along stream edges or in meadows. When cut by ranchers for wintering livestock this sedge is known as wild, or swamp, hay. If you can find some, it will not take you long with your belt knife to cut a generous bundle or two. Lay it out to dry, and, with luck in the weather, it will be ready for use by evening, particularly if you turn it a time or two and keep it thinly spread.

I doubt there is a farm- or ranch-raised boy who did not at some time worm his way into and otherwise contrive to cover himself with hay to keep warm. You can do the same. You must, of course, protect yourself and your hay from possible rain, so you will lay the hay inside a shelter, either your triangle tent or a double brush lean-to. You make this sort of lean-to by constructing two facing roofs which meet at the common ridge pole. You will want plenty of brush over the ridge pole to keep out rain.

You will find it easy to use the hay as a mattress, but more difficult to arrange it above you as a cover. The sides of whatever shelter you use will help to contain the hay. If you make the shelter of brush, you then can use the fabric sheet, folded, between the mattress hay and the covering hay to form an envelope which you can get into with minimal disturbance of the hay.

Of course, as your farm-raised youngster well knows, you can crawl into the hay without benefit of a folded sheet, but this means at best much hay stuck to your clothing and more likely a good deal of itching besides.

If you can find the necessary sedge with which to make hay, this shelter and bed will keep you warm through some very cold nights without any need of tending fire. In case it has occurred to you to wonder, the technique does not work with brush instead of hay as brush is too heavy for the topside insulation. Brush does not seem heavy as you handle individual bough ends, but enough to do the job of insulating weighs so much that you can't squirm into your fabric envelope after the brush is laid above it.

There is another insulating material which you may sometimes use to keep safe at night. It is found near large, mature, sheltering coniferous trees, such as pine, spruce, or fir. This material is squirrel trash, the residue of chips cast aside as the small creature tears apart the outer cone to reach the edible core.

You will sometimes find large trees which let through virtually no rain and which have around them on the ground a huge accumulation of this trash, often to a foot or more in depth. The trash will be very dry, and though the ground itself may be frozen, the trash remains loose.

You shelter in this trash by simply making a trench long enough and deep enough that, when you lie down in it, your top side is roughly at the original surface level of the trash. Then you heap the trash you took from the trench over yourself, starting at your feet and working up your body until only your arms, shoulders, and head are free.

Now, this is far from a comfortable way to spend the night. For one thing, you cannot move about without disturbing your covering of trash. Nonetheless, you will be safe if you are adequately clothed to start with, and this is a fast method of sheltering without fire in the early winter before there is enough snow on the ground to build a snow shelter.

Ground-warming Techniques

Then there are some methods in which you use fire to keep warm, but at the same time do not maintain fire through the night. Whatever variant you use, the principle is the same: you store the heat in the ground or in stones and then draw on it while you sleep.

The simplest variant is to build a fire about seven feet long by three feet wide, in a *safe* location and handy to a fair amount of fuel. Start the fire as soon as you are committed to make camp, then feed it well until you want it to die down for preparation of your bed.

At the same time that you have the fire burning, gather brush for a mattress. When the time comes to go to bed, you clear away the ashes of the fire, which you have by then let burn down, and make your brush mattress on the heated ground. You lie on the brush and draw over yourself anything you have with you which will help to contain the heat.

A bear once killed a calf on spring range in the ranching country in which I grew up, and I lay up near the kill to try to get the bear. The bear came late in the day, as bears often will, and in the impatience of my youth I shot too soon and without sufficient care. I missed altogether, but spent the remaining daylight searching along the track to be sure of that fact. Only at dusk did I make my way to a nearby water hole and get a fire going. I heated the ground for two to three hours, then passed a cold spring night in fair comfort with one thin blanket, a tatty bit of canvas, and no brush. At first I was much too warm, then I was warm below but cool above, then I was cool altogether but comfortable enough until morning.

This ground-heating technique will not work on thoroughly wet ground, and there are better ways to proceed when the ground is frozen to depth. You must never, of course, attempt it where there is any accumulation of organic forest debris overlaying the soil. There is no danger of setting your mattress brush on fire, because you let your fire burn out and then you remove all your ashes well to the side. Your brush goes onto the hot, cleaned ground surface, not onto residual ashes.

The Domed Hut

Another way of using stored heat is to build a dome-shaped hut, like a sweat house, and keep it warm with hot stones. You light a fire and place a number of stones in and about the fire to heat. The stones should be as large as you can handle. While the stones are heating, you build the hut. The next set of sketches (Figure 5:4) will give you an idea how to proceed. When I was a boy, my brother and I built huts of sapling frames, which we thatched after a fashion with the leafy ends of aspen branches. It was many years later that an old Indian man from Sugarcane near Williams Lake in British Columbia told me how to make a similar but more securely roofed hut, and how to heat it with stones. He offered it specifically as a way to avoid having to tend fire through the night.

With little in your kit to work with, you can prepare yourself for a very chilly night, provided you leave enough time before darkness falls for making this camp.

If you think you will need them, you can heap your fire with additional stones when you go to bed and bring them in should you grow chilly in the small hours of the morning. This calls for good judgment and experience in banking the fire with green wood to keep it going, as otherwise the stones in the fire will long since have cooled by the time you want them.

Of much greater importance is that you heap on plenty of moss or ground trash for the insulation and that you do a thorough job of

A Dome-Shaped Hut Heated with Stones

Make a frame of supple saplings about ten feet long, overlapped and tied at the top of the dome. Set the butts well into the ground.

Cover the dome with brush followed by moss or ground trash. You may need to weave in some light willow saplings on the horizontal to get the cover material to hold.

Here is the floor plan showing the bed of boughs and the stones laid in after being heated in the fire.

Handle the stones with this pair of sticks.

Hold here with one hand or lash together.

Hold here with the other hand.

Flatten the sticks with your axe.

Figure 5:4

blocking up your entrance. At first you'll be too hot if you close the entrance, but when the time comes, your comfort for the remainder of the night will depend on it.

The Double Lean-to with Open Ridge

If you decide to maintain fire through the night in order to sleep in its warmth, you already know about the brush lean-to with the long fire in front of it.

A variant of this, particularly useful to two people out together, is the double lean-to with an open ridge. This is made by selecting a pair of trees a suitable distance from each other and using two ridge poles, one on each side of the trees. The space between the ridge poles is left open for passage of smoke from a fire in the centre. Figure 5:5 illustrates this shelter.

You do not need a large fire, and when your mattress brush is fresh it presents little fire hazard. You can help to keep it from drying out from the heat of the fire by using a stout green log to retain it.

Use the best dry fuel you can find, as half the battle with the smoke is won if you do not make much of it to start with.

Yet nothing is ever quite as simple as we would like, and often any one of your choices is a compromise of some sort. The double lean-to is very cozy and pleasant while you cook over your small fire and chat together to pass the evening, provided that a contrary wind does not come along to blow all the smoke back in on you instead of letting it rise out through your carefully contrived opening. But you can't have a huge fire, and so you must constantly wake up to feed it, though with two of you you can divide the night into watches.

You can extend the fire's holding time by adding green wood, but that means you have more smoke. Still, as long as you keep your head at ground level the smoke might be tolerable and you might reckon the warmth is worth it.

SHELTERING WITH A SLEEPING BAG

Now we have considered a number of methods by which you might, in these seasons without snow, keep safe through the night without a sleeping bag. This is the sort of circumstance which will confront the day-hiker who must spend an unexpected night out.

Double Lean-to with an Open Ridge

Roof well
brushed on both sides.

Green logs to retain
bedding brush and
reduce fire hazard.

Figure 5:5

If you go down in an aircraft without your sleeping bag, you will need to consider everything that has already been said. Also, you will want to have a pretty serious talk with yourself, because you have made a very grave error. When you travel by air, the time you are pinned down may last a long while, and into the bargain the aircraft carries the bag for you — *provided you put it on board.* There is no excuse.

So you're down, and you have your sleeping bag and the rest of a sensible outfit lashed to a packboard. The first significant advantage you have is that, with adequate clothing and an adequate sleeping bag, you will not need to maintain fire through the night.

The situation when you are downed in an aircraft can vary considerably: you may be the only survivor; there may be a group of survivors; you may have a proper outfit, while the others may or may not be equally well equipped. Bush aircraft are required by regulation to have sleeping bags and other survival gear and supplies on board; this aircraft may be in compliance or it may not. Your companions may be, as you are, both knowledgeable and confident; or one or more may be quite unprepared and ready to panic.

There is no set situation, and so, once more, I will offer ideas on which you may draw according to the demands of the event itself. For now, I am still concerned with sheltering techniques for the seasons without snow and heavy frosts.

Again, the single and double brush lean-to shelters are both a possibility. If there is canvas on board, this may be used in conjunction with the brush. Still, anything you can do with material from the bush frees the gear from the aircraft for other uses. If you can keep the weather out with brush, you can use the canvas in other ways, perhaps to supplement a short supply of sleeping bags. One sleeping bag, opened out, will cover two people, who can then keep warm underneath with folded canvas over a brush mattress.

The Tipi

A double lean-to large enough to accommodate a group of people is a possibility, but you might also consider building a brush tipi, as the circular ground space is more convenient. The best way to understand the tipi is to look at its construction in canvas, since the brush tipi will be an adaptation of it.

A tipi, or plains lodge, is, in essence, a conical frame of poles with a canvas stretched over it, a door opening at the bottom front, and a smoke vent at the top front. Two flaps, one on either side of the smoke vent, assist critically in inducing the smoke from the fire to leave through the vent.

If you make a half-circle of paper and then bring one half of the straight side to coincide with the other half you get a cone. The cover of the tipi is also a half-circle, but with slight variations and additions. The true tipi is a tilted cone, steeper down the back than the front. This is so that the fire, when placed just in front of the tipi's centre, will be well under the smoke vent. It also ensures more head room at the back of the lodge where most of the living is done.

The space in a lodge increases at a surprising rate as the diameter increases. For light hunting-camp purposes, two people can manage in a thirteen- to fourteen-foot lodge, while a group of six, in a survival situation, would be well off in a sixteen-foot lodge. One reason for this is that a sixteen-foot diameter makes it possible to swing the bed directions.

Figures 5:6 and 5:7 show something of the construction and use of the tipi.

The final use of space will depend on how many people there are and what gear must be accommodated, but these two floor plans will give you an initial idea.

It is highly unlikely, unless you have parachutes on board, that you will ever have enough fabric material to make a regular lodge in a survival situation. It is still worth knowing how to go about it (Figures 5:8a-e), but you should note that a rectangular tarpaulin, to do the job, needs to be as wide as the proposed lodge diameter and twice as long.

A lodge cover laid out on a radius of sixteen feet will result in a lodge of that diameter. When you are making a lodge up from rectangular material for an emergency shelter, it is scarcely worth trying to achieve the tilt. Make the lodge as a true cone, but set the fire as well forward of centre as you can without interfering with the doorway.

You will need twelve frame poles and two smoke-flap poles for a small lodge of up to fifteen feet in diameter, fifteen frame poles and two smoke-flap poles for anything larger. Cut all poles at least one foot longer than the diameter of the lodge.

To set the frame for, let us say, a sixteen-foot lodge, mark a circle on the ground sixteen feet in diameter and proceed step-by-step as shown in Figures 5:8b-c. Keep the back of the lodge to what, in your

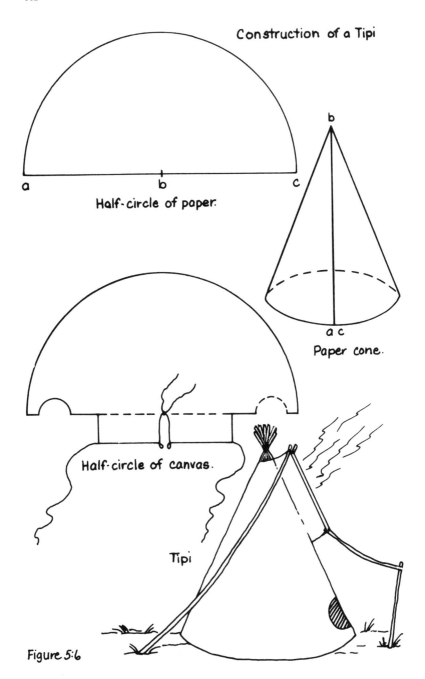

Construction of a Tipi

a   b   c

Half-circle of paper.

b

a c

Paper cone.

Half-circle of canvas.

Tipi

Figure 5:6

Use of Tipi Interior

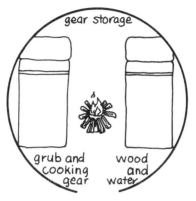

Two-person lodge.

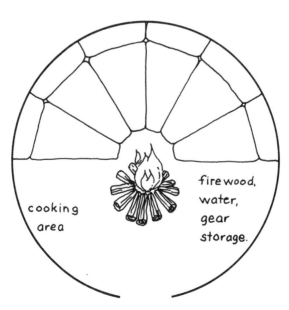

Figure 5:7   Six-person lodge.

114

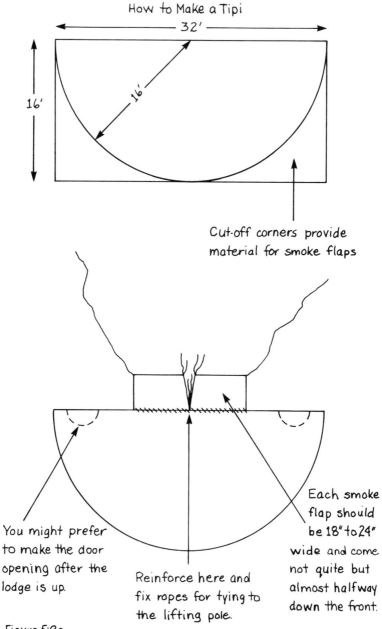

How to Make a Tipi

32'

16'

16'

Cut-off corners provide
material for smoke flaps.

You might prefer
to make the door
opening after the
lodge is up.

Figure 5:8a

Reinforce here and
fix ropes for tying to
the lifting pole.

Each smoke
flap should
be 18" to 24"
wide and come
not quite but
almost halfway
down the front.

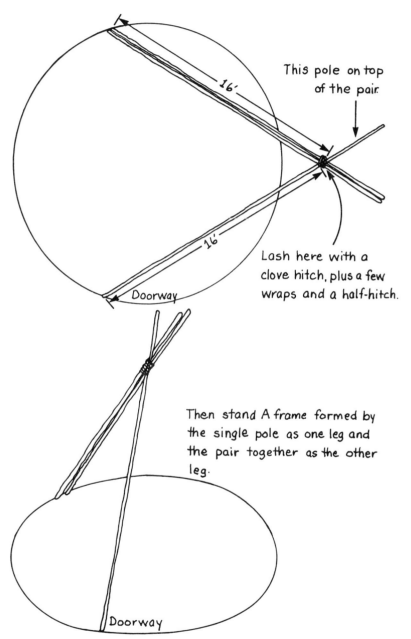

This pole on top of the pair.

16'

16'

Doorway

Lash here with a clove hitch, plus a few wraps and a half-hitch.

Then stand A frame formed by the single pole as one leg and the pair together as the other leg.

Doorway

Figure 5:8b

116

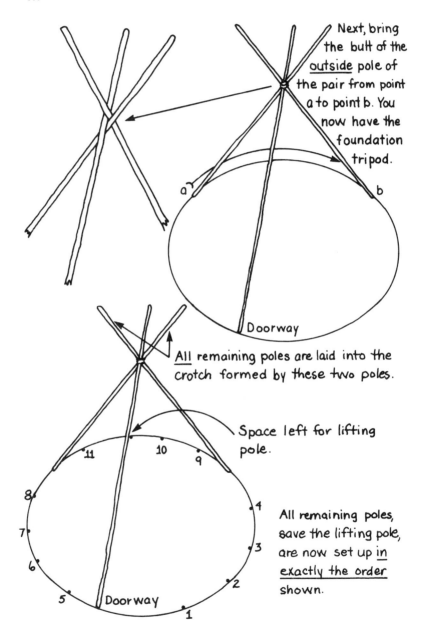

Next, bring the butt of the outside pole of the pair from point a to point b. You now have the foundation tripod.

a

b

Doorway

All remaining poles are laid into the crotch formed by these two poles.

Space left for lifting pole.

11   10   9

8

7

6

5   Doorway

4

3

2

1

All remaining poles, save the lifting pole, are now set up in exactly the order shown.

Figure 5.8c

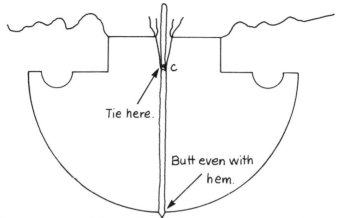

Lay your remaining pole on the lodge cover as shown and tie securely at point c.

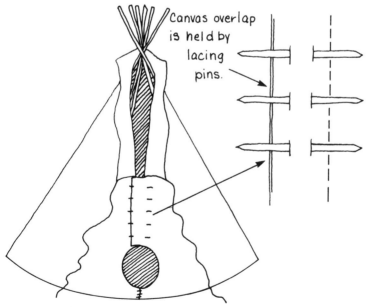

Canvas overlap is held by lacing pins.

Stand the lifting pole and cover together, then bring the cover around the frame and lace up at the front.

Figure 5:8d

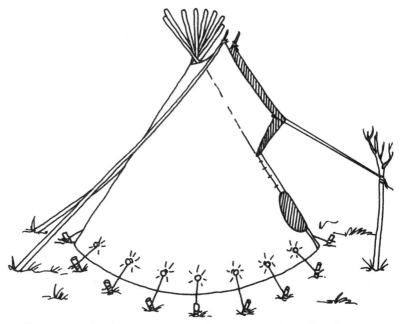

With the smoke-flap poles and the ties, position the flaps.
Then peg down the hem of the cover.

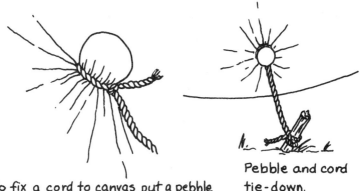

To fix a cord to canvas, put a pebble
on the bottom side, then gather
material around it and tie, collar-fashion,
with the cord. An excellent technique
with plastic covers.

Pebble and cord
tie-down.

Figure 5:8e

estimate, is the prevailing wind, and as much out of the strike of the wind as possible. Be sheltered!

As you go through the steps illustrated in Figures 5:8b and c, you should keep the following points in mind.

When you lay the pole that goes next to the doorway across the other two poles of the tripod, make sure the distance from the butts to the tie is in fact the radius of the lodge cover.

As you stand this A frame up, stand beside the leg composed of the pair of poles. This puts you in position, when the A frame is upright, to grasp the *outside* pole of the pair in order to swing its butt into location to form a tripod out of the A frame.

The remaining poles must go up in the order shown and they *all* go into the crotch formed by the two poles which began together as a pair in the initial A frame. This procedure has the most efficient result possible. It places the bulk of the poles in the front where the smoke vent will be, reducing the bulk at the back where the lodge cover must be brought around.

Standing the lifting pole with a heavy cover attached to it can be a bit of a struggle until you get the knack. After the cover is securely tied to the pole as shown (Figure 5:8d), gather the cover to the pole and tie it around at the bottom and again six feet up to keep it compact and fixed to the pole as you raise it. Put the pole end in place and walk toward the tipi, raising the pole in front of you. Also, you will find that a stake or other obstruction to prevent the butt from slipping as you begin to bring the pole upright is quite helpful.

Lacing pins are the best method for securing the front of a regular lodge, but, for a lodge improvised when you are lucky enough to find sufficient material on board a downed aircraft, you might do as well to lace up with cord (Figure 5:8d). You won't then need the overlap, and this is likely a structure that you will be using only once.

You can make an improvised ladder in order to tie the smoke-flap poles to the top corners of the flaps. Alternately, if there are other hands in the party, these poles can be tied before the cover goes up, since one person can keep moving them up while another raises the lifting pole and cover.

To operate the smoke flaps, follow the rule that if the wind blows across the lodge, you raise the near flap against the wind and drop the other, if it blows from the back of the lodge, keep both flaps up but more spread apart than straight out at the tops, and if the wind blows front-on, drop one flap completely, then bring the other across the opening to block the wind, leaving room behind it for smoke to escape. You can handle any wind well, save a dead-on front wind — and even that can be managed with some success. Now, that tells you about the basic lodge you could build if you had the canvas, and since I live in one in indolent comfort, I have no hesitation in praising it to you. However, if you should decide to make one for your use outdoors, as against simply having it in mind in an emergency, please do not build from these instructions but obtain a book by Reginald and Gladys Laubin called *The Indian Tipi* (Ballantine Walden Edition 22339). You will then build a tipi with superior detail and the correct tilt of the lodge toward the back.

Given a survival situation which looks as though it could last for some time, you may decide to build a brush tipi (Figure 5:9) in preference to a double brush lean-to. Now that you know the basics of constructing the real thing, you're better than halfway there.

First, decide how much ground space you need for the number of people to be sheltered. The rule for any shelter is to make it large enough, *but not one inch more than large enough*. In doing this, you conserve material at the time of construction and require less fuel later to keep warm. In cool and cold weather, this rule is increasingly critical to success. I suggest no more than a fourteen-foot-diameter lodge for two people, and a seventeen-foot-diameter for a small group; the latter will be large enough that people may sleep at the back of the lodge with feet toward the fireplace and heads toward the perimeter (as in Figure 5:7).

Mark a circle of the desired size on the ground in the best location available to you. Do a proper job of drawing the circle by using a stake driven in the centre of the area and a length of line tied to it to span the radius. Scratch the ground thoroughly with a stick to define the circumference.

Cut poles which are a foot longer than the diameter of the circle. Select three *stout* poles and set up your tripod as you would for a regular lodge, lashing thoroughly. In the brush lodge there will be more weight on the structure altogether, and the tripod is the key to holding it all up — so make the tripod *strong*.

Lay in all your remaining poles in the regular way — except that you won't need a lifting pole. Put up all remaining nine or twelve as the case may be.

A short distance from the apex you will need to lash in some strong pieces on the horizontal. Regardless of the size of the lodge, you should put these in about two feet below the tie (see Figure 5:9a). You will need to improvise a ladder so that you can do this work, and details for this are given later.

Having attached the horizontal pieces, you can now lay in many additional poles with their butts on the ground in the circumference and their tops leaning on your horizontal pieces, overreaching by about four inches (Figure 5:9b). It is important that *all* poles and these cross-pieces be of green material, and if you cut from young spruce or fir, the branches you trim off will all be used in the brush cover. You *may* use lodgepole-pine brush, but spruce or fir (Douglas fir or alpine fir) are preferable. In the north you won't have Douglas fir, and spruce is more likely to be available than alpine fir. You can lay in virtually as many poles as you have room for. You will need to lash the butts of the shorter intermediate poles above the door to a cross member.

When you lay on your brush cover, it becomes obvious that this is no shelter for a quick one-night camp, as an enormous amount of brush is wanted for the cover. On the other hand, it is a good shelter, and well worth while if the chance exists of a long stay. Also, if you are building a larger lodge, it is even more suitable because there are several of you, and with all hands helping you can gather the brush at quite a rate.

If you make a light-weight cover (Figure 5:9c) you may need to weave in some saplings of willow or something similar to help hold the brush. If you go for a heavy-weight cover, this won't be necessary.

You can use the lodge once the cover is on and you have your bedding brush in, but you will have much better smoke management if you have one piece of canvas to use for smoke control (Figure 5:9d).

In a cloudburst you may get some drip through the brush and some dribble down the poles, but a bright fire will soon dry things out again. You will find life a good deal more cheerful in your lodge around the fire than in any white man's tent in which you can't build a fire at all. You might find it better in the long run to build a good lodge and use any tent that might be in the aircraft supplies to meet other needs for canvas rather than for shelter. Of course this would depend on other factors, such as the number of people there are in relation to the size of the tent, and whether or not there are available a small woodstove, stove pipe, and safety device for passing a pipe through canvas.

If all hands have adequate sleeping bags, you won't need to

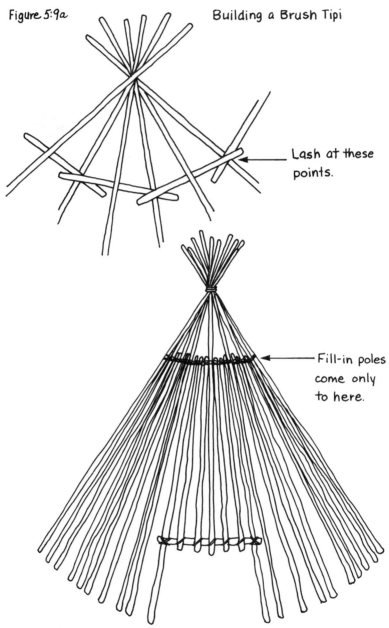

Figure 5:9a

Building a Brush Tipi

Lash at these points.

Fill-in poles come only to here.

Figure 5:9b

Figure 5:9c

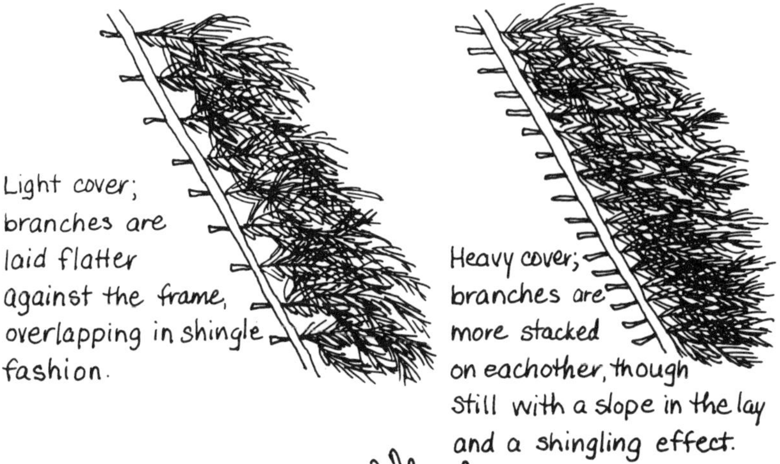

Light cover;
branches are
laid flatter
against the frame,
overlapping in shingle
fashion.

Heavy cover;
branches are
more stacked
on eachother, though
still with a slope in the lay
and a shingling effect.

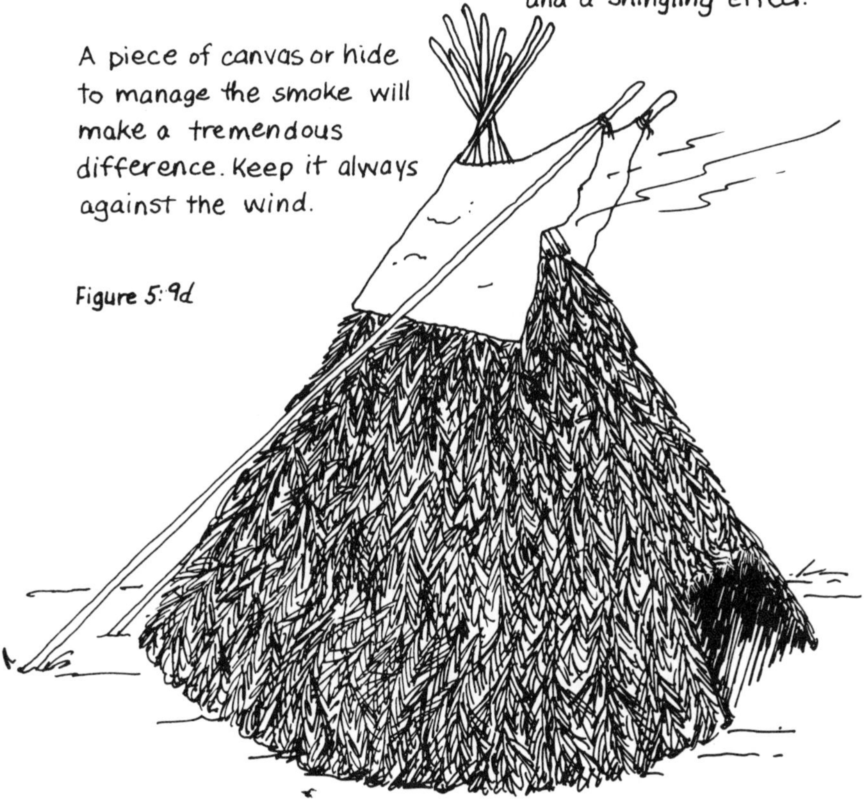

A piece of canvas or hide
to manage the smoke will
make a tremendous
difference. Keep it always
against the wind.

Figure 5:9d

keep fire through the night. If a fire is necessary, rotate your sleeping in watches with one person always awake to tend fire and be alert to any thrown embers that might land on bedding.

■ WINTER SHELTERING

All right, we have considered a variety of ideas for sheltering in the seasons without snow, both with and without an adequate sleeping bag.

Let's now go to winter and begin by observing two fundamental facts: first, we have snow to work with and that's an advantage; second, temperatures are colder, with the potential to be dangerous, and that means there are no mistakes allowed. An oversight which leads to discomfort in the milder seasons may lead to death at $-40°C$ ($-40°F$).

Yet go in the bush in winter with the right clothing, with a light pack containing the right bits of gear, and with the confidence born of understanding what you are about, and you will go well.

Much winter sheltering makes use of methods we already have discussed. Let's begin with the simpler things we can do to get safely through the night, assuming that we are without a sleeping bag.

JUST SITTING

When caught short, how about just sitting? Yes, it can be done, and in surprisingly cold temperatures, depending on your health, vigour, and clothing.

For example, if I go in the bush when the night temperatures are likely to run to $-30°C$ ($-22°F$), I might choose a combination of my best cold-weather moccasins, light wool long underwear, wool trousers and shirt, and my best parka. I will wear good winter mitts and will have in the pack spare socks and a second layer of long woollen underwear which will fit easily over the first. I will have other gear in my kit as well, including my fabric sheet.

If need be, I can find a place well out of any wind, pack the snow under a likely tree with my snowshoes, put brush on the snow, and then sit, knees drawn up and my sheet partly folded beneath me where I sit and partly giving extra protection to the back of my thighs, which for some reason tend to grow cold in this position.

I can sit like this and keep reasonably warm, forearms around my knees with my head resting on them, and even catch a little sleep. Note that the central core of the body is well protected in this position, while my head is well protected by my parka hood.

A main reason why this works for me is the generous cut of my parka. I open the front of it, and when my knees are drawn up, it comes around on each side to almost meet in front of my knees. Where it doesn't meet, my folded arms cover the gap.

I don't lean against the tree, as that would make my back cold and prevent my folding up my body as compactly as possible.

Figure 5:10 shows this position.

I have been told, by a reliable informant, of an Inuit woman who was caught in a sudden blizzard with no hope of returning to the safety of her igloo and who kept safe by adopting this sitting position in the lee of an old stream bank. As the wind blew the snow over the bank, it drifted around and over her until, in a short while, she was completely covered. Because she was dressed in fine caribou-skin clothing, she was protected from the immediate cold of the snow, while the snow in turn protected her from the vastly greater cold of the wind-driven air. She would have known the nature of the type of snow that drifts in the lee of a low bank and that she could break out of it and go home after the storm was over — which she did.

My problem in this position is twofold: in time I grow uncomfortably stiff and, unless I'm tired enough to doze, I get terribly bored with it. I can alternate, therefore, between sitting in this fashion and lying on my side, but in basically the same position, knees drawn up and hands folded around them. Then I can use my sheet under me from hip to shoulder, folded as many times as its size will allow. When you lie on brush freshly gathered and put down on snow, you notice the heat loss where your body weight compresses your clothing.

Now, quite frankly, that's a dull way to spend a winter's night, but it's perfectly safe and at worst uncomfortable, not by any means miserable, *provided that* you can fold up, that you have the clothes for it, and that you know your individual capacity.

Obviously, the next step is to sit on brush under your tree with a fire going and with the sheet of material over and around you but open at the front. Make sure you start out with enough wood to last all night. Since you have the fire, you won't need to fold up to protect your body core, and so you can shift your position enough to

A Simple Sheltering Position

Figure 5:10

relieve stiffness. You may not catch much sleep, particularly if your fire worries you with the occasional thrown ember, but you will come safely through the night.

LEAN-TOS

Again, as in other seasons, you can build a brush lean-to and a fire in front of it, then feed the fire between intervals of sleep. Some people do not bother with a shelter if the weather is clear and cold, preferring to build two long fires and lie on brush between them. Obviously this plan requires that you have extensive experience in managing fire.

My own conviction is that the fastest way to shelter safely in the bush in very cold weather is to carry a sheet with which to make a lean-to or a triangle tent, preferably the latter. This goes up quickly, and all remaining time can be spent gathering fuel. With a good camp-axe you can have an abundance, including some good-sized rounds, which will burn for long intervals without tending. Even after dark you can often continue to gather fuel in the immediate camp area by the light of the fire. Remember that once the fire is well established, you can burn green wood as well as dry. We will have more on fire management later.

Two people out together might choose the double lean-to and take alternating watches of, say, three hours each, one sleeping while the other keeps fire and guards against thrown embers.

Once more, you may choose to carry a space blanket in your kit. These products can be useful in helping you through the night, provided you are adequately dressed to start with. With brush beneath you, the space blanket over and around you will definitely reflect back a measure of body heat which would otherwise be lost.

I find these plastic blankets of little or no use in preventing downside heat loss, and once more I emphasize that you must determine from your own testing what these products will and will not do for you. And you should carry out these tests long before you depend on the products in an emergency.

SNOW SHELTERS

To avoid having to keep a fire through the night and yet maintain safety in extremes of cold you can use snow as an insulator. Again, the point of these techniques is to slow down the rate of heat loss, at least to the point of safety, and to the point of comfort if possible. Heat moves from a warmer body to a colder one. Lie naked in the snow and you will experience a painful rate of heat loss. However if, like the Inuit woman, you have enough insulation to protect you from the snow, the snow in turn will protect you from the much colder air outside. Also, since we are dealing with *rate* of heat loss, protection from cold air includes protection from the movement of the air. Movement of air increases the rate of heat loss from any warmer body exposed to it, and the heat loss is greater as the movement increases. The still air in the snow shelter will cause a far slower rate of heat loss from your body than air outside at the same temperature but blowing at fifteen miles an hour — or at one mile an hour for that matter.

In addition — and this is significant — the air temperature inside a well-built and properly closed-up snow shelter will be warmer than the air outside the shelter (irrespective of wind chill — we are talking only of temperature now), even without a heat source in the shelter. What happens in fact is that the well-built snow shelter traps and holds some of the heat which is constantly being lost from the ground below — even from ground frozen for many feet down.

The following differences in air temperature were reported by Alan Innes-Taylor of the Yukon Territory in a survival guide prepared for the Scandinavian Airlines System. The experiments were conducted during February and March of 1956.

Time of day.	Outside air temperature three feet above surface.	Interior temperature of unoccupied shelter taken at centre, door well closed.
1530	−17°F	+18°F
0815	−36°F	+20°F
0800	−40°F	+21°F
0800	−36°F	+19°F

One hardly needs to point out that, no matter how well you are dressed, the problem of staying alive is much simpler at 20°F (−7°C) than at −40°F (−40°C). At the level of adequacy of dress of great numbers of people who go into the bush for winter recreation, the difference is that between a moderately comfortable night and a miserable death.

My own experience is that, with brush on the floor as the only supplementary insulation to the snow of the shelter itself, I can, with the winter dress I use, lie down in a snow shelter in complete safety and moderate comfort. I will feel the heat loss where my body weight compresses my clothing beneath me at my shoulder and hip, but not to an extent that is troublesome.

If you are without a sleeping bag, or without one sufficient to the season, the snow shelter is a main road to safety.

In bush country, except rarely in a place such as a drifted area on a frozen lake surface, you will not find snow from which you can make blocks for construction of a shelter, such as the traditional igloo. Other methods must be used, and you should know something of them, even if on balance you decide that fire and a heat-catching shelter are your first choice. Even those who rarely venture above the timber line may one day need to shelter where snow is abundant while fuel is scarce.

Now you cannot toss together a snow shelter in a few minutes just before dark. Even when snow conditions are better than average, you must expect to put an hour or more of diligent work into the task. It is likely that in your first practice attempts you will be quite disenchanted with the whole undertaking, but do stick with it. A snow shelter can be a lifesaver, and a remarkably comfortable one at that. Some knowledgeable outdoors people become so proficient at the art of building such shelters that they will choose them even when abundant fuel is all about.

There is a feature of snow at colder temperatures which is critical to any sort of building with snow: if loose, dry snow is stirred in such a way that it mixes, it will harden and set if left a while. Wind blowing across a frozen lake surface will stir the snow and heap it in drifts; you may later find these drifts and discover that you can cut snow blocks out of them which are quite durable enough to use for building. If, at −18°C (0°F), you make a mound by gathering up into a heap the loose snow around the site, and then let the mound sit for half an hour, you can dig into the mound to make a cave with no fear of the roof falling in. Generally speaking, the colder the air temperatures the more rapid the process and the firmer the set.

More often than not, in making a shelter in bush country you will need to mound the snow to some extent before excavating. This serves two purposes: it gives you depth enough to work with and at the same time alters the loose snow to this desirable, set consistency. An important step in shelter construction is finding something else useful to do after mounding up, but before excavating.

Now what about tools? A snowshoe makes an excellent shovel for gathering the snow into the mound, and even your feet, used sideways, can push together a useful quantity of snow. If you use a snowshoe, do work with great care and watch out for fallen stems on the ground. A damaged snowshoe is a very bad business, and you do not want it. Do not scrape all the way to ground level when using a snowshoe.

If you wear large gauntlet mitts, you can move much snow with your hands. The drawback is that, even in quite cold weather, the warmth of your hand inside the mitt, along with the friction of the activity, may result in wet mitts. You will need a fire, if at all possible, to dry your mitts after your work is complete.

If you ski, you can now buy a small but effective shovel blade to attach to a ski pole, specifically designed for use in snow sheltering.

A sharpened stick is useful during excavation to loosen snow which can then be moved by hand or with a snowshoe or ski-pole shovel. A billy can is quite useful during excavation.

As warm air rises, the air temperatures inside a snow shelter develop a marked gradient from floor to ceiling. It follows that the closer you are to the ceiling when you lie down to rest, the warmer you will be. For this reason you should always build into your shelter a sleeping platform above floor level. Any height will help, but try to have the sleeping platform at least a foot above the entrance level. It is also important that there is no more room from platform to ceiling than is essential for moving about. The floor area should be much less than the platform area, and we call this floor area the "well". Here the cold air pools as the warm air rises. The entrance should be at this lowest level to keep to a minimum the loss of warm air on use of the entrance. The sketch which follows (Figure 5:11) will help to illustrate the principle.

The most effective snow shelters are those entirely of snow, but when either an insufficiency of snow or a shortage of time warrants hurrying up the job, a useful shelter can be built by making the walls of snow and the roof of either two overlapping reflecting blankets or of any fabric sheet. Also, one can make a roof of snow, supported during construction by sticks laid across from side to side with the sheet laid over these.

If there is sufficient snow on the ground and it is of a strong consistency, as in a drift, you can excavate into the snow as you find it. If there is not sufficient snow you must first heap enough into a mound and then, after it has set, make your excavation. In bush-country snow conditions, some heaping up of the snow is usually necessary.

If you propose to excavate a shelter leaving snow in place for the roof, you must gather a large enough mound that, after the cave is made inside it, the roof and walls are thick enough that they will hold in place and insulate effectively. At least a foot at the thinnest locations is advisable.

The Snow Cave

Let us first consider an excavated cave, complete with roof (Figure 5:11). Choose a site where the ground is level and free of fallen growth for a good distance all about. Then, by working around and around the location of the proposed shelter, move snow toward the centre. Make a mound that is more than five feet high and at least ten feet across the base, preferably somewhat more.

Snow Shelter

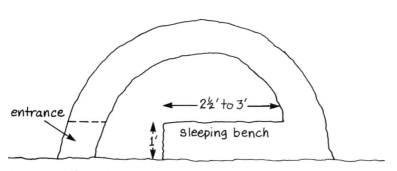

Cross-section of a snow cave excavated out of a gathered mound.

Figure 5:11

When you have enough snow in the mound, leave the work. Spend half an hour gathering brush for the sleeping platform, perhaps lighting a small fire near by, and gathering extra fuel as well. You will likely sweat at your work and get snow in your clothing into the bargain, so the fire will be useful for drying out afterwards.

When you reckon the snow has set, return to work on the shelter. Even up a vertical face on one location on the perimeter of the mound, then begin tunnelling into the mound at ground level. Work through as small an opening as you can and work patiently. Do not try to hurry the job. Much snow has to be removed and working alone is awkward, but still you will find it easier to keep to a fairly small entrance throughout the work than to repair an oversized opening later.

Once you are into the mound about a foot you can begin to enlarge the excavation upwards and sideways, and by now you will have discovered the most difficult part of the job: contriving to move all that snow out through the opening. You soon wish you had a companion outside clearing it away as you push it through the entrance. A usual method is to excavate with your hands, while at the same time using your feet to push the snow out.

The cave need be only so large as to provide a ground-level area immediately inside the entrance in which you can get to your knees, and, immediately beyond that, your sleeping platform of about two and a half feet in width and seven feet in length.

Your final job is to bring brush into the shelter with which to cover the sleeping platform, and you will now find that an important function of a brush mattress in snow sheltering is that, if snow is carried on your clothing onto the sleeping bench, it will settle through the brush and out of the way.

You can block the entrance in several ways. Often by the time you are ready to occupy the shelter you will find that you can cut some half-decent small snow blocks from around the edges of the mound. A perfectly functional snow knife can be whittled from a dry sapling stem with your axe and belt knife, and it works well to cut the blocks. These, along with your pack, may block up most of the entrance, and extra snow can be gathered inside near the entrance to finish the job.

Now, what were the problems?

The main difficulty was getting such a large volume of snow out through that small entrance. Even putting the brush in for the platform was awkward. However, if we boldly open up the whole side of the mound to make things easier, we then will find it quite difficult to rebuild the wall with a small entrance that will hold together. We really would like to find an easier way.

Trench Shelters

If I have in my kit in these cold winter months a rectangular sheet, at least nine feet long by whatever-I-reckon-is-useful wide, I can put it to use now to make a snow shelter with much less difficulty (Figures 5:12 & 5:13).

First I gather the heap of snow, but now I need just enough that my heap is a good three feet deep and covers an area of six feet by twelve feet. I let the snow set while I gather brush and perhaps some fuel for a fire and then I take a huge leaping step into the middle of the heap and work around myself to make a trench nine feet long by three feet wide. It should be three feet deep at what will be the entrance end of my shelter, but perhaps only two feet deep

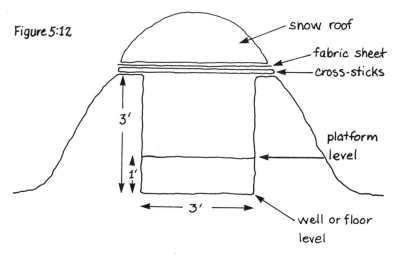

Cross-section end view of a trench shelter with snow roof supported by cross-sticks and a fabric sheet. Again, the snow was first gathered into a mound.

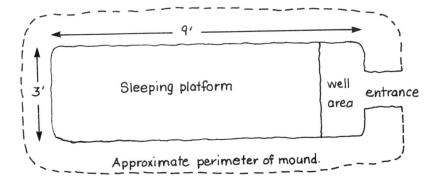

Figure 5:13

throughout the remainder where the sleeping platform will be. I end up standing in my trench, of course.

Then, with as little damage to the trench wall as possible, I take a big leaping step out of the trench. Now I can put my brush in with much convenience.

While I was waiting for the snow to set, I had time, in addition to gathering my brush, to cut eighteen or twenty light sticks about five feet long. These I now place across the top of the trench at about six-inch intervals. Then I throw my piece of fabric over the cross-sticks and, given the size of sheet I carry, I just cover the trench on the length but have plenty of overlap at the sides. If I put snow first on the overlap at the sides and then some extra sticks at the ends to secure the fit, I can proceed to cover the whole shelter with enough snow to make an insulating roof. The snow which came out of the trench will do for this, but it may have to be loosened up a bit because it will have had time to begin to set.

Now, to complete the shelter I need only tunnel through from the end, making the smallest entrance I can crawl through.

There is, in addition, an even faster way to make a roof: carry in your kit two of the lighter style of plastic reflecting blankets and place these over the trench. No sticks will be needed for their support. Put enough snow on the overlap of the plastic on the wall tops to hold them in place and allow as much overlap of one blanket over the other as their size permits. One sheet is not convenient, as your trench is nine feet long and these reflecting sheets are only seven feet long.

Any snow shelter properly put together will, without any sup-plementary heat source, provide temperatures not much below the freezing point, even though outside air temperatures may be run-ning to forty or more below. The shelter traps, not only the heat loss from the ground, but also much of the heat from your body. As unlikely as it sounds, the quick roof of reflecting plastic is quite effective. It is arguable, in fact, that this is the only truly useful purpose for these so-called emergency blankets.

Now this trench with the quickly made roof is a popular, fast way to shelter, and certainly requires less work than does the excavated cave. Much less snow needs to be brought into the initial mound, and if you want the roof of snow supported by the cross-sticks and a fabric sheet, you have at your disposal the snow you took out of the trench.

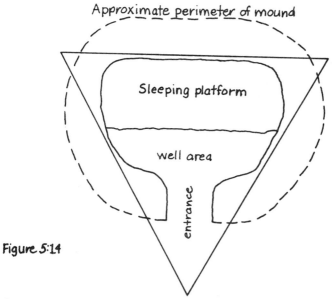

Figure 5:14

Floor layout of shelter where the triangular sheet is to be used over cross-sticks to support the roof. The sheet must be at least eleven feet to the side, but twelve feet to the side is better. The point of the triangle over the entrance helps in closing up.

But suppose you have decided to carry, for its several emergency purposes, a triangular rather than a rectangular sheet. The solution is simple: you make a different shape of shelter, one which is easily roofed over with cross-sticks and the triangular sheet. Such a quick shelter is simply a pit in the snow with a roof over it, and you can easily change the shape of the pit. The accompanying sketch will give you the idea (Figure 5:14).

Many knowledgeable people carry in their kit a survival candle — a candle designed to burn for about twelve hours. If one of these is burned in the well of the shelter, the temperature on the sleeping platform can be raised to above freezing. Since most emergency camps, other than an aircraft camp, are of only one night's duration, you can see that the candle is a very useful item indeed.

You should experiment with different shapes and sizes of shelters, but do remember that the sleeping platform is integral to success. In your trials you may not wish to cut brush every time, and an ensolite backpacker's mattress is excellent on the platform.

Size is important. Obviously the smaller the shelter the more effectively it will warm up from your body heat and your candle, if you use one. On the other hand, if the shelter is too small, you are bumping into the walls and the roof whenever you shift about, and the task of blocking the entrance is made quite awkward.

If you use a fabric sheet over sticks to support a snow roof, there is a way to retrieve the sheet after the snow has set. When you cut the sticks you must make them smooth and cut them long enough that when you lay them across the trench they project well out on one side. Then, when you lay the fabric, fold it to a size which is just an inch or two larger than the opening of the roof of the trench. You will have to place the snow on with care until the edges are secure, and then you must pile on plenty of snow so that the roof is well heaped up.

After the snow has had time to set, you can pull your sticks out by the protruding ends. Then, from inside your shelter, you can retrieve your fabric sheet. Some snow will come loose with it, but no more than will settle out of the way through the brush. Only experience will teach you how long you must wait before retrieving the sheet, but the trouble is worth it. You can use it at once for other purposes, and you will be saved having to take apart a firmly set shelter the next day to retrieve the sheet before you leave the site.

If you find snow drifts of substantial depth in the lee of a river bank or at the edge of a frozen lake surface, it takes little imagination to see how easily you may make a shelter where the snow is already of a firm, set consistency. You can excavate a shelter on its length into the drift, then fill up the open side with snow blocks after you have completed the interior. Use the whittled snow-knife I discussed earlier. Practice, before ever you are in the emergency, is the key to success. I rarely come across a drift offering snow suitable for making building blocks without stopping to cut a few blocks. Then, even if I don't complete it, I begin a structure of some sort — in spite of the fact that, as a long-time fire-and-lean-to man, I have little skill in the snow-building arts. Anyone who takes these opportunities to develop skills will soon know how to make a functional shelter, rough-hewn though the first attempts may be.

The Igloo

Why not build an igloo, as this is undoubtedly the finest of snow shelters? The answer to that lies in the nature of bush-country snow: snow of building-block quality occurs so seldom that the igloo cannot be considered a practical bush-country emergency shelter. Yet, with that recognized, there is nothing to prevent you having a shot at building one if you do come on a drift which offers the snow. I once took enough blocks from a drift in a driveway in Whitehorse in the Yukon Territory to make an igloo for my small children to play in. Two people could have sheltered in it in reasonable comfort.

The next set of sketches (Figure 5:15) will help you to get started, but let me emphasize that igloo construction is largely a matter of learning by doing. Once you get the knack of setting a block so that it holds in place, you need only time and snow to complete a structure. When you have finished the first one, you will see what improvements you want in the next. My instructions are only to get you started. Within a few hours, your own experience will overtake everything I say here.

The snow-knife I mentioned earlier will work quite well, and if you own a machete or an extra-large butchering knife, these will serve. Cut blocks about eight inches thick and at least twice as long as wide, up to a maximum of about forty-five inches. There is no advantage to small blocks and the work goes faster with large ones, but the quality of the snow will often limit the size of block you can make.

Set your first course of blocks in a circle the size of the structure

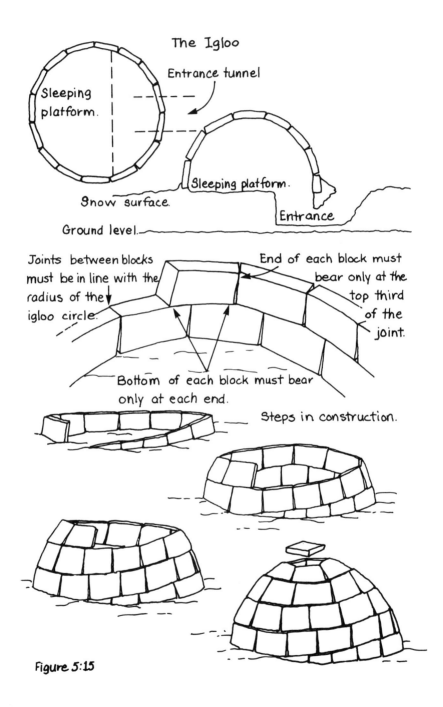

The Igloo

Sleeping platform.

Entrance tunnel

Snow surface.

Ground level.

Sleeping platform.

Entrance

Joints between blocks must be in line with the radius of the igloo circle.

End of each block must bear only at the top third of the joint.

Bottom of each block must bear only at each end.

Steps in construction.

Figure 5:15

you hope to complete. Use full-sized blocks for this first course and lean them slightly inward.

You will find that to bring the wall up in a narrowing spiral you must trim each block so that it is shorter along the top edge than along the bottom. This is necessary even on the first course, and the final shaping of each block must be done as it is placed in the wall.

After the first full course is in place, trim the tops of about a third of the blocks to form an incline (as pictured).

The vertical joints between the blocks must always be trimmed in line with the radius of the igloo circle.

Do not attempt as you place each block to have it fit uniformly along its bottom edge with the top of the previous course, or uniformly on its end in contact with the last block in place. Should you accomplish such a uniform fit, not only would you waste time in being so fastidious but the block will fall out of the wall into the bargain. With each course you must move the blocks inward and incline them considerably. *When you trim a block into place on the wall it must bear on the bottom only at each end and be in contact with the previous block only at the top third of the joint* (see Figure 5:15). Ignore that rule and you will get nowhere; follow it, and you will be astounded to find, as the spiral closes in to form the roof of the dome, that a block will stay in place even when it is almost on the horizontal.

You can make a temporary entrance for passing in snow blocks (except for the first course or two you can build only from the inside), then block it up when you are finished and ready to excavate the entrance tunnel.

The blocks lean inward only a little at first, then progressively more as the wall changes into a dome-shaped roof. When only enough room is left for one more block, you will find with a little juggling that you can pass a block endways through the opening, then fit it as you settle it down in place. Once you get this far, the last block will not defeat you.

A feature of first attempts is that the dome is not drawn in quickly enough, and the igloo is higher than it should be in relation to the base diameter. This is easily corrected in the next attempt as you become confident about placing the blocks close to the horizontal for the roof portion of the structure.

The spaces left in the joints between the blocks can be sealed with snow on both the inside and the outside. When you press snow into and against the joint, you need hold it in place only a short moment for it to set enough to stay in place.

Do not forget to make a small vent-hole in the roof before you occupy the igloo and block up the entrance. You and your candle both need some air.

Although the igloo is not a bush-country shelter of much significance due to the nature of bush-country snow, you should add it to your inventory of ideas if you can. Check the next snowdrift you see to determine if it contains building-block snow.

Now we have looked at a variety of sheltering methods for use, with or without a sleeping bag, in all the seasons.

It remains for you to consider the question of sheltering in relation to your style of travelling in bushland and the material which your particular stretch of bush has to offer. When you have decided how you would shelter if you were caught out unexpectedly, you should follow that up with some practice camps in which you actually do stay out overnight.

Practice moves you up from thinking you can manage to knowing you can manage.

When you know you can manage, you will go very well in the bush indeed.

SIX

Fire Management

We have discussed already the use of fire in connection with sheltering, but the subject of fire management requires attention in detail. Skill in making and keeping fire is a vital part of safe venturing in the bush.

■ MATCHES AND FIRE-STARTING TOOLS

To begin with, carry plenty of matches and keep them dry. I would settle for no less than four hundred matches in an aircraft survival pack. This apparently large number of matches makes no allowance for such wasteful habits as using two to light one fire.

I suggest that you have some matches in a pocket in a waterproof container, more in your core kit, and the remainder in your pack, in a sealed container. You can also purchase matches which are individually waterproofed and will light even after immersion for a length of time in water. The ones I have seen must be struck on a striking strip on the side of the box. On balance, I prefer a "strike-anywhere" match, and I accept the necessity of keeping it dry. I have never seen an individually waterproofed strike-anywhere match.

Once you have made camp, you must break the seal on your main container to move matches to your smaller container for regular use. A re-sealable main container is clearly an advantage, and it should be stored in some place where dampness, loss, or damage is virtually impossible.

One method of match care I have seen requires a little more preparation than a container, but is worth considering. Tear an old sheet into long strips a little wider than your matches are long. Pass the strip through melted wax and then lay it on a table or counter top. Quickly lay individual matches crossways onto the strip with about a match width between each and, while the wax is still soft, roll up the strip. When you have a good-sized roll, wrap more wax-soaked cloth around the roll in all directions to seal it completely.

To use, you peel down to the matches, saving the waxed wrapping for ensuring your fire starts. Also, you tear away a little of the waxed strip with each match, which increases the flame volume and duration of the match.

In addition to protected matches, I recommend small starter-strips of waxed lamp-wick. You buy the lamp wick by the foot, and then pass it through melted wax. After it has set, you cut it into pieces about four inches long. Each time you make fire, you light the starter strip with the match and then the fire with the starter strip. Once the fire is secure, you can snuff out the starter strip for use again. If you select good tinder and lay your fire carefully, you will light many fires from each strip and never use more than one match per fire.

There is a strong argument in favour of having a supplementary means for making fire in your kit. However much care you take, mishap may ruin your matches or, in an exceptional instance, you may finally use up the supply.

There is commonly available, through sporting-goods stores, a magnesium fire-starting tool, which consists of a small block of magnesium with a sparking insert fixed to one edge. First you make a small pile of magnesium shavings by scraping the block with a knife blade, then you ignite these shavings with a fast stroke of the blade down the sparking insert. Of course, you have assembled some good tinder in position to be ignited from the short-lived but very hot flash of the magnesium shavings. This is in fact a flint-and-steel method, with the magnesium acting as initial tinder.

■ STARTING A FIRE

Now, you don't have these aids to fire-making so that you may then be careless about preparing your tinder and smaller pieces of wood. You must always begin with plenty of fuel that is sure to ignite and blaze up quickly and with larger pieces immediately at hand with which to build the fire up once it is going. If there is any movement of air, however slight, you must also be well sheltered from that before you strike the match to light your starter strip or throw the spark to ignite your magnesium shavings.

There are several sources of good starting-fuel.

Look for well-branched, large spruce, pine, or fir trees. On the lower trunk, below the green branches, there will be small, dry, twig-sized branches, many of them no larger than your matchsticks. Gather several handfuls of the smallest branches from directly beside the main trunk. Then gather an abundance of some a little larger, and then some larger yet, until you have enough fuel from this source to burn for around fifteen minutes if you were to add nothing more.

Lay the fire with the smallest twigs on the bottom and the rest above in increasing size, but be sure you can reach under the small twigs with your flame. I usually put down two thick sticks a few inches apart and pile the smallest twigs across these. Then I can reach beneath the whole pile quite easily.

Even in a run of wet weather, twigs gathered from the main trunk of a large, spreading conifer will light up readily, but please remember my qualification that I am talking of interior and northern bush-country, not of rainforest. Starting a fire in rainforest during the wet seasons is altogether another problem, and so critically different that I must repeat my qualification that I am not writing about the rainforest situation.

Another source of starting fuel in bush country is in pitch-laden wood. If you are in bush where Douglas fir is common, look about for a large, ancient tree, long since fallen to the ground. You will find that most of the wood has been reduced to a long pile of reddish-brown, crumbly remains. If you whack about in this crumbled material with the back of your axe, you will frequently find streaks of solid wood which, soaked with resin, have survived intact. A few shavings of this pitch wood, followed by three or four kindling pieces, will be quite enough to get your main fuel going. Don't, of course, use this pitch wood as your main fuel. Gather all you can find and keep it for fire-starting.

If there is yellow pine in your vicinity, find one that has fallen and go to its top, both to the main stem and to the branches close to the knot by the stem, and you can gather very pitchy wood with a few strokes of your axe.

If you have lodgepole pine, a very common tree in bush country both in central regions and a long way north, look for a tree long gone down, with its root system torn up. Try the exposed roots. These won't always be useful, but often they will be very pitchy, and if cut into fine bits, will start easily.

Also, look around for birch bark. Where some outer layers have begun to peel away from the tree, gather an abundance. They will usually start quite readily, though in damp weather I prefer to find pitch wood and then to go to the inside of the piece just to be sure.

Learn to make shavings from a kindling stick with a sharp knife.

Figure 6:1

Do keep this one very important fact about wood in mind: not all dead wood is dry wood, and standing dry wood is invariably better than fallen dry wood. It is quite true that a tree which has fallen some years back, and is propped off the ground by previously fallen material, is still reasonably sound and will burn. You may use much of this material. However, for top-grade fuel go to your standing dry, the tree that has died on its feet, as it were, and has not yet fallen over.

If you don't find any of the starting material I have described which looks satisfactory to you, then bring down as large a standing dry tree as you can with your axe, best of all a pine, but spruce and most others will do. With your axe chop into the trunk with a wide bite, so that as you go down into the notch your chips will have some length. Take the chips from some depth into the trunk and split these into kindling sticks, making some that are as small as twigs.

Make shavings from some of your kindling sticks as shown in the diagram (Figure 6:1). It takes practice to become deft at this, but it is a skill well worth developing. Use a very sharp knife and shave the wood off in long, thin strips, leaving each strip anchored near the base of the stick. For best results, cut on the edge of the grain, rather than on the flat of the grain.

I never go to bed in camp on a winter's night without preparing a supply of these shavings for making a rapid fire in the chill of the morning!

With these shavings and kindling pieces a fire will start readily. I have used such a source of starting fuel in wet country in a wet season when only the inside wood in a cedar snag was still dry. It will work in rainforest if you know what you are about, and it's a sure-fire method in bush country.

■ MANAGING A FIRE

For your main fuel you must go to the best of what is at hand that you can gather with your axe. In the milder seasons, you may choose to go with a belt axe, but in winter change to a medium-sized camp axe in order to make fuel-gathering just that much easier when your need will be greater.

The best dry fuel — the "standing dry" — is for use at start-up and during cooking with an outside fire. Lesser-quality dry wood, which is often easily gathered in quantity just by hand, and freshly cut green wood will serve to keep your fire going for warmth. Green aspen, spruce, pine, and fir will all burn without further additions of dry wood once you have a sufficient base of coals and provided you add new fuel well before the fire has dwindled to coals alone. You can make a fire last longer by using extra-large pieces. Large logs, say a foot or more through and six feet long, though tedious to make with a light axe, will burn quite a long while, and two at a time, laid parallel and close together, will keep burning at a steady rate. Do avoid wood that is obviously resinous, however, as it will burn very hot and be gone very quickly. Dry pine is fine; pitchy, dry pine will drive you off while it burns and leave you looking for fresh fuel much too soon.

For a long-burning, steady fire try using green wood in rounds as large as you can cut conveniently with your axe. Lay the pieces parallel because green wood maintains fire along the contact between the pieces. Make your fire a good six feet in length. It will burn hotter and faster toward the centre, and when you rebuild you will have the unburned ends to throw in on the main coal-bed to help the next lot of green to start up.

Do not go into the night without some tinder and a large reserve of good dry wood at hand. You may sleep until the fire is down too far for green wood to catch again without dry wood to help it.

Particularly in cold winter weather one is anxious to have the fire burn for long intervals and not go out, even when burned down to little more than a heap of ashes. A useful method is to find a dry, standing snag as large as you can handle with your axe, then fell it, leaving a generous stump. Buck the felled trunk into lengths for the fire and set your fire hard by the stump. Of course, you then set your shelter and bedding brush in a suitable position to the fire, rather than the other way around. You will gather additional fuel from the surrounding growth, and should you sleep so soundly that your fire dies down and you wake up feeling cold, the stump will still be burning beneath the ashes and will quickly revive when fresh logs are thrown on it.

In some country you will find willows growing to twenty feet high and to four or five inches on the stem. They occur in clumps, and the clumps spread over large areas of flat land adjacent to water. Each of the clumps will consist of green stems with many dry stems interspersed. It is often convenient to make your fire right in the midst of a larger clump of stems, and to gather additional fuel from the surrounding clumps. The mix of green and dry stems in the clump will keep your fire going for many hours with only occasional additions of further fuel.

If you are camped in very deep snow you may choose not to clear away to ground level for your bed-and-fire area, particularly if you are on skis and have no snowshoe for a shovel. In such a case you will lay your bedding and walking brush on top of the snow, and then will prepare a fire base to prevent the fire sinking out of sight as it melts the snow below.

To do this, cut long green pieces of wood, as thick as possible with the time and equipment at hand, and lay these side by side, placed as much as a foot down into the snow. You'll need to clear away some snow beforehand, and then back-fill on top of the green pieces to the surface level with green branches and snow mixed. Then top this with another layer of green pieces placed side by side. The whole bed should be a foot or two longer and wider than the proposed fire, say eight feet by four feet.

If you decide on a double lean-to or a brush tipi for sheltering, you will rely on your best dry wood as much as possible to reduce the smoke problem. However, you may be forced to use green wood due to a shortage of dry. If so, save the dry for those times, such as when you are cooking and drying clothes, when you will want to be moving about in the shelter. Use the green for keeping the fire going while you are resting on your bedding at ground level. Even with quite smoky wood, the air near ground level is usually tolerable, as the smoke rises. Discover by trial how much cold air you must let in at the doorway to keep the green burning and to scour out the smoke.

■ FIRE SAFETY

In all those seasons when there is no snow on the ground, you have a primary responsibility to be impeccably careful with your fire so that it does not spread into the bush. The fact that you are in an emergency camp, with your safety in some measure dependent on fire, does not remove that responsibility.

A fire in a small clearing of green grass or in deciduous bush is safer than a fire in coniferous bush. A fire beside a stream is safer than a fire some distance from a stream. The farther any fire is from dry ground-trash, the safer it is. A small fire is safer than a large one. Stop to think about fire safety from every point of view before settling on a location for a fire. If you must compromise other desirable elements of a campsite for the sake of fire safety, do so. In a prolonged dry spell, when the whole bush is explosively dry, you can invariably do without a fire for a short camp of a night or two. Better a little discomfort than to live the rest of your life with a forest fire on your conscience.

If you have decided that it is safe to light a fire — most times it is — and if you have chosen a site in the timber, clear away all organic ground-trash over a sufficient area that your fire will have adequate clearance of three feet minimum in all directions for a small cooking fire and five feet minimum for any larger fire. Clear the fire bed down to mineral soil.

In a green, grassy opening or at a stream edge, this precaution may not be necessary, and in rainy spells you may find safe ground in the timber without quite so much preparation, but the onus is on you to be sure that what you do with fire is no hazard to the forest. Millions of dollars' worth of prime timber goes up in smoke annually, a great part of it from the carelessness of people who venture into bushland. Let's not be part of that.

If you propose to sleep beside a fire, you want safety from embers and a steady heat with long intervals between refuelling.

It is difficult to give advice about safety from embers. Spruce, both green and dry, seems consistently hazardous. Lodgepole pine is often quite safe, yet in some growing conditions will throw embers. Dry aspen in some locations is completely safe, in others wholly unreliable. I have found that an ember from dry aspen will persist long enough to ignite cotton cloth, while usually an ember from lodgepole pine will not. Trial of the wood at hand is your best guide.

When you are done with your fire, drown it. It is unforgivable to walk away from any fire, however burned out it may appear, without drowning it. Pour on twice as much water as you think necessary, then stir the ashes and coals into a thoroughly muddy mass with a stick. Pour on more water and stir again. Repeat this process long past the point at which the fire seems absolutely dead. *That* is the sort of fail-safe conduct which is wanted in fire management in the bush!

To go well in the bush is to take care that you will have the bush to go into again.

SEVEN

Food and Water

You now know about clothing and footwear, about not getting lost through use of fundamental map and compass techniques, about sheltering, and about fire. You have some ideas for keeping warm, dry, and rested, and with any luck you'll soon be out, since you know which way to go to get there.

If you can't get out right away, which might be the case with a downed aircraft, or if you aren't disposed to go without water and food, even for a night, you will want to do something to meet those needs.

■ FINDING WATER

Water is a fairly immediate imperative. You can go longer without food than water, and also the absence of water puts a constraint on the use of fire.

Fortunately, water is usually easily found in the boreal and sub-boreal forests of North America — those great stretches of country we call the bush. In winter it is all around us for the melting, and in other seasons it is generally quickly located. It is seldom that you will not come to water within a reasonable time simply by walking downhill.

Only two factors are likely to force you to camp without water:

injury so serious that you must shelter where you are as best you can, or your own carelessness in acknowledging too late in the day that you aren't going to get out by nightfall.

If you acknowledge in good time that you are going to spend the coming night under the big sky (a matter of no anxiety and perhaps even of pure adventure to the competent person in the bush), your first search will be for water.

Use your map. You know roughly where you are. Is there a stream, pond, or lake shown anywhere near? You may not know your position closely enough to hit a small pond by compass bearing, but you can surely cut across a watercourse or larger lake. If a watercourse turns out to be dry at this season, follow it downhill. It will lead in time to a more consistent stream course, and you will have water.

If you are in gently undulating country of the sort that the map can't define in close detail, you may get little help from the map. You may be as far from a defined watercourse as you are from the road you aren't going to reach before dark.

Often the simplest solution is to go back to where you last crossed water. However, if that is a matter of some hours' travel, then assess the ground and work downhill. When you come to a distinct draw, follow it. It may be dry, but it will be a tributary to a larger draw or depression, and if that too is dry, it will be tributary to something else. Usually, sooner rather than later, you will come to water or to swampy ground.

Your best bet is a running stream or an obviously fresh pond or lake. Failing these, and finding still water or muddy ground in a swamp, make a shovel-like stick with your axe and do some digging. Swamp water filtered through a few feet of soil is better than water from a stagnant pool.

If in any doubt about the safety of the water, boil it.

You will have noticed by now that the factors which determine your choice of a campsite are becoming clear. You need water, firewood, camp brush, and shelter from the wind. But the first of these is water.

■ FOOD

Then what about food? Should you carry it with you or gather it in the bush or do some of both? If you gather it, should you rely on edible plants or game or both? If you rely on game, how do you secure it? Do you snare or do you hunt? What about small game versus big game? Should you go prepared to hunt for moose or caribou if your aircraft goes down or should you concentrate on setting rabbit snares? How about fishing?

For the day-hiker whose time out will seldom exceed a night or two, the problem is easily handled by carrying a small supply of light rations. Two or three pouches of freeze-dried food weigh but a few ounces. On the other hand, what goes into an aircraft survival-pack should be decided according to the type of wildlife environment you will be flying over and your own set of skills.

CARRYING FOOD ON A DAY HIKE

Let's consider day-hiking first and begin with the observation that most people in good health can carry on at a fair level of physical activity for two or three days without food and do themselves no harm in the process. There is an initial interval during which the body converts to drawing on body reserves of fat for producing energy. During this period, one feels rather weak and may need to avoid sudden fast movements, but after the adjustment is made, most people in good health will have the energy to cover quite a distance every day. On the other hand, the unpleasantness of this experience could be greatly reduced by simply carrying a little food in the day pack.

Principles of Nutrition

What should you carry? Without exception the manuals that I have read on the subject recommend relying in large measure on food with high sugar content as a way to get the most calories for the least weight. I disagree strongly with this view, but when I do I know I tread on difficult ground. Amateur and professional nutritionists alike are unable to agree on this question, so I do not expect my views to be regarded as authoritative. I am a woodsman, not a nutritionist. I simply pass on to you what seems reasonable to me and what has worked in my experience. You should then consider the question in the light of your own convictions and decide what is best for you.

On one thing we can all agree: we do want to carry the most food value possible with the least addition of weight to the pack.

If by food value you mean simply calories, then I suppose you should carry refined sugar and nothing else. However, I don't think anyone supposes that straight sugar is sensible nutrition, even for one day or one meal, which illustrates my first main point: what constitutes good nutrition doesn't change because you happen to be in the bush. You may indeed need more calories, but these should still be obtained from wholesome sources, not from candy bars and other junk food. Even plain chocolate without a candy filling is heavy with refined sugar.

When I asked the Canadian Department of National Defence for material used by that department in survival instruction, I received written material containing, among others, a recommendation that one carry "a package of wholesome hard candy"! Wholesome, if it means anything at all, is precisely opposite to junk food of any kind, high in calories or otherwise.

A suggested ration kit for two people for fourteen days included, among other items, 9 ounces of raisins, 1 pound of sugar, 4 ounces of Pream, 12 ounces of coffee or cocoa, and 12 chocolate bars. What an incredible waste of weight! Do these people realize that they are talking of something so vital as the preservation of *your* life?

Let's consider energy production. In order to supply fuel to the individual cells where the fuel is burned to produce energy, the body must, through digestion, reduce the food which is eaten to a simple sugar that can be carried in the blood for delivery to the cells.

Consider at the same time the requirement for energy. The daily activity of most people requires a constant level of energy throughout the day and this is certainly the case for most physically active pursuits, including travel on foot in the bush. One does not want a great surge of energy just after a meal, followed in turn by a dearth of it two hours later. One wants a steady and adequate level of energy throughout the day.

Consider what happens when you eat a meal consisting mainly of sugar and other highly refined carbohydrates which, already so close in structure to sugar, convert almost instantly to sugar in digestion — for example, a breakfast of those atrocious processed cereals to which, as if the sugar added by the manufacturers were not enough, most people add yet more. In such a case, the whole energy potential of the meal comes onstream at once, not evenly over a period of several hours, and the body simply cannot use it. The body is forced to get it out of the way and moves it off to storage in the form of fat. Thus a short interval of sufficient energy is followed by a long interval in which you don't have enough. Large numbers of people go through their days in this pattern, adding to their fat storage, which is what they do not want, yet failing to get an even level of energy production, which is what, presumably, they do want.

Protein is essential to the growth and maintenance of body tissue and is also important as a regulator in the production of blood sugar from ingested food. A meal consisting of carbohydrates, fats, and a generous supply of protein will not produce an initial blood-sugar level that is too high, but will maintain an adequate blood-sugar level over a period of many hours. Doubtless the quality of the carbohydrates is also important in the process. Unprocessed, unrefined carbohydrates, such as a porridge of freshly cracked whole grains eaten without sugar, will convert more slowly than cornflakes with sugar. However, there is a growing belief that the regulating effect of protein on energy production from other foods eaten with it is an important factor.

Now let me step into the eye of the storm. There are many who argue that the best diet for both weight control and energy production is one which is high in protein, generous but not as high in fat, and very restricted in carbohydrate. No chocolate bars in your pack here, and no raisins either.

I have been impressed for much of my life that the Inuit, the people we erroneously refer to as Eskimo, though living in a harsh environment which demanded constant physical effort to survive, did so well on a diet of fat meat with, for the most part, no carbohydrates at all. In fact, since they have begun to lean heavily on carbohydrate foods imported to the North in trade, their health has deteriorated alarmingly. We must keep in mind, of course, that this may be as much the fault of choosing the wrong carbohydrates as of the shift from protein and fat. I am sure that a family eating a little food from the land and quantities of whole grains would be in vastly better health than one eating the same limited amount from the land and large quantities of straight white-flour bannock.

However, I consider it instructive that the Inuit did live so well on a diet which often for long periods included no carbohydrate at all. It seems instructive, too, that on a diet exclusively of animal tissue the Inuit ate prodigious quantities of fat with the lean; in fact, they ate every scrap of fat they could secure apart from that which they had to spare to burn in their lamps for heating and allow in the ration for their dogs. They ate their meat raw, wasting no fat in fuel for cooking. I have read no reports of obesity among the Inuit or of an insufficiency of energy when they were on the aboriginal diet. We know that pemmican was widely used by Indian people and by Europeans on the frontier, people who required vast amounts of energy day in and day out. The men employed to paddle the freight canoes and carry cargo over the portages during the fur trade were heavy users of pemmican. Most pemmican was made from only lean, dried meat and rendered fat, although dried berries would be added occasionally. Instructions on how you can make your own pemmican will be given later in the chapter.

My conclusion is that whatever position one takes on the high-protein, low-carbohydrate diet as it is advanced presently for weight control, one must acknowledge that many people have lived successfully on a diet high in meat and fat with little or no carbohydrate for long intervals, and that we can do the same if circumstance requires it. We may also, if we choose, use proteins and fats for concentrated trail food in preference to the highly refined carbohydrates which are so often recommended.

What To Take

So back to the day hike. What are we to carry against the chance of being out for a longer time than expected?

Why not a few pouches of freeze-dried food of the sort prepared for the backpacking trade? These are expensive, admittedly, but we are talking of only a few meals, and food preserved in this way has a long shelf-life. You can select your foods according to your convictions about nutrition. One failing of these foods is that you must have water for their preparation, and they will be of little use if an injury forces you to camp without water.

I often toss in three or four tins of the less expensive sardines in oil, along with a can opener. Here is a mix of protein and fat which keeps me going remarkably well, notwithstanding how little volume of food is found in each tin. I'll wager it is a better choice than chocolate bars any day.

I would take any dehydrated soup from the supermarket shelf ahead of a chocolate bar if that were the only choice, but I doubt whether these are a source of good nutrition. You might disagree, and they do make a quick hot drink, very welcome on a rainy day.

I have in my kit of core items a commercially prepared emergency ration, labelled SR Ration, from Compactas of Bergen, Norway, which is often used by bush-line aircraft. A two-hundred-and-fifteen-gram (seven-and-a-half-ounce) package contains one thousand calories and is ready to eat. I carry it for its convenience, although I believe it leans rather too much to carbohydrate. I also carry snare wire!

Dried lean meat, known as jerky, has long been a standby. I know of no commercial source of *good* jerky but you can easily make your own. Cut lean beef from the round into long thin strips, about the thickness of your finger, and dry them thoroughly by any fairly fast means. In the sun in a wind strong enough to keep off the flies is perfect, but your oven at a very low setting with the door open will do. A box with racks in it to hold the meat and a light bulb for heat, with holes in the box for a continuous flow of air, will also work. Be absolutely certain that the drying is complete. The finished jerky should break with a fairly crisp snap and crumble somewhat when chewed. There must be *no* moisture left. If someone suggests to you that a body can't go well in the bush for a few days on no other food but jerky, that person is contradicting the experience of countless Indians and frontiersmen.

If you favour whole grains for a healthy diet, you can take your chosen mix of grains and perhaps unpolished rice and soy grits. All these are easily cooked in a billycan over an open fire, and a pound or two goes a long way.

I would like to suggest that, quite apart from the possibility of being delayed a night or two in getting back to base, a little bit of low-weight food in the day pack along with some simple cooking utensils — there are some excellent one- and two-person mess kits available or you can assemble your own — can make your venturing into bushland more enjoyable when all goes well. You don't have to wait for an emergency to light a fire to cook a meal and make some tea, especially in the colder weather when a hot meal is so much better than sandwiches. Have enough of your trail food in your pack that you have some for both your lunch today and the emergency which might occur.

In addition to carrying foods of good nutritive value yet little weight in the pack, you might also consider gathering from the land as well as, or instead of, carrying your food. If it is berry season, berries and jerky make a better meal than jerky alone. If you can snare a rabbit or get a fool hen with a stick, by all means do so. I have eaten many a grouse when a meal hour caught me unexpectedly away from camp and my main supplies.

On the other hand, if you are delayed on a day hike, the chances are that the time you would spend gathering food from the land, with the exception of berries in season, is about the time it will take you to finish your journey. Also, most edible plants are mainly carbohydrate foods, and if you believe in the need for protein you will have to set snares as well. Then again, for a day or two you won't suffer from a lack of meat to go with wild edible plants.

My own choice is to carry food on a day hike and supplement it with food from the land if it is not too much trouble to do so, but I do not spend much time at it. I would as soon spend the time on the journey out.

FOOD FOR A LONGER JOURNEY

We turn now to the question of food for the longer stay you might have to make should you, for example, go down in an aircraft. In such a case you would do well to remember that a number of factors may make survival on a diet of edible wild plants alone quite difficult.

Limitations of Wild Plants

For one thing, wild plants are seasonal and very few are usefully available in the winter months. It is true that cattail root and rock tripe, a lichen, can sometimes be secured in the winter, but they are a last resort. Indians of the northern bush, when speaking of the old days, have emphasized that if the dried foods stored in the previous summer and fall ran out in winter and game could not be located, starvation was the certain outlook.

Second, even when available, wild plant foods do not provide the strength of diet needed for the vigour of bush life. The contribution to protein requirements is so slight as to be negligible. As a supplement to meat and fish they are, of course, an excellent means of securing additional vitamins, minerals, and the otherwise-absent carbohydrate, but I caution you not to look on them as sufficient in themselves.

The third caution is that the availability of edible plant material varies from one area to another, although there are some useful plants which occur so widely as to appear in almost all the bushlands of the northern United States, of Alaska, and of Canada. However, the use of wild plants as food must be studied with the region in which you are interested in mind, and with the help of the best texts on the subject that you can secure. Avoid relying on survival manuals which at best are second-hand sources and will not give you the authoritative detail that will enable you to become proficient in locating and preparing wild plants suitable for food. Go to the texts which specialize in this subject and, with the texts in hand, go into the bush to learn by direct experience.

Having said that, I do not propose to deal further with the subject here, although this is not to discount its value. Wild plant foods can be a useful supplement to animal and fish sources, but the latter are the key to survival over any period of time and with these I will deal at length. The specialized texts are the best source for wild-plant-food information.

Let us return to the question of a longer stay in the bush, necessitated by, for example, a downed aircraft, and leading to perhaps many weeks of reliance on what you have brought with you and what you can shoot or take in a snare, deadfall, or fishnet.

Being Prepared

Transport Canada publishes regulations requiring certain equipment and supplies to be carried on aircraft during flights over sparsely settled areas. The food requirement is specified in terms of calorific value only, calling for ten thousand calories per person to be carried on the aircraft. If this is rationed at two thousand calories per day, it constitutes a five-day supply.

The same regulations require that equipment for gathering food from the land be carried as well, specifically snare wire and gill-net. In the event that the downed aircraft is not soon located it is clear that gathering from the land will be the means of surviving. The snare wire and fish-net will be your key to staying alive.

I do not know what the statistical probability is that any one flight, out of the thousands of flights made by bush aircraft every year, will go down, but it clearly is not a high risk. Assuming that the forced landing is survived by the occupants of the craft, an early pick-up by search aircraft is a reasonable probability. Clearly the odds are slight that you will need a substantial supply of food with which to keep alive as a result of misadventure when travelling as a passenger in a bush-line aircraft.

The point of preparedness, however, is to provide for the statistically unlikely yet potentially disastrous event. I can think of no situation I should enjoy less than to have survived a forced landing only to suffer and perhaps die for want of food, knowing all the while that the choice had been mine to put both food and food-securing equipment into my pack before I boarded the aircraft. When you board a bush-line aircraft you are entitled to carry with you at least as much equipment as you can strap to a pack-board. I travelled extensively in this way in the Yukon Territory and northern British Columbia and only once did a pilot express concern that I should be adding such weight to the load. Although I had been one of the first passengers to book for the flight I offered to stay behind rather than go without my pack, even though this meant waiting several days for another flight. I eventually went on board, along with my pack, but after that, when booking a flight, I always specified that I would have baggage in the form of a loaded pack-board.

Such a pack should contain both food and food-capturing equipment, although in what proportions will depend on how much you want to depend on carried rations and how much on hunting and fishing. There is no one right answer to this question. You must reach your own decision through assessment of the sorts of foods you can carry, the nature of the wildlife habitat which you fly over, and your own knowledge and skills in capturing food from the land.

Food To Take Along

Let's consider some choices. Freeze-dried foods weigh little. Data from one manufacturer suggests they contain about two thousand calories to the pound for eggs, meat, and main courses of a meat-and-vegetable mix. (That is, two thousand calories to the pound as carried, before reconstituting with water.) You can hold out for a long time on two thousand calories a day, which suggests that twenty pounds of this food would give you a useful margin of time in which to develop your ability to live off the land.

Don't overlook some of the old standby hard foods much used by trappers and others on the frontier: dried beans, rice (unpolished of course), and cracked whole grains (not your instant rolled oats, please). A few pounds of these go a long way, in both total calories and sound nutrition, and all are easily cooked in a pot hung over an open fire.

Pemmican takes time to make beforehand but, as mentioned earlier, it is a highly concentrated protein- and fat-based food with a strong historic endorsement in the fur trade. You can make your own pemmican. It consists of pounded jerky mixed with rendered tallow. Make jerky by the method I have described, then pound the jerky into a fine crumble. Mix this crumbled jerky with hot, melted tallow and pack the mix into tins of a convenient size of the sort which have a plastic, snap-on lid. No special seal is needed. The jerky in the pemmican won't spoil, and the tendency of the tallow to go rancid can't be prevented by any canning or bottling process.

My suspicion is that pemmican is at its best in its first season and grows increasingly rancid as it gets older. You can help to keep yours fresh by purchasing your fat as lard or beef tallow to which preservatives have been added to prevent rancidity. One may not care for the additives, but they are less harmful than the rancidity which they prevent.

Now, all dried and preserved foods, if used as the only diet over a lengthy time, will lead to scurvy and other vitamin-deficiency diseases. You might wish to consider a fairly complete vitamin supplement as part of your food pack, and at the very least I would take a supply of Vitamin C. At the same time, even with vitamin supplements, I don't suggest that you should, to any avoidable extent, live exclusively on these carried foods.

I suggest you begin at once to capture game and fish and look on these as your primary food source. Resort to your carried foods as little as possible. Live off the land and keep your carried foods against some later emergency or use them sparingly to balance a meat supply which is too lean to be sufficient in itself, such as a supply of varying hare alone.

CAPTURING WILD GAME AND FISH

There is a surprising variety of game to be found throughout the bushlands of the northern contiguous United States, Canada, and Alaska. Not all animals are found everywhere, and it sometimes happens that there will be a virtual dearth of any game, but in most situations a supply of useful animal food-sources does exist.

Here is a partial list of small game, much of which may be taken with snares: snowshoe, or varying, hare; rock rabbit or pika; marmot or woodchuck; yellow-bellied marmot; hoary marmot or whistler; Columbian groundsquirrel; Parry groundsquirrel; Arctic groundsquirrel; red squirrel; beaver; muskrat; porcupine; grouse and ptarmigan; various waterfowl.

The following large game animals may be found and hunted,

depending on the particular situation: caribou, moose, sheep, goat, bear.

There are also a number of the predator species, seldom thought of as food, which can quite well be eaten in time of necessity. Some of these can be taken in a baited deadfall, though many of them are seldom taken by any means. I refer, for example, to the fox, coyote, wolf, cougar, lynx, bobcat, mink, marten, fisher, wolverine, and otter.

Before we talk about how to snare or shoot these animals and birds we'd better be clear on one point: all species of larger game and most of the smaller are protected by law against being taken for either much or all of the year, depending on where you happen to find yourself. It goes without saying that if you are merely delayed in the bush for a day or two from a day hike you have little legitimate reason to contravene a game ordinance and certainly not to take down large game.

It also goes without saying that if you are down in a remote region, perhaps some distance off course, if you have been unable to make radio contact with anyone on the outside, and if search conditions are poor, then you had better bring down as much meat as you can and deal with the legality of it later if the question should ever arise.

Unless radio contact has been made I would, for my own part, always take game at the first opportunity, the larger the better. Ten pounds of varying hare will require a number of successful captures by snare sets and is very desirable; seven or eight hundred pounds of moose meat is a jolly sight more desirable and, if the moose are there and you know how to go about it, may not take any more time and little additional energy to secure.

The equipment for securing fish and game breaks down fairly clearly into categories defined by the nature of the supply itself. Let's consider these before deciding what should go into the kit.

In summary, large game is taken with certainty mainly with a large-bore rifle; small game may be taken mainly with snares, a small-bore rifle, or a shotgun; fish may be taken with hook and line but usually in greater abundance and with more certainty by gill-net.

Choosing Firearms

During the years in which I travelled extensively in the north as a passenger in bush aircraft, I lashed to my pack, always, a large-bore rifle, and I carried in the pack a hundred rounds of ammunition. The rifle weighed nine pounds, the ammunition seven. Where big game is a possibility, this equipment, I am convinced, is a necessity. What sort of large-bore rifle should you choose? To the novice this can be a baffling question, made only more so by the incredible array of makes, models, calibres, and chamber dimensions which confront him or her on inquiry at the local sporting-goods store. Let's sort this out so that anyone may arrive easily at a sensible choice.

What actually brings down the meat you badly need for your survival is the bullet. Bullets come in many sizes, and we refer to bullet size first by calibre, which is the diameter of the bullet in inches or millimetres, and secondly by weight, which we define in grains. We may, for example, choose a .30-calibre bullet of 200 grains in weight.

A bullet of any calibre is driven by the force created when a propellent powder of a particular burning rate is ignited within a brass cartridge case in the chamber of the rifle. The rapidly expanding gases force the bullet to travel out the barrel at a velocity which will depend on more factors than we need to consider here — factors such as bullet weight, case capacity, and the burning rate and amount of powder used.

A bullet of any given calibre may be matched with a brass case of many different shapes and sizes. The combination of bullet and brass case with its propellent charge we call a cartridge. The size and shape of the brass case is a main determinant of how fast the bullet will travel and over what distance it will remain effective.

There may be a profusion of cartridges based on one calibre. All these cartridges carry a bullet of the same diameter and often of overlapping weight ranges. One cartridge may push a given bullet at a muzzle velocity of twenty-two hundred feet per second while another will move the same bullet at three thousand feet per second.

Cartridges are variously labelled, which adds to the confusion, although all do make reference to the bullet calibre. In .30 calibre, for example, we find among others these cartridges: the .30-30 Winchester (.30 calibre with an original load of 30 grains of black powder); the 300 Savage (.30 calibre on a case brought out by the Savage Arms Company); the .30-06 (.30 calibre with a case size and dimension adopted by the U.S. government in 1906); the .308 Winchester (.30 calibre with a case adopted by the NATO Alliance and known in military parlance as the 7.62 mm NATO cartridge but brought out as a sporting cartridge by Winchester Repeating Arms); the 300 H & H Magnum (.30 calibre with a very large case by Holland and Holland).

No wonder the novice is confused! But add to this profusion of cartridges, even within one calibre, a further profusion of rifle manufacturers turning out many firearms based on the bolt action, the lever action, the slide action, and the self-loading or semi-automatic, variously chambered for one or more cartridges, and you really start to shake your head.

Calibres vary from .22 inches to some old blockbusters of black-powder days of .50 inches. In each of the calibres there will be one or more brass cases which, together with that bullet diameter, constitute a cartridge.

Rifles come in considerable variety as well. A rifle, by any manufacturer and based on whatever basic action, is simply an instrument by which you direct and fire the cartridge. Each of the many rifle manufacturers produces a variety of models, and each model is chambered for one or more cartridges (including any popular cartridge brought out by and bearing the name of a competitor, such as the bolt-action rifles by virtually all other makers which are chambered for the .270 Winchester cartridge).

The selection of equipment with which to shoot big game *begins with the selection of bullet calibre, which is followed by the selection of a cartridge*, and only after these have been settled do you consider such questions as action type and manufacturer's model.

The bullet should be chosen for its ability to reach out over a long distance with sufficient delivered energy to kill a large animal, and to get there on a trajectory of minimal drop so that it is possible to estimate roughly where the bullet will strike. You also want the recoil created by the sudden pressure of the fired propellant to be tolerable to you, as you will never shoot accurately if it is not.

Experience has shown that bullets of too-small diameter and too-little weight, though they may be driven at very high initial velocities, do not deliver energy well over a distance. Bullets of large diameter and great weight, unless driven at velocities requiring enormous initial pressures, cannot hold velocity and drop markedly below the line of sight at a relatively short range.

There is a fairly general consensus among experienced riflemen that the optimum calibre for big game in North America is in the .270 calibre on the smaller side and in the .30 calibre on the larger.

Within the .270 calibre, only the .270 Winchester cartridge is available. Between the .270 and .30 calibre, a variety of cartridges are available in 7 mm, which is .284 calibre when expressed in inches. The 7 × 57 Mauser approaches the .270 Winchester in ballistic performance, but the remainder, except for the 7 mm Remington Magnum, fall well short of it.

Once into .30 calibre you have a great many choices, but one cartridge, the .30-06, gives clearly the best performance, unless you opt for magnums.

I recommend against magnum cartridges in 7 mm and .30 calibre, however, and, for that matter, against any magnum cartridge for the purposes we are concerned with here. Only in very long-range mountain or tundra shooting do they offer an advantage and, unless you are experienced and practised in dealing with the recoil they create, you won't shoot accurately enough to gain the advantage. A competent hunter, armed with the .270 Winchester or the .30-06 cartridge, can usually accomplish whatever needs doing. If he is not competent, a magnum cartridge isn't going to help.

The popularity of magnum cartridges in North America has little to do with ballistic necessity and everything to do, I'm afraid, with a misguided male ego which equates bigger, stronger, and noisier with better. In .270 calibre, then, choose the .270 Winchester cartridge, and in .30 calibre I suggest the .30-06 as it has the best ballistics within the calibre at manageable levels of recoil. You might wish, however, to go to the .308 Winchester (the cartridge adopted by NATO), since it gives you the choice of a lever-action rifle and performs almost as well as the .30-06 ballistically. As a bush-country cartridge, it has much to be said for it.

The profusion of choices is now reduced to three: the .270 Winchester, the .30-06, and the .308 Winchester.

In these calibres, I recommend the following bullet weights and styles: a 150-grain pointed soft-point in the .270 cartridge; a 180-grain pointed soft-point in the .30-06 cartridge; and a 165-grain pointed soft-point in the .308 Winchester cartridge. These will serve you until your own assessment and experience lead you to a different choice.

It remains then to select a rifle. There are four basic actions: the bolt, the lever, the slide, and the self-loading, or semi-automatic.

The strongest of these actions is the bolt action, and for accuracy it is widely accepted as the best. With one or two exceptions, only bolt-action rifles are chambered for the .270 Winchester and the .30-06 cartridges. Remington does chamber a slide-action rifle for the .30-06, and this has a distinct advantage for the left-handed shooter.

Some people have a strong preference for a lever-action rifle. No lever action is strong enough for the .270 Winchester or .30-06 cartridge, and it is doubtful if any lever action will deliver the same accuracy as a good-quality bolt action. Still, you can obtain perfectly satisfactory bush-country accuracy in lever actions. If you want a lever action, then go to the .308 Winchester cartridge for which at least one lever-action rifle is chambered — the Savage Model 99C.

Avoid self-loading rifles. Some of the pressure which is wanted for driving the bullet must be drawn off to operate the mechanism, and both accuracy and velocity are affected. Once again, some men mistake the rapidity of fire possible with these rifles for superiority, either in the rifle or in themselves, and they waste both good meat and ammunition in the process.

Do not buy an old, worked-over military-surplus rifle. Buy a new rifle by an established sporting-rifle manufacturer or a used rifle of similar origin which has been checked and test-fired by a competent gunsmith. The superior quality of a top-grade sporting rifle over a military clunker is too great an advantage to be done without.

Sighting equipment is also important. Undoubtedly the most accurate available is the telescope with cross-hairs or cross-hairs and post. However, for a survival-equipment rifle I suggest you purchase a rifle which can be equipped with a hunting aperture sighting system. Such a sight system is far more rugged and, in a situation where you can't have repairs or replacements made in the event of damage or malfunction, you will be much more certain of continued service. Excellent accuracy is possible with an aperture, and the risk of damage during transport is negligible. By contrast, the risk of damage during transport to the telescopic sight is considerable.

Finally, with the guidance of an experienced rifleman, learn to handle your rifle with absolute care and safety and to shoot it with knowledgeable competence. In virtually every community in North America, there is a rifle club or fish-and-game association through which you can find someone willing to help you get off to a good start.

I have two pieces of advice on handling which your adviser might not give you. First, in cold weather do not bring your rifle into the warmth of the fire or of the interior of the shelter. Leave it out in the cold. The change in temperature will cause condensation which leads to rust. This can occur inside the barrel near the muzzle and destroy accuracy. Second, in any weather do not oil the mechanism but keep it impeccably clean with solvent. An oiled mechanism will frequently fail to fire in cold weather, whereas an impeccably clean mechanism will function at temperatures as severe as any in which you are likely to go out to hunt.

If four people are travelling together in a bush aircraft there is no need for more than one survival rifle with ammunition on board. Many, but by no means all, pilots will see to this need in any aircraft assigned to them. All you need do is ensure that this requirement is met by the pilot, by another passenger, or by you.

The choice of weapons for small game is not quite so straightforward. Much small game may be taken with a shotgun, with a small-bore rifle using a .22 rim-fire cartridge, or with snares. Some small game is taken more readily by one type of equipment than the others and no one choice is best across the board. The varying hare in winter can be taken in quantity with snares yet be seen so seldom as to make shooting a futile undertaking; the willow grouse may be taken readily with a small-bore rifle or shotgun but not easily by snare; ducks and geese are difficult to secure in most circumstances except by an experienced hunter with a shotgun.

The shotgun can be eliminated immediately as a possible choice, since shotgun shells are very bulky in relation to their meat-securing potential. The small-bore rifle is the next alternative. Several hundred rounds of .22 long-rifle ammunition can be carried for the weight and space of twenty shotgun shells. As the rate of expenditure of either is usually one successful shot for each meal secured this also helps rule out the shotgun.

The question facing you now is, do you take the small-bore rifle with a supply of ammunition or not? The answer will depend on the circumstances. If you feel that you should take only one firearm as part of your kit, then you must decide which kind to take according to the type of wildlife habitat you will be flying over. In some stretches of bush, and perhaps in some seasons more than others, you can live well with the aid of a small-bore rifle. In the late summer and early fall of an excellent year for willow grouse, you could live moderately well with a small-bore rifle on this game alone. On the other hand, with a large-bore rifle for big game and snare wire and twine for small game you have a chance for success in both categories.

If you do decide to take a small-bore rifle as part of your kit, I suggest a bolt-action repeater chambered for the .22 long-rifle rim-fire cartridge, and this time I suggest using a telescopic sight with the iron sights left on as a back-up. The scope can be mounted in such a way that if it should be damaged it can be removed and you can carry on with the iron sights. A scope sight on a good-quality .22 rim-fire rifle makes exceptional accuracy possible, and you may take your game not only with a single shot, but also with the chance of a shot to the head to avoid wasting meat.

Hunting Techniques

Now to the larger question: given these sorts of equipment for capturing food, how, exactly, does one go about it? How do you hunt the moose or snare the rabbit or fill the gill-net with a load of nourishing char?

How, indeed? The successful hunter goes far afield and returns often enough with meat, but if you ask him precisely how he achieved this result, he will probably be unable to tell you except in the vaguest way, referring frequently to luck. Others, ardently desiring success, may speak of the ways of the game, of the wind, of the habits of the bull in rut, of the freshness of the track, and of the manure still steaming by the morning bed, but will come back dispirited and empty-handed.

I cannot with certainty illustrate the path to a sure kill and a camp abundant with meat. Even so, there are better and worse ways to apply yourself to the problem, and if you have some sense of what to do and what not to do, your chances of success will increase. The basic steps and principles for the capture of game may seem obvious; they are, nevertheless, the foundation of good hunting. You must also bear in mind, however, that the habits of game differ widely from species to species and you must adapt the basic principles to the type of game and the habitat with which you are immediately concerned.

The steps to a kill are these: first, the determination that game useful to you *may* exist within hunting reach of your camp; second, confirmation that such game is *in fact* utilizing ground within your hunting reach; third, locating the game itself; and fourth, getting a view sufficient for a killing shot or setting snares in such a way that capture is assured.

Whether you seek groundsquirrels or moose and whether you have been hunting for an hour or two weeks, the steps remain essentially the same. You can develop your competence by considering each step in turn.

First, how do you determine that game useful to you *may* exist within hunting reach of your camp?

You do this by assessing how well the habitat fulfils the needs of the animals known to occur in your general area. Moose occur throughout most of British Columbia, the Yukon Territory, and Alaska, and in parts of the northern Prairie provinces, Ontario, Quebec, and the Maritimes. However, for any particular location in the fall and winter, the presence or absence of moose hinges almost entirely on whether or not the specific vegetation essential to their fall and winter diet is found in the area.

If you know the habitat requirements of bears, and you find yourself in need of meat in the berry season in mountain country, you know at once that game useful to your survival is very likely within hunting reach of your camp.

Of course, I cannot possibly give here all the detailed information you will need to manage this first step successfully; the number of useful species of animals and the variability of habitat throughout all our bushlands are both much too great. *You* must prepare *yourself*. In doing so you will discover, if you haven't already, a most vital dimension of this bush into which you venture or over which you travel — that is, the extensive and varied life which thrives there.

Few will deny that there is pleasure in a day out on cross-country skis on a well-marked trail, even if your attention is absorbed primarily by how fast you are travelling, how fit you are, and how brilliant the snow-clad landscape is in the winter sun. Yet the adventure will be enhanced tenfold if you discover, perhaps while breaking new trail beside a meadow and along a frozen stream, traces of otter and mink and beaver; or observe that on yonder south-facing slope, which supports a stand of mixed fir, pine, and aspen, there is an undergrowth of upland willow, young birch, and red osier dogwood on which moose have been feeding.

You can develop the knowledge of animals in their habitat which enables you to make an effective assessment of the ground you might someday need to exploit for survival by reading, by listening to people experienced in a particular habitat, and by direct study in the field.

The biology departments of provincial and state universities are a rich source of titles for your reading. Extensive field research on all the big-game animals, as well as on many of the fur-bearers and smaller game, has been done in the last few decades and has broadened significantly our understanding of the dependence of animal species on their habitats. To understand what an animal must find on the land around him in order to live and procreate is to know, among other things, where there is a chance that *you* will find *him*.

Talk to the people who are experienced with the wildlife in the particular type of bush in which you are interested, especially those who live in some measure by hunting in that bush. Then go afield to confirm by your own observation what animal life thrives there and what use each animal makes of the ground in the different seasons in order to survive and procreate. When out in the field you will find that steps one and two — assessing the habitat for game possibilities and confirming the presence of game — are inseparable. The same excursion which confirms the likely quality of the habitat brings the delight of discovering fresh signs. Ripe berries on the mountainside tell you that bear may be about; piles of fresh dung, found within moments of casting about between the bushes, tells you that bear *are* about and perhaps, as the Indian women of the Yukon do, you should sing a berry-picking song to warn the bears of *your* presence in order to avoid a too-sudden confrontation in the thickets.

Take with you on these study trips those texts which you believe will be most useful. In moose country you might wish to carry a booklet which identifies food species by seasons. I also make constant use of the *Field Guide to Animal Tracks* by Olaus Murie in the Peterson Field Guide series. This, along with my copy of *The Mammals of British Columbia* by Cowan and Guiguet, is dog-eared from frequent reference.

If you harbour the soul of the true outdoors person I promise you that your excursions into the bush will reward you, whether or not you ever take an animal for food. The meaning the bush holds for you will deepen with every new discovery. Here in the night the deer were feeding. By this pond a family of otter lives. On this sidehill in the winter the moose fed in number, though there is no sign of them now. The edge of this field is a veritable homestead of yellow-bellied marmot. A bear passed this way perhaps two days ago, and so on.

When you become adept at identifying likely habitat and then confirming by tracks, manure, and other signs that certain animals are about, you begin to realize that this is the easier end of the hunting skill. More difficult is to locate one or more specific animals, and most difficult is to get a view sufficient for a kill, whether or not your life actually hangs on killing the animal for meat.

You must learn to judge the freshness of sign. Last week's track is of interest for what it tells you of recent use of the ground; a track made a few moments ago holds the immediate promise of meat on which to survive — if you make the right movements over the next little while.

Think about the sign you see. A fresh track has a crisper quality to the print, a sharpness about the edges, which the older track has lost. If it rained overnight, only this morning's track will be unworn by the rainfall. If leaves are falling, the older track has a leaf or two fallen into it, the fresher one has only the leaf imprinted into the track by the footfall of the deer. If a trace of pellet snow fell at daybreak, only the freshest track will be without it. In cold weather, the loose snow which falls back into the moose track as the foot lifts out will set firmly in a few moments; if your finger finds it still loose, the track is very fresh indeed and, in fact, you probably frightened the animal off.

In a short while you become skilled at gauging the freshness of manure. Freshly dropped, it has a bright appearance, whatever its colour. As it ages, the brightness fades. This morning's droppings are distinct from yesterday's and yesterday's from last week's. Droppings made since the last rain are distinct from those made preceding it.

In cold weather, droppings freeze. Those made moments ago are still warm; those made a little earlier are chilled; those made earlier yet are beginning to freeze; those made several hours ago, depending on the temperature, are frozen. Most often on rising from a bed a large animal makes droppings before moving off. The skilled hunter habitually takes a pellet between thumb and forefinger to test its freshness. Is it still easily compressed and warm to the touch? Is it chilled yet? Is it beginning to freeze? The manure tells him how long ago the animal moved off and how far, therefore, he may be from his quarry.

Though tracks and manure are the most common signs to look for, you learn to recognize others as well. Freshly browsed osier tells you moose are present; chewed bark — most often pine, though other trees may show sign as well — tells you that porcupine are about (though you must distinguish between different bark-chewing signs as moose and elk eat bark at some seasons too); green pine twigs nipped off and bark chewed from very young pine trees that have tender growth near ground level suggest the varying hare; during the rut, a pawing place, freshly used, will indicate deer or moose, depending on the size and the associated track; a wallow speaks of elk; all the antlered animals work the velvet from their racks as the rut approaches in the fall, and bushes used for the purpose will show the characteristic rubbing marks.

Pay close attention to what you see on the trail today, for if you come this way tomorrow, you want to recognize new sign. A moose's hooking on a sapling where you know with certainty none existed yesterday tells you that moose are using the ground and that your search for meat is narrowing.

When the frequency of fresh sign tells you that the animals you seek are clearly in the vicinity, you must alter your method of travel (if indeed you continue to travel at all) in order to make the most of your chances for a useful view. When you are in the stages of scouting, both for likely habitat and for signs within the habitat, you may move along at a steady pace with the idea of scouting as much ground in a day as you can. However, once you find enough fresh sign to know that game is in the vicinity, you must slow down and move silently; you must work into or across the wind if at all possible; you must take full advantage of cover and must search with your eyes *and with your ears* with totally concentrated attention. You may spend hours in a quarter-mile of ground if you are certain that game is there. If you spot the game before the game spots you, your chances of success are far better than if matters develop the other way about.

Now it is impossible to give fixed rules for how to proceed at this stage of the hunt. Exactly what will work best depends on many factors: on the species being hunted; on the nature of the terrain and cover; on the conditions of wind and weather, and on the season of the year; even on the question of whether this particular ground is hunted heavily in the season by recreational hunters or not.

None the less, some general ideas are useful so long as you use your own initiative in applying them. I will offer you observations and suggestions which, at some times and in some places, but never in all of either, will prove useful.

Try this rule: if the game is moving, remain still; if the game is not moving, stalk it. Daybreak and dusk are feeding times for most game, and if you sit motionless with a good view over likely ground, you may see more game than if you are on the move, however cautiously. You will also have the best chance for a rested and accurate shot. Also, if food is running short in camp and you are on tight rations, you will use less energy sitting than moving, however slowly.

Deer, more than moose, elk, and caribou, are night-feeding animals. Remember that if there is a bright moon up through much of the night, deer will rarely move in daylight. On the other hand, a black and stormy night will keep most game down, and if the weather lifts in early morning, the game will be on the move.

Large game often beds up in the daytime in draws and gullies, and some terrain is characterized by a series of draws lying in roughly the same direction. Hunt up or across the wind, whichever lets you also hunt across the direction of the draws. As you come over the rise to search in each successive draw, proceed with absolute caution.

In good tracking-snow you may decide to trail an animal, having found track so fresh that you know you cannot be far from a view. Most game is very alert to anything following on its back trail, and you are better advised to make large half-circle departures to the downwind side of the trail than to stay dead on it. Come back to the trail at intervals, working up the wind with caution. When you intercept the trail, assess its freshness anew, then make another wide half-circle. If your quarry is travelling in earnest, you will be outdistanced, but if it is stopping to feed or to consider a bedding place, you may get a view as you approach the trail from one of your circling manoeuvres. The animal you trail may also lead you to others, increasing your chance of a kill.

If you startle an animal which you see too briefly to shoot (or perhaps only hear as it strikes off through a thicket), it will often be useful to abandon caution and attempt a very fast circling action to the downwind side. Make all the noise you need in order to move quickly. Move so as to overtake the animal on its downwind side and then come up toward what you reckon to be its line of movement. The point of this manoeuvre is that if the animal keeps moving you won't see it again anyway, but if the animal stops to follow the sound of your movement while attempting to get your scent, you will often get a view as both you and the animal search for each other.

Another theory is that you should stop as soon as you realize you have startled an animal and remain dead still for a long while — as much as half an hour or more. The animal may circle back to discover what startled it, and you may get a shot. Mule deer particularly seem to suffer from curiosity. I prefer the fast-circling action, but I make no claim that it is superior.

When moose are on pond feed, you may hunt with great effectiveness at daybreak and again at dusk by making a small raft and drifting on a pond within shooting range of the shore. Try to take your game as soon as it appears on the shoreline, as it is very difficult to recover a carcass from the deeper water in which moose quite readily feed. A distinct side benefit to this procedure — the mosquitoes are usually less numerous out in the middle of the pond than in the brush on shore!

Two people hunting in co-operation can often more than double their individual chance of success. If you know that game is almost certain to be found in a specific location from the signs you have seen there, one hunter may sit in wait at one side of the location while the other comes through from the opposite side. Need one add that this co-operative hunting requires totally responsible safety behaviour by both hunters? Either will shoot only with a positive view of the game *and the ground behind the game*.

Should you go down in an aircraft in remote bush there is a good chance that any game you find there is not heavily hunted by recreation hunters in the season, often not hunted at all. This fact will greatly affect your success. There is no doubt that game which is not ordinarily hunted can be taken with much greater ease than game subject to regular hunting.

Recreation hunters, seeing no game, often complain that all the game is gone and heap criticism on the government department responsible for management of wildlife resources. People opposed to hunting often make the same complaint, though from a different motive. Undoubtedly there are places where game was once abundant and is now scarce, but the scarcity is primarily due to *loss of habitat to human activity*, rather than to hunting, and *where habitat still exists, game still exists*.

In some of my favourite haunts, in the past, I rarely hunted more than a day or two, often only a few hours, in order to take meat meat with assurance. Hunting those same haunts now I might spend two or three weeks in diligent hunting, yet come away empty-handed. Still, I suffer no great disappointment, for I discover, daily, that *an abundance of game is still there*, although it has grown ten times more wary than it used to be. This should be reassurance enough that the remoteness of the bush you may go down in is much in your favour for, other things being equal, remoteness means an absence of hunting and game that is consequently much more easily found and killed.

The next step to consider is planning the shot. Here the hunter has two basic choices: a shot to the vital organs or to the head and neck.

A skilled marksman, shooting from excellent advantage, will place a killing shot into the head-and-neck area, thereby taking game with virtually no bullet damage to usable meat. However, a slight error in placing this shot can mean a clean miss at best, and a miserable death for the animal, which you will probably never recover, as a distinct possibility.

If well placed, the shot into the vital organs will ruin little meat; if poorly placed it will ruin more meat *but still bring the animal down*. The effective target area in this shot is much larger than in the head or neck shot and is without question the best choice for the survival hunter.

The shot is easily placed from a full side view and can still be placed if the animal is partially turned away. In this case the shot enters on an angle but will still be effective. Placed from the front, the shot is, in essence, into the full of the chest at the base of the neck.

If the camp is in desperate straits for food and the vital-organs shot cannot be made, you must hit the animal in any way that is likely to bring it down. A survival situation is not a sporting proposition; you must get food however you can, and if this means crippling an animal in the hope of tracking it down for a final kill, that must be accepted.

In any case you must search thoroughly for any animal at which you shoot that does not go down at once — or even appears not to have been hit at all. A large animal may travel a surprising distance after being hit fatally with a shot to the vital organs, and unless you search diligently, you could return to camp in the belief that you have failed when in fact you might have had meat in abundance.

The following sketch (Figure 7:1) shows the target area for the vital-organs shot.

Using Snares and Deadfalls

Snaring is often a more certain way to take an animal than shoot-

Placement of a Vital-Organs Shot

Figure 7:1

ing; moreover, snaring of large game is possible, even though it is more usually used to take small game.

Ingenuity is the mainspring of survival, and never more than in the use of the snare. Your stock of ideas is your sleeveful of tricks, and if one doesn't work perhaps another one will. The more you know of the ways of the game and the more accurately you read the sign that the game leaves, the more certain you are to devise just the set to catch what you need for the pot.

At its simplest the snare is a noose of strong line or wire securely anchored and set in such a way that the desired animal will be caught by the neck (occasionally the foot) and either die there or be held until you arrive to kill it. You should always carry snare wire. Snare wire — and twine as well — takes up so little weight and space and can be so useful that it should be taken along as a matter of course.

There are many variations to the snare and some essential principles in its use which should be considered.

An unbaited snare must be set where it is likely that an animal will pass and in such a way, at the point of the set, that you can judge pretty accurately where the animal's head will go through.

A baited snare differs only in that, by placement of the bait, you will induce the passing animal to put its head through the noose to get at the bait.

A trail in frequent and *current* use, which is constricted at places by natural growth, offers an ideal place to set a snare. However, where a natural constriction does not occur you can make one.

The burrow entrance of a ground-dwelling animal can be a successful location for a snare. In summer the groundsquirrels and marmots are usually the animals most easily taken in assured quantity. In winter, on the other hand, the rabbit is much more vulnerable because its winter trail reveals its location.

You cannot count on catching an animal in every snare, every night (or day as the case may be). If you find you are taking an average of one rabbit for every eight snares set, then you should set forty snares and a few for good measure in order to count on five rabbits for the daily ration.

A description of rabbit-snaring in winter serves as a good primer. (This animal is actually the varying, or snowshoe, hare, but is usually called the rabbit.)

Search in likely locations. Because the rabbit is such an adaptable herbivore his tracks will be found in abundance in a variety of places with a variety of forest covers. (It must also be a favourable time in the population cycle, for at or near its bottom there will be hardly a track to be found for miles in any direction.)

There will be definite trails at the edges of thickets, where the stems of young conifers or of willows or alder grow tightly together and some further low growth and old debris help to thicken the ground cover. Each trail is used for many rabbit excursions in the course of the night.

At a naturally constricted place on a trail set a simple wire snare. If necessary, improve the constriction with upright sticks planted in the snow at either side of the set, and also, if no stout low branch of interlodged stout stick is handy for anchoring the snare, install a stick for this purpose. Figure 7:2 gives an idea of what the snare should look like.

The snare should be about four and a half inches in diameter and about three inches above the surface of the trail. It is best to make it of a soft brass wire which will hold the shape into which it is bent, but if necessary you can make it of cord. If you do you will have to use twigs to hold it in shape (Figure 7:3). The wire stands a lot of twisting before it breaks, an important feature if the rabbit is poorly caught and spins about for some time before it dies.

The rabbit comes in and out of the thicket in its search for food. If you find a deep growth of willow along the edge of a stream, you might conclude that there are plenty of rabbits about but will still not be able to decide exactly where to set the snare.

If there is lodgepole pine in the vicinity, cut a young sapling growing out in a nearby small clearing. This tree is preferred because a young pine growing out in the sun will probably be more attractive to rabbits than one growing with difficulty under the canopy of the thicker forest. Lay the sapling a few yards out from some likely-looking gaps in the edge of the willow thicket. Then leave that place alone for two or three nights while you continue to set snares in other naturally occurring sites.

Very probably, when you come back to look at the small pine, you will see rabbit tracks around it in profusion, evidence that needles and bark are being eaten in abundance, manure all over the snow, and a well-packed trail at every likely place for a snare at the edge of the thicket — a sign of steady traffic. Now you may set snares confidently. Moreover, since this technique has worked once, you should cut some more small pine and start several such feeding stations.

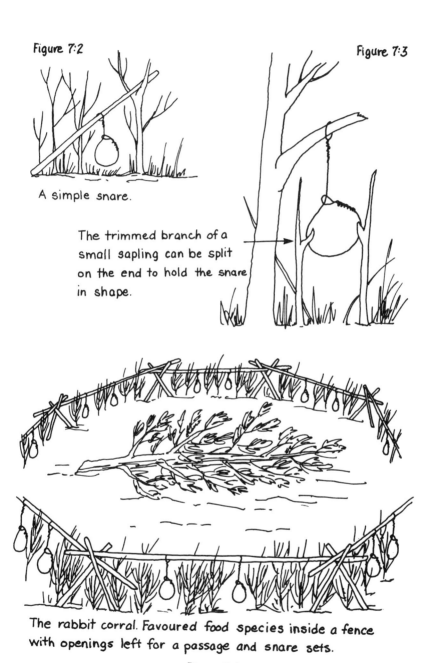

Figure 7:2

A simple snare.

The trimmed branch of a small sapling can be split on the end to hold the snare in shape.

Figure 7:3

The rabbit corral. Favoured food species inside a fence with openings left for a passage and snare sets.

Figure 7:4

It may happen that you don't find any undergrowth or thickets where the rabbits are obliged to use any one trail repeatedly. Tracks may go everywhere but not often in the same place twice. This might happen in the sort of forest that consists of a mixed stand of lodgepole pine, alpine fir, and the odd Engelmann spruce. In such a case you might resort to a rabbit corral. First, cut a few small pines for bait and pile them on the snow in a likely small clearing. Then build a fence around them as shown in Figure 7:4. Use crossed sticks driven into the snow — or any other handy method — to hold up the ends of the horizontal main fence poles which will be the anchoring poles for the snares. These poles should be about ten inches to a foot from the surface of the snow. Then stand spruce or fir branches against the fence to make a solid covering, except for a space every few feet that is just the right size for a rabbit to pass through.

Leave this corral for a few days until the rabbits are coming in number. Then set snares in the spaces, well anchored to the horizontal pole. If you find that you are taking a couple of rabbits a night with a modest little corral, make as many more corrals as you need, perhaps fifty to a hundred yards apart through the wood.

Lodgepole pine appears to be a favoured food of rabbits, and so is the bark of many deciduous trees. I have seen young aspen cut down in the Yukon Territory to attract rabbits with great success.

Some rabbits may be lost after they have been caught in the snare, because they twist and break the wire. Sometimes, too, a rabbit will be caught by only a foot or by both hind feet. This points up the fact that, however carefully we make our sets, not all rabbits are caught by the neck, and the ensuing struggle results in loss of both game and precious wire.

The sets may be improved by the use of a toggle and toss-pole. The toggle provides a triggering action, and the toss-pole lifts the snared rabbit up in the air. This method of lifting the captured animal enables you to use cord if wire is in short supply, since once it is off the ground, the rabbit cannot get at the cord to chew through it. Any method which snatches the prey upward on capture results in far fewer losses.

Figures 7:5 through 7:7 show the essential features of the toggle system. I find that a toggle about four inches long seems right for length, and the main skill is in finding just how far back around the anchor pole you must set the snare end of the toggle to ensure that the other end just safely holds the wrap of the toss-pole line in place and no more.

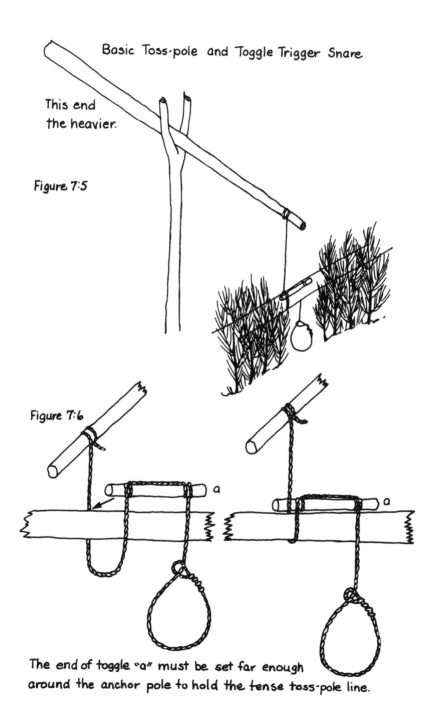

Basic Toss-pole and Toggle Trigger Snare

This end
the heavier.

Figure 7:5

Figure 7:6

a

a

The end of toggle "a" must be set far enough
around the anchor pole to hold the tense toss-pole line.

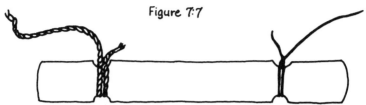

Figure 7:7

Toggle with cord one end, wire the other. Note notches.

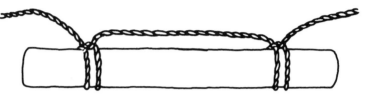

Toggle attached to continuous line. No notch needed.

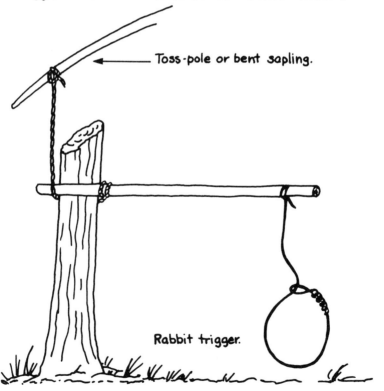

Toss-pole or bent sapling.

Rabbit trigger.

Figure 7:8

It takes longer to set out a given number of these toss-pole snares than it does to set simple snares. In a situation of pressing need I recommend getting out a large number of simple snares immediately in the best natural locations available, following up as soon as possible with many toss-pole snares. Do make corrals, as well, if there is any shortage of good natural locations. For one thing corral sets are always easy to locate, whereas simple sets can be very hard to find, especially after an overnight snowfall.

Check your snares every morning; most rabbit movement occurs at dusk, through the night, and at daybreak. And remember, this is a numbers game! Set every snare with all possible care, but at the same time set many, many snares.

There are other methods for triggering a snatch-up action and a few of these are shown in Figures 7:8 through 7:11. Methods requiring a peg to be driven into the ground are obviously not useful when the ground is frozen.

Tree squirrels may be taken with wire snares attached to a pole which can either span between two trees or lean from a low branch to the ground. Again it is important to set the pole where you see evidence of squirrels — or the squirrels themselves. If there is an established run between two trees, set the pole between those trees and a few feet from the ground. Several snares may be set on one pole. The snare diameter should be about two and a half inches, and the wire should be long enough so that the squirrel, when caught, will hang well below the pole. This snare is shown in Figure 7:12.

Groundsquirrels are light enough that a sapling, stuck well into the ground and then bent over, will serve to snatch up the snare. Since you don't have an anchor pole you can hold the sapling bent over by a simple hook-and-peg system (Figure 7:13).

Heavier marmots will require a toss-pole balanced over a stout forked stick securely driven into the ground. Generally speaking, a sapling bent over is only good for quite light game, and then not all saplings will straighten up promptly if they have been held over in a bent position for many hours. In cold weather most saplings simply freeze into the bent position. You will have to discover the limitations of the saplings available to you and use toss-poles where necessary.

Wire which can be salvaged from a downed aircraft makes good snares. Particularly for predators and beaver, the snares made from wire should be double-looped so that when they tighten they will

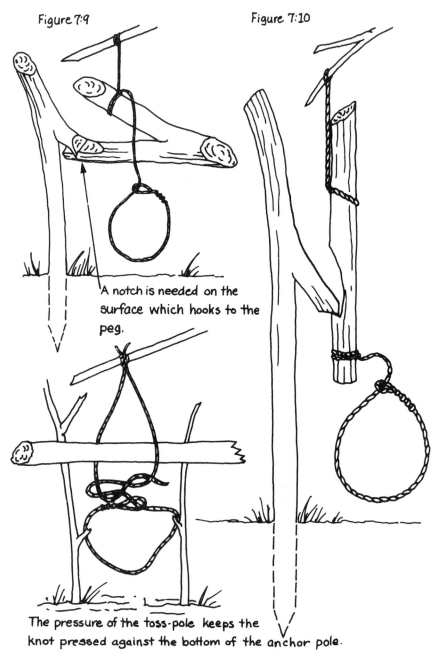

Figure 7:9

Figure 7:10

A notch is needed on the surface which hooks to the peg.

The pressure of the toss-pole keeps the knot pressed against the bottom of the anchor pole.

Figure 7:11

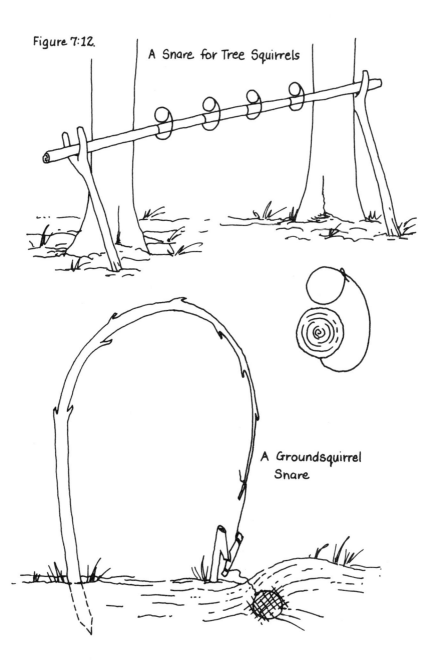

Figure 7:12.

A Snare for Tree Squirrels

A Groundsquirrel Snare

not again slacken. In a single-loop snare the line goes through the eye once, then directly wherever it is secured. In a double-loop it must go around the loop formation a second time and through the eye a second time.

Also for any game larger than rabbits, the snares made from line of whatever weight should be set with a slip knot in the eye which will close up as the snare tightens to prevent the snare slacking off should the animal pause in his struggles; see Figure 7:14.

Many of the predator species such as the lynx and the members of the weasel family may be taken in a baited snare. The lynx particularly is good eating and affords considerable meat. Rabbit offal is a source of bait. Figure 7:15 gives you a front and side view of a baited snare. Make sure that the enclosure around the bait is high enough that the animal must go through the entrance where the snare is set, and also so that birds don't get at the bait. Adjust the size of the set according to what animal you intend to capture.

A variety of small birds often gather about a camp, and in a situation where you are pressed for food, you must see them either as food or as a source of bait for fishing or for the baited predator-snare. The bird snare takes practice to adjust so that it sets and works, but you will manage this with patience. Figure 7:16 will get you started.

The important point is to make the perch stick and the trigger hole just the same size, and bevel the end of the perch stick slightly. Then the tension of the snare line will just keep the perch stick in place until a bird lands. Also, you can make your hole directly in an upright sapling that has been cut off and flattened, and tie a weight to the tension end of the snare line rather than use a bent spring stick.

It is also possible to snare beaver. When ice is on the beaver pond you can set snares through a hole in the ice (Figure 7:17). Stay entirely away from the lodge but set near feeding locations. Cut a hole in the ice and put fresh willow branches into the water, anchoring the butts securely to a dry log on the ice. Put two or three snares in the water beside the willow branches and anchor these as well. The beaver will come to cut off the willow branches and while at work will become fouled in the snares.

Beaver can be taken in an underwater set (Figure 7:18) during open water and when the ice is not too thick to manage the set. Choose the nearest point upstream of their dam, where the current is slow but the stream is not too wide or deep to work in. The snares should be about eight inches in diameter.

Figure 7:14

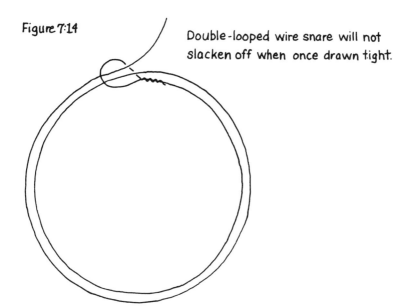

Double-looped wire snare will not slacken off when once drawn tight.

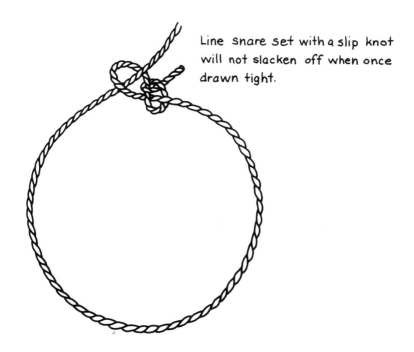

Line snare set with a slip knot will not slacken off when once drawn tight.

Figure 7:15

The Baited Predator Snare

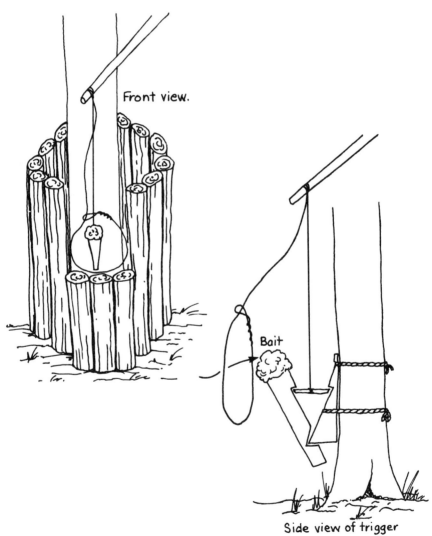

Front view.

Bait

Side view of trigger
mechanism.

Figure 7:16

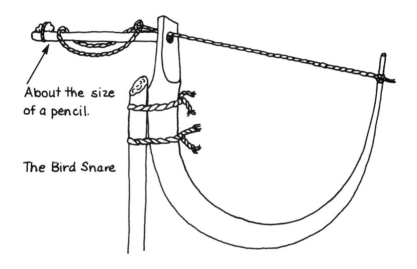

About the size
of a pencil.

The Bird Snare

Figure 7:17

A Snare for Beaver When There is Ice on the Water

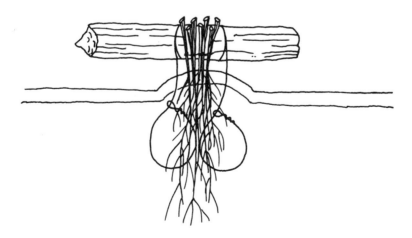

Figure 7:18

Cross-Section of an Underwater Snare for Beaver

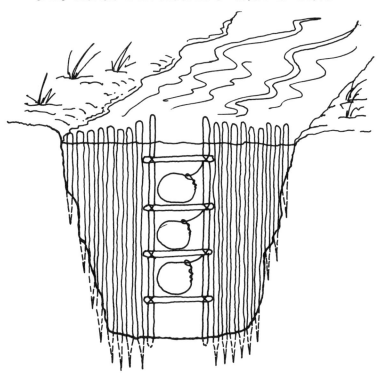

As I suggested earlier, big game, too, may be taken in snares. At one time or another, the Indian people of the bush country caught virtually all large game in snares. Indians in the Yukon Territory made superb rawhide ropes with which they snared moose. Unfortunately, although the odd such rope survives, the practice itself has been given up, and no wildlife management authority in North America would allow you (or me) to try it on an experimental basis. Nonetheless, we know it can be done, and in case of urgent need you can turn to it, if you must, to preserve life.

The principles remain the same. You must find a well-used trail, in current use. In some types of forest cover, the game does not use well-defined trails on a consistent basis; in others the trails are regularly used and you may predict the passage of an animal every night or two with confidence.

You will of course need strong line. Polypropylene or nylon rope are as likely as any to be on board an aircraft and have enormous strength for their weight. I would set for mule or whitetail deer with a three-eighths-inch rope, and for moose with a half-inch rope and be quite confident about the rope being suitable.

If the signs are favourable, look for the naturally constricted places in the path where the snare may be set. The diameter and the height of the noose will be determined by what animal you hope to take. Remember that animals do not carry their heads as high while they walk as you may think from seeing them in an alert attitude. Most game that you sight sees you, and the head is up to search the wind, the ears are out, and the body is gathered for instant flight. Deer in undisturbed travel may have their heads centred about two and a half feet from the ground. A snare two feet in diameter and about eighteen inches from the ground at bottom will be about right, save for snaring a buck with exceptional antlers. An excellent technique is to set the snare where an animal must duck slightly to go under an overhead obstruction. You can set the snare immediately below the obstruction and be certain that the animal's head will be well directed.

Figure 7:19 will give you the basic idea for this kind of snare. The leaning log is important. It should be as heavy a log as you can manage and should be propped against the tree with as little secure purchase as possible so that the initial struggles of the animal dislodge it readily. Also you must do a thorough job of disguising the snare loop with brush.

Particularly with deer, but also with most other large game,

Large-Animal Snare

Figure 7:19

your best chance of success comes at night. Therefore you must visit every such snare *first thing in the morning* to minimize the time between the death of an animal and dressing out. Cavity contents left in, particularly in mild weather, can sour the meat in a very short time. You must do all you can to avoid this.

The deadfall is another in the inventory of devices for capturing game. At one time Indian people made much use of this device too for taking game, particularly during the early years of the fur trade, but it is difficult now to obtain accurate details on its successful use as it has been replaced everywhere by the steel trap and in most jurisdictions is now illegal.

As with any device for capturing game, the deadfall must be triggered when the animal is in the vulnerable position and must be dependable in its action. Generally speaking, the simpler the mechanism, the more reliable the result.

Because of its illegality, I have not taken game with the deadfall, but I have constructed and tested the action of many, and have no doubt of the potential usefulness of a well-made deadfall in practical application.

It seems to me prudent to make any deadfall with a ground log as well as a fall log, and to provide guide stakes for the fall log to ensure the accuracy of the drop. In the style which I describe here, the fall log is raised at one end and descends in a scissor action onto the log below, trapping the animal between in order to injure and hold it, if not kill it outright.

The deadfall may be triggered by a trip line or by disturbance of bait. Since small herbivorous animals are best taken with snares and very large game such as bears or moose are best shot, the deadfall is most useful in trapping the small- to medium-sized predators and the smaller ungulates such as mule and whitetail deer. Bait will be the practical method of bringing any predator into the deadfall. Deer may be taken by setting a trip-line deadfall on a well-used trail, carefully camouflaging enough of the structure so that it appears as no more than a natural interference along the way.

The size of the deadfall is in relation to the size of the animal you hope to capture. For deer, this means you will need the heaviest log two people can contrive to manage with lines and levers; for predators such as lynx and coyotes, I would use as heavy a log as I could manage alone.

Opinion varies as to how well animals can sense a trap and thus

avoid capture. Many trappers go to considerable lengths to camou-
flage human scent and the physical outlines of the set trap. In a
survival situation you won't be able to do much about scent, but
certainly with brush and twigs and ground trash you can do a good
job of hiding the main outlines of your deadfalls and your snares.

Given the persistence of the small predators in getting into my
winter meat cache, I have no doubt about the practicality of inducing them into a baited deadfall. One winter I lost quite a few
pounds of moose meat to a mink before I even discovered what
creature was getting into the cache; on another occasion a weasel
came into my lodge by the light of my evening lamp to contest with
me the possession of the meat I had brought in from the cache for
the next day's stew-pot. Members of the weasel family may not be
your first choice for the entrée, but in a survival situation every
animal is a potential meal.

Various deadfalls are illustrated in the order in which I will deal
with them. Figure 7:20 is a trip-line deadfall requiring rather a lot
of line. You choose a tree which is right beside the trail and make
sure that the crotch of the branch over which the line must pass is
well smoothed out for free passage of the line.

Do some trials with the trigger mechanism. The notch faces
which bear on each other are critical to the sensitivity of the
mechanism; by altering the angle of these faces you can go from a
connection which no amount of pressure will trip to a connection
that won't hold at all. My trials suggest that the bearing surface of
the notch should be just a shade more open than at right angles to
the centre line of the stick from which the trigger is made. There
will be sufficient friction to hold the two halves of the trigger
together in the set, yet they will release on very little pressure from
the trip line.

Figure 7:21 illustrates a trip-line set requiring less line than the
previous set. I refer to this as the broken-knee set. The trick here is
to cut the notch in the support stick so far through that only a thin
strip at the back still holds and then to support it in place with
a wedge that is precisely thick enough that only enough of a bend
backward from the trip line to keep the stick upright is achieved.
Very little pressure on the trip line is then necessary to bring the
knee forward to the point of sudden collapse.

This deadfall may also be set with bait. Tie the bait securely
to the support stick just above the notch and wedge. Brush in all
around the set, leaving access only at the end farthest from the

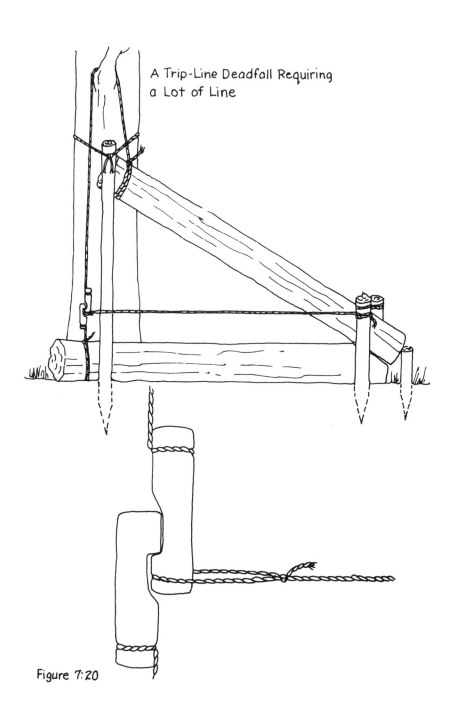

A Trip-Line Deadfall Requiring a Lot of Line

Figure 7:20

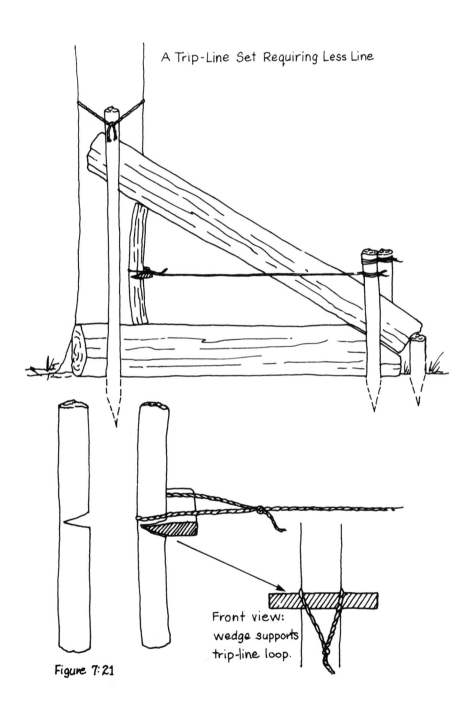

A Trip-Line Set Requiring Less Line

Front view:
wedge supports
trip-line loop.

Figure 7:21

baited support stick, which is placed toward the ground end of
the fall log. This will ensure that the animal will be standing on the
ground log while tugging at the bait.

Figure 7:22 illustrates a baited deadfall with a minimum requirement for line. The key to success here is the bevel on the top
end of the support stick to which the bait is tied. You should use
logs with some rough bark, and you should set the support stick
back into the set almost but not quite to the point of balance of
the fall log. The support stick can be made to hold when leaning
slightly forward at the top and with the bevel cut to conform to the

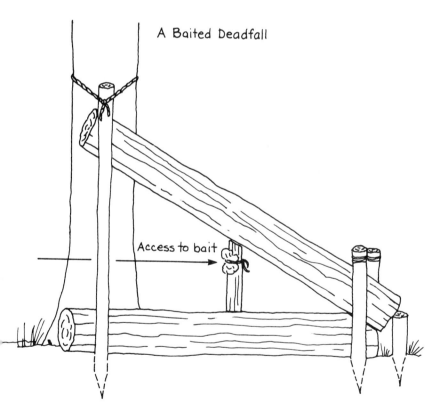

A Baited Deadfall

Access to bait

Figure 7:22

angle of the fall log. In order to hold, the stick will bear the weight of the fall log mainly toward the peak of the bevel. Very little tugging at the bait, which is tied securely to the support stick near the top, will produce a quick collapse. You can test the set with a long string tied to the top of the support stick. Stand in front of the set and pull in the direction from which the animal would approach the set. You will soon find the particular adjustment which on the one hand holds the log up yet on the other permits sudden collapse with only a moderate tug on the bait.

Now, with any baited deadfall you must complete the set by fencing up around the whole structure in such a way that the only opening left ensures access to the bait from the effective direction — in this case from the front end. Dead sticks, pieces of bark, and brush leaned against the fall log will do the job, but be careful that nothing will interfere with the drop.

Figure 7:23 illustrates an important mechanism for triggering a deadfall. It is important because, with a little practice, you can build it quickly, it is reliable, and it requires no line apart from the little you would need to secure the bait. Also it can be used with a trip stick instead of a trip line, and this could be critical for capturing a deer when you are short of line.

It is easier to set the mechanism on the end of the fall log than on the side, but both are possible. In a side set you may need an upright stake to prevent side-sway and premature triggering of the mechanism; see Figure 7:24.

It is important to have the main upright stake in the mechanism close to the end or side of the fall log to ensure a clean action. I set this stake as close to the fall log as is possible without interfering with the drop.

Look at Figure 7:23 again. The top of the upright stake "a" is shaped with a sharp knife into a wedge, the edge of which should be precisely horizontal to the ground when the stake is upright. The supporting lever is then notched accurately at a right angle "b", and with this lever then set firmly onto the wedged top of the stake one can mark with accuracy the bevel "c" wanted at the top end to hold the fall log, and at the bottom end "d" to fit the notch in the trigger stick.

If you set this mechanism as a trip stick, use a light, dry stem for the trip stick and support the far end of it with a light forked twig (though this latter step is not always necessary). It seems that the mechanism will trip better from one direction of strike than the

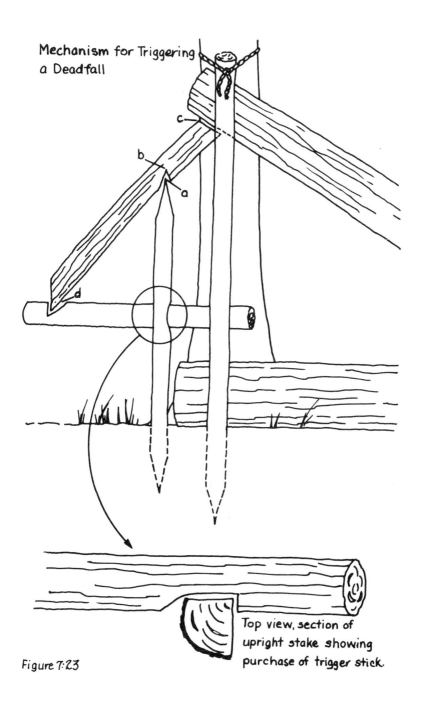

Mechanism for Triggering a Deadfall

c

b

a

d

Top view, section of upright stake showing purchase of trigger stick.

Figure 7.23

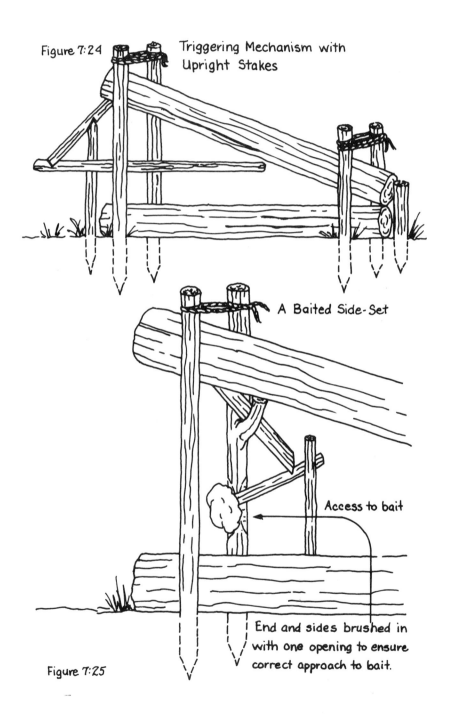

Figure 7:24   Triggering Mechanism with Upright Stakes

A Baited Side-Set

Access to bait

End and sides brushed in with one opening to ensure correct approach to bait.

Figure 7:25

other, but if properly set, it takes little disturbance from either direction to get a collapse.

Figure 7:25 shows a baited side-set. The alternative is to set from the end, again with the bait secured to the end of the trigger stick. Although the tugging on the trigger stick may not appear to be as effective as in the side set, the disturbance will still bring about the necessary collapse. Whether setting a baited deadfall with this triggering system on the end or on the side, it is critical to cover with brush around the set, with an opening left at one side toward the back. The objective is to have the animal standing full length on the ground log when tugging at the bait.

Now the mechanism in the deadfalls in Figures 7:23 to 7:25 is perhaps at its most useful as a trail set for deer, with a trip stick when you are short on line. You will need a large version of the set, well camouflaged and with the light, dry trip-stick set high enough that the deer will likely disturb it. Remember that deer are clean-stepping animals and, given line for it, I would use a snare for deer ahead of a deadfall.

This mechanism is a little slow in getting the collapse underway and for a baited deadfall I would choose the broken-knee set or the bevelled support stick with the bait securely tied to the stick in both cases.

Figure 7:26 shows a trail set that is good for beaver, but not likely to work for clean-stepping animals such as deer. It is probably one of the best trail sets, easily assembled and rapid in collapse. The forked sapling selected for the trigger mechanism must be very strong, as only the force of the fork pressing the fall log against the upright keeps the log in place. The longer stem of the fork must be just barely caught by the trip stick so that the least downward disturbance of the trip stick will release everything. This deadfall is ideal for a well-used beaver trail leading from the stream bank to where the beaver are cutting feed.

Figure 7:27 shows an effective bear trap. If a bear is coming around camp to threaten the safety of your food supply, you must try to add him to the larder. If you have no rifle, this trap is your best alternative. It will take time to build and the fall log must be so heavy that you will need to use levers and blocks of wood to raise it. After the fall log is set on the trigger mechanism, you add the additional leaning logs for greater weight.

You will see in the sketches that much use is made of stakes driven into the ground. Obviously, in the winter months when the

A Trail Set Suitable for Beaver

Figure 7:26

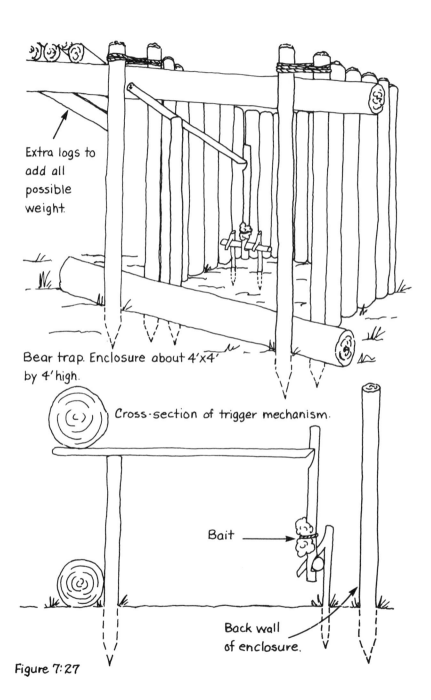

Extra logs to add all possible weight.

Bear trap. Enclosure about 4'x4' by 4' high.

Cross-section of trigger mechanism.

Bait

Back wall of enclosure.

Figure 7:27

ground is frozen this presents problems. A partial solution is to make sets where trees are available a convenient distance apart. The requirement for stakes is reduced and if you position such stakes as you do need, and then pack snow around their bases thoroughly with your feet as well as tamp a little with the end of your axe handle, you will find that half an hour later they are quite firm due to the refreezing of the disturbed snow.

Once more I urge practice. While it is not legal to set out a deadfall with the intent to capture game, there is nothing to prevent you from constructing deadfalls and testing the trigger mechanisms, provided you disassemble everything when you are done. It is only through this trial-and-error process that you will discover the techniques which make for both a secure set and a sudden and certain collapse.

The next sketch (Figure 7:28) illustrates a useful trap for small game. It works particularly well with grouse. Some sort of bait such as bread crumbs or seeds must be placed so as to lead up to and inside the trap. The creature enters easily by pushing through the bars, but cannot readily escape as the bottom ends of the bars are against the inside of the bottom horizontal piece. It will take time and patience to build the trap, but grouse may be taken repeatedly in the same trap.

Fishing

In many ways fishing presents far fewer problems than trying to obtain land game. First, if you come on fish in waters seldom touched by the sports fishery, the odds are good that these fish will be easily taken. Second, when you are unrestricted by regulations, you may find yourself faced with an eye-popping abundance.

When travelling extensively by bush-line aircraft over the sparsely settled stretches of northern British Columbia and the Yukon Territory in the nineteen-sixties, I had always in my pack some fishing line, some leader material, a few hooks and commercially tied flies, and, finally, a generous length of gill-net in a mesh size suitable to trout and smaller char, whitefish, and the occasional large grayling. You might also want to check with the local fish-and-game administration to see what species and size of fish you can expect.

You could include, if you wish, a light sectional rod, but for survival-fishing a satisfactory rod can be improvised from a willow

A Small-Game Trap

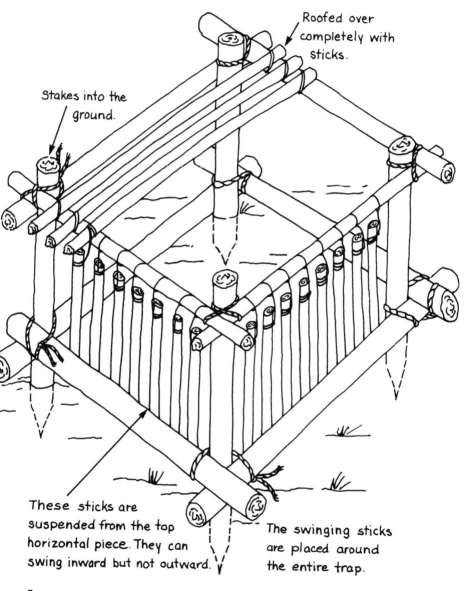

Roofed over completely with sticks.

Stakes into the ground.

These sticks are suspended from the top horizontal piece. They can swing inward but not outward.

The swinging sticks are placed around the entire trap.

Figure 7:28

stem. Ferrules are not essential, but it is worth having a good eye at the tip of the rod through which the line will pass with ease. Either a safety pin or some snare wire can be made to do the job. With the butt of the rod in one hand, the fishing line in the other, and the reserve length of line loosely coiled on the ground, one soon develops techniques for rudimentary shore and stream fishing.

At its simplest, your fishing can begin with rod and line with six feet of leader, on the end of which you have a baited hook suspended in the water of a pond or stream. In unfished water you might do remarkably well at this, using virtually anything at hand for bait: worms, grubs, grasshoppers, or any scrap of food from your kit.

A float is often very useful in bait-fishing. When you have determined the depth at which you are likely to get the best result, you can keep your baited hook at that depth by adjusting the length of leader below the float.

If you are bait-fishing in a stream, you will usually have the best result if the bait can be moved along the stream bed by the current. If you adjust the leader length to just short of the stream depth and at the same time attach a few pieces of split lead shot to the leader to hold it straight down from the float, you can drift your bait along a stretch of stream bed by letting the float drift with the current on the surface. I have had splendid results in steelhead fishing with this technique.

Fly-fishing can be particularly productive in unfished water, and a crudely improvised fly may do just as well as the outrageously priced creation from the store. Grayling are often voracious about any likely speck that hits the surface, and for this reason are easily fished out in accessible water. Whenever I have travelled to remote grayling water, I have found that even an old fly reduced to little more than a few threads on the shank will fetch a panful of fish in a few minutes. Figure 7:29 shows some basic equipment.

If you are down in an aircraft and the outlook for an early pick-up is doubtful, don't hesitate to put your net in the water. Figures 7:30 through 7:32 give some ideas for an effective set. Use sound, dry pieces of wood for the float line and stones for the lead line. Find stones of an irregular shape so that they may be tied securely. Also, it is important to use many moderately sized stones rather than a few very heavy ones.

For open-water sets, the lead line should exert enough force to set the floats firmly into the water, but not below the surface. When

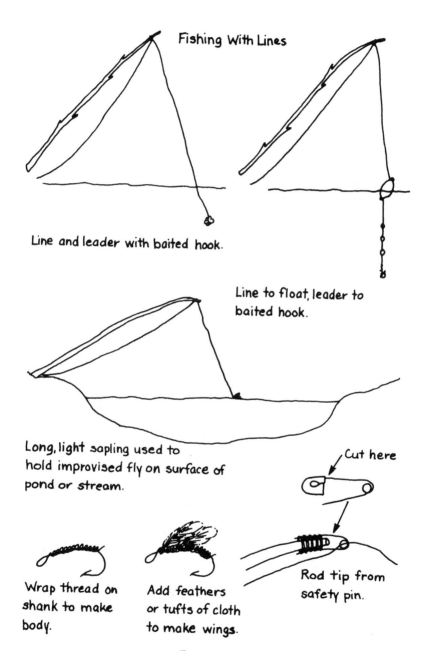

Fishing With Lines

Line and leader with baited hook.

Line to float, leader to baited hook.

Long, light sapling used to hold improvised fly on surface of pond or stream.

Cut here

Wrap thread on shank to make body.

Add feathers or tufts of cloth to make wings.

Rod tip from safety pin.

Figure 7:29

Fishing With Nets

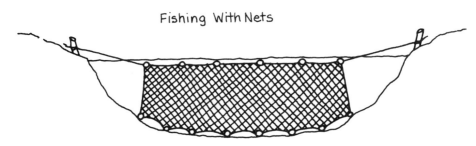

Block the whole of a smaller stream with a net.

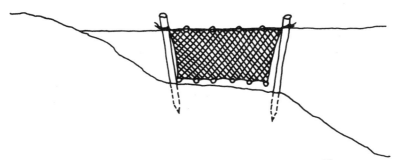

Set between the beach and the main drop-off
in a lake.

Figure 7:30

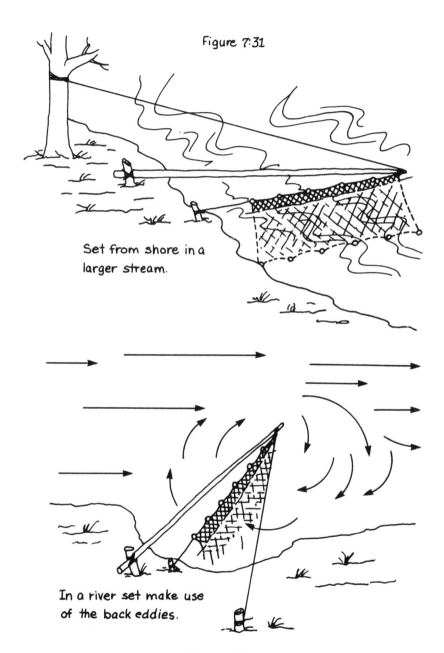

Figure 7:31

Set from shore in a larger stream.

In a river set make use of the back eddies.

Figure 7:32

you see the floats bobbing a good deal and a few of them being drawn under you know that fish have hit the net. Pull the net as often as your success rate requires, but never less than once a day. Setting a net below the ice is demanding, but in early winter before the ice is too thick this is often the surest way to get a food supply. The sketches in Figures 7:33 and 7:34 will give you the idea. As long as you can manage the ice, you can manage the fishing.

The net requires a float and lead line like any other set, except that the balance between the two must ensure that the float line does not rise to settle against the ice. If it does it will be frozen in as the ice thickens, and you will have a tedious and wasteful job getting it free afterwards.

In the sketch, the drawing lines have been left attached to the net and simply brought up through the hole in the ice along the stake. In very cold weather it is best to remove these lines after the net has been secured to the stakes. The freezing-up of your access holes means that you must chop them out every day when the net is drawn, and there is real danger of cutting the line in the process. The drawing lines can be attached as required each time the net is lifted.

In very cold weather you may also have difficulty with the net freezing into a heap on the ice as you draw it out the hole to clear it. I have known Indians in the north to make a practice of lighting a fire near by when lifting the net, and of boiling a container of water to pour over the net immediately prior to drawing it back under the ice.

Where ice is not a consideration, fish can be taken in quantity by constructing traps. You must choose a location where the stream is shallow enough in which to work safely and wide enough that the current is dispersed and manageable. A simple trap can be made with stakes driven into the stream bed, as illustrated in Figure 7:35, or a more complex trap can be constructed, as shown in Figure 7:36. In either case a good deal of work is involved which will only be warranted where plenty of fish are in evidence and you think you will be stranded for some time. There is also a size limitation with a trap. You cannot close off the current, and the trap is of no use for fish smaller than the spaces which must be left in the trap fence for the water to flow through.

The simple stake trap is used in conjunction with a drive, and again the stream must be of a size and gradient which makes this possible. All hands go upstream a considerable distance, then wade

Figure 7:33

Setting a Net Under the Ice

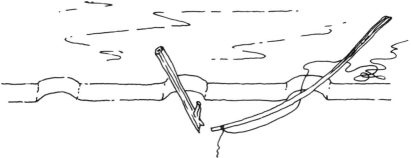

To set beneath the ice, first get a line drawn.

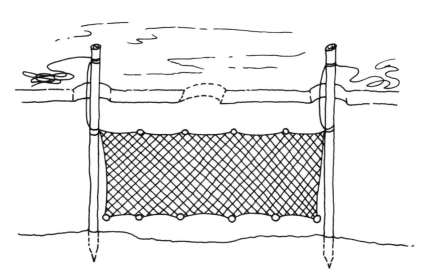

Keep the float line well below the ice. Set the stakes lightly.

Figure 7:34

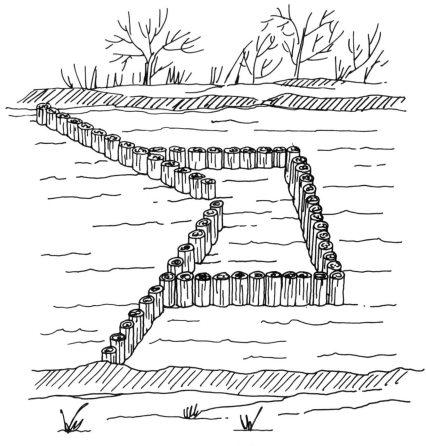

A simple fish trap.

Figure 7:35

A More Complex Fish Trap

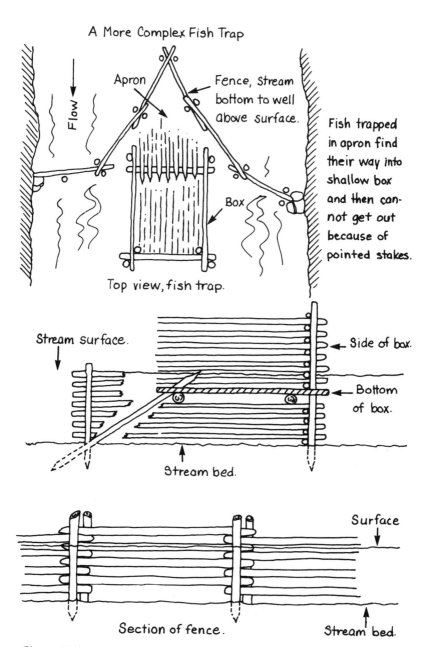

Flow

Apron

Fence, Stream bottom to well above surface.

Box

Top view, fish trap.

Fish trapped in apron find their way into shallow box and then cannot get out because of pointed stakes.

Stream surface.

Side of box.

Bottom of box.

Stream bed.

Surface

Section of fence.

Stream bed.

Figure 7:36

down, beating the water with sticks as they go. When the beaters converge at the trap, the entrance should be blocked and the fish taken out with a dip net or gaff.

The trap in Figure 7:36 is more complex and is highly successful in a stream in which migratory fish travel in runs. This was the trap used by Indians in the Yukon Territory to catch salmon in the Alsek river system which reaches the northern Pacific directly through the mountains of the southwest part of the Territory. The relentless upstream surge to the spawning grounds brought the salmon into the trap and no drive was required.

The sketches will give you some ideas to work with, and once more your own study and familiarity with the terrain you travel in is essential. Know the habitat, know the fish, and know the proven fishing techniques, particularly those used by Indian people who now or in the past may have lived on the land around you.

You should now have a good idea about what types of food to carry, how to hunt efficiently with a rifle, how to capture game with snares and deadfalls, and how to take fish.

If you have reasonably good fortune as well, you will be supplied with an abundance of protein, a good measure of fat, and, apart from what you may have carried with you, not much carbohydrate. If the time out stretches over a number of weeks you could be many days on a carbohydrate-free diet. At worst, a carbohydrate-free diet is a sight better than no diet at all; I personally believe it to be a positively good one. The experience of northern Indians and Inuit and of the many non-native people who have lived on the native diet for extended periods suggests that a healthy individual can maintain vigour on a meat-and-fish diet over a considerable period of time, some would say indefinitely.

If you go in the bush and you succeed in the hunt, you will go well in the bush indeed.

EIGHT

Camp Management

If we were concerned only with information vital to survival through
the commonest hazards in the bush we would be almost done. A
review of clothing, footwear, and emergency shelters, which we
have considered, and of signalling and first aid, which we will look
at in the next two chapters, could be said to be the core of it and
all the rest extraneous, however interesting.

Yet surely we are concerned with more than bare survival;
surely to go well in the bush is to manage in such a way that
survival may be taken as assured and our attention can be given to
comfort and enjoyment as well. Hence I am not satisfied with the
argument that since search-and-rescue operations, with exemplary
technical capability, will have me out within days, and since there
is two weeks' grub in the aircraft, I need not be concerned about
gathering food from the land. I know, in fact, that I can survive
many days with no food at all, but I have no intention of putting
myself through that if any alternative exists. I will try to use my
snare wire, rifle, and fish-net with such diligence that the two
weeks' or five days' supply of food on the aircraft stays in reserve.

I am concerned here, too, with some basics of camp management, a review of information which, though it will not be a
comprehensive dissertation on every aspect of campcraft, will none-

theless go a long way to making camp life more comfortable and
secure.

■ SITING YOUR CAMP

A good camp begins with a good site, and the factors which make
for a good site tend to vary with the seasons.

We have mentioned already the need for water, fuel, and camp
brush. In summer you must find water in rivers, lakes, streams, and
ponds; in winter you have it all about as snow for the melting. In
summer you need just a little fuel and a bit of camp brush; in
winter you want both in abundance. Yet these constants — water,
fuel, and camp brush — are not the only factors that you look for in
a good site.

In colder seasons wind protection is vital, particularly from
the northerly winds, but to a great extent from other winds as
well. A south wind at − 5°C (23°F) may seem balmy after a couple of
weeks of forty below, but you still do not want it pushing through
the middle of camp.

Because the most effective protection from wind can also block
out most of what little sun the season affords, a related factor in
mid winter is the desire for sunlight. While one hopes to be outdoors through most of the daylight hours, there is still much
cheer afforded by sunlight falling on tent canvas and about the
camp vicinity.

My choice for a winter camp is on the north side of a small
clearing. The camp lies hard by the timber on the north side and
the north wind is barely felt, though one hears it pushing at the tree
tops. The small clearing to the south of the camp effectively lowers
the horizon of trees so that the winter sun may reach the camp, yet
the clearing is not large enough to let the southerly winds strike
with force.

I recommend this choice, provided that you have a well-made
camp and plenty of fuel. If the camp is deficient in fuel, then you
must go right into the timber for maximum wind-protection and
forgo the sun.

In hot weather you want protection from the sun, yet you would
like some breeze, both for its cooling effect and as a deterrent to
mosquitoes. Among a few aspen trees on a windy point along a lake
or river can be an ideal site. The aspen trees afford shade, yet let the

breeze through at the same time. In high mosquito-season I will live in the wind, even if doing so causes much inconvenience in other respects.

A camp needs well-drained ground, and you must have your mind on this, particularly if, on the day you choose the site, there has not been a drop of rain for weeks. Heavy soils which will pool water on the surface in a downpour will have you in a dismal mess in wet weather. Light, gravelly soils will absorb the water as fast as it falls, even around the perimeter of the shelter, where it is gathered by the shedding roof. Do not set camp in a depression of ground, however absorbent the soil appears.

Be wary of riverbank sites. These are often the best sites for access to water and to the mixture of shade with some wind that one wants in the summer. However, camps and the people in them have been swept away in the night from such sites by flood-waters originating so far away in the headwaters as to be totally unexpected.

The general rule is that rivers originating in large lake-systems rise and fall gradually, while rivers rising directly in mountain country with no lakes in the system are capable of flash flooding. One exception to that rule, of course, is flash flooding due to ice jams during break-up. Seasoned river-travellers do often camp on bars and exposed gravel beds below the main banks, but they know their rivers and never adopt the practice along a stream where flash floods are possible. They also often set a small stake at water's edge immediately on coming ashore so that, when they inspect it a few hours later, they will know whether the river is rising or falling.

■ WASTE DISPOSAL

As soon as you have decided on a campsite and on the exact location for construction of your shelter, decide also on where you will dispose of waste. No waste should ever be discarded into a stream or lake. When the ground is not frozen, all body wastes and camp refuse should be buried *immediately they occur*. A common practice is to dig a short trench at the beginning, and each time that waste is dropped in the trench, it is well covered with soil dug out of a small extension of the trench.

There are two obvious reasons for *immediate* burial of wastes.

First, flies cannot settle on the waste one moment and on food in camp the next. Second, bears are attracted by the smell of decomposing waste foodstuff. Waste foodstuff buried immediately sets out far less odour than the same material buried a day later.

The waste-disposal site should be well away from the main camp area — a hundred yards is a reasonable minimum — with an exception made only if one member of the party has been injured and requires a special facility.

If you lack a shovel, the necessary digging can be accomplished with a somewhat flattened and sharpened stick. The job will be tedious, but it can be done, and is so important that it must be done.

■ STORING EQUIPMENT AND SUPPLIES

You must safeguard equipment and supplies. However much or little you have with you, it is all you have for the duration of the time out and you cannot afford to lose any of it.

A large tree with a spreading canopy and many sound, dry branches near ground level makes a good tool shed. Cut off the lower branches a few inches from the trunk and you will be delighted to find how much of your equipment and supplies may then be hung around the tree. You will need a small hanging thong on each item to be stored. There is much to be said for fixing a hanging thong to most camp and emergency gear beforehand as a matter of course.

Storage of preserved food and some equipment, such as anything made of leather, requires care to protect them from animals. There are many ways to make a safe cache, and much depends on what you have to work with. A platform high off the ground is effective, particularly if you have some light sheet-metal of any sort to fix around the trunks of the supporting trees or posts to prevent rodents from climbing them.

The next sketches (Figure 8:1) will give you ideas from which to work. Check your cached supplies constantly, and if any animal is gaining access you must apply your ingenuity to defeat him. Consider the use of a snare or deadfall by which to add the creature to your food supply.

Birds can be a serious threat to food supplies, particularly in winter months. Food on a platform or other open cache will need to be in containers or be wrapped or covered.

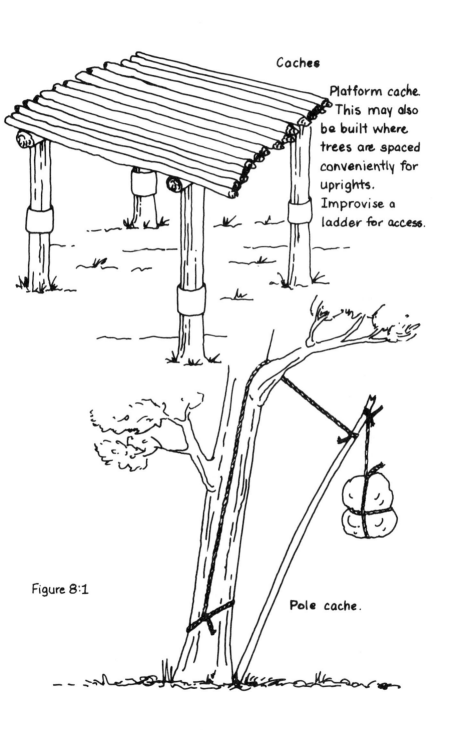

Caches

Platform cache.
This may also
be built where
trees are spaced
conveniently for
uprights.
Improvise a
ladder for access.

Figure 8:1

Pole cache.

218

■ PRESERVING MEAT

SKINNING AND DRESSING

In addition to the question of safe storage comes that of preservation. It is of little use to kill a moose if, within a few days in warm weather, the meat is going rotten.

In winter months there is clearly little problem. Most bushlands enjoy sufficiently cold winters that meat supplies can be kept safely for weeks or months with no fear of spoilage. In severe northern winters it is even advisable to cut large meat into pieces convenient to the cooking pot immediately following the kill, since solidly frozen meat is terribly difficult to cut.

In warm and hot weather there is a clear advantage to concentrating on small game, if it can be taken regularly and with certainty. Each kill will be consumed before spoilage becomes a problem. Nonetheless, if there is any question at all of needing the food for maintenance of health and vigour, large game may be killed in hot or warm weather if you take immediate action against spoilage.

The animal must be dressed and skinned without delay. For the novice faced with a large moose this can be a formidable task, but one must get on with it.

The animal should be turned fully or as far as possible onto its back. Slit the skin only, taking care not to go through immediately to the cavity, from the windpipe to the anus and then down the inside of each leg to the initial slit.

The skin should then be drawn and separated from the flesh until a clear path down the length of the first slit is exposed. The sketch in Figure 8:2 will show you the basic skinning action to use with hands and knife.

Now the muscle sheath of the cavity needs to be opened, *without penetration of the cavity contents*. This can be accomplished by careful, light slicing until an opening exists through the sheath, after which the knife may be turned and the opening completed, *with the contents depressed away from the knife point with two fingers*. The sketch in Figure 8:3 will help.

You must cut around the organs which pass through the pelvic opening so that these are free to be drawn out with the cavity contents. As well, you will want to open and free the windpipe along the neck and inward above the brisket so it will come through to the cavity. All these steps are summarized in Figure 8:4.

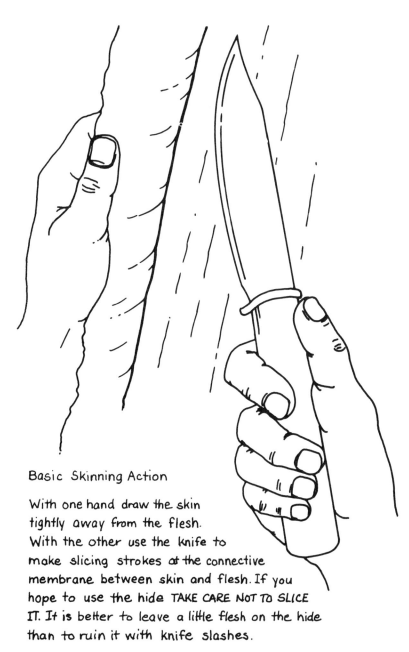

Basic Skinning Action

With one hand draw the skin
tightly away from the flesh.
With the other use the knife to
make slicing strokes at the connective
membrane between skin and flesh. If you
hope to use the hide TAKE CARE NOT TO SLICE
IT. It is better to leave a little flesh on the hide
than to ruin it with knife slashes.

Figure 8:2

Opening the Sheath of the Body Cavity

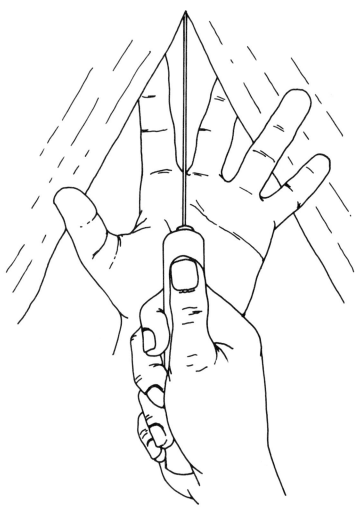

Use two fingers to depress the cavity
contents while the knife blade is run
under the sheath to open it.

Figure 8:3

Figure 8:4 Initial Steps in Dressing Out an Animal

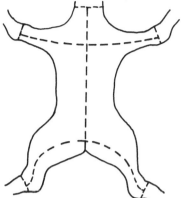

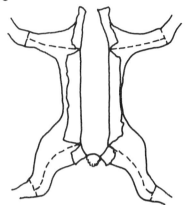

1. Slit the hide only as shown by the dotted lines.

2. Skin back a clear path from the centre line. Leave external genitalia attached to organs which pass through the pelvic channel.

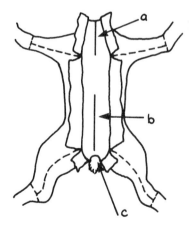

3. a.- Open the neck from the brisket forward to free the windpipe. Cut around it to loosen it where it passes into the lung cavity.
   b.- Open the stomach cavity from the anus to the brisket but DO NOT PUNCTURE THE CONTENTS.
   c.- Cut around the anus to free the organs which pass through the pelvic opening, pulling them through into the cavity.

4. Turn the animal on to one side and proceed to draw out the contents of the cavity.

With the animal now on its side you can start removing the contents by grasping and drawing with both hands. Once some room is made, you will discover by feeling where the contents are connected along the backbone. Careful severing there and around the ribcage to free the diaphragm will gradually loosen everything enough that you will be able to clear it out. Even experienced field hands do a fair amount of grunting and feeling about and incremental cutting before the job is done. With a mule deer or small caribou you can be done in moments; with a large moose, the sheer volume and depth of cavity make the task cumbersome.

If you are going to skid the animal a short distance to a suitable place for initial hanging, then do the skidding while the hide is on. This will be possible with deer or small caribou. If the meat is to be packed some distance to a hanging place, then proceed at once with the skinning. In any case, in warm weather it is vital to get the skin off at once, and only a short skid should delay skinning.

Using the skinning action shown in the sketch (Figure 8:2) complete skinning one side, then roll the animal over and finish up the other. With care the meat can be kept on the skin and the flesh will remain clean of ground debris.

There are two methods for the initial breaking of the carcass into manageable pieces. One involves cutting through bone and requires at the least an axe and preferably a meat saw; the other can be done mainly with a knife, but you will need some knowledge of the skeletal anatomy.

The standard slaughterhouse break is accomplished by splitting the full length of the backbone to produce sides, then severing the front and hind quarters so that the two last ribs are left in the hind quarters. You *can* do this in the field, using an axe to handle the long split of the backbone, but if you are not precise with the axe, you can also make an awesome mess.

The next sketch (Figure 8:5) shows a more convenient method for use in a lightly equipped field situation.

If you are not familiar with butchering you will undoubtedly make something of a hodge-podge of extra cutting and probing as you search for the way through a joint. This cannot be helped. Just be sure you do not throw any meat away on account of it.

The ribcage, loins, and neck which are left may be manageable now by cross-cutting the backbone, and this you can do with an axe to help sever the bone.

It is often the practice, particularly with meat that will be cut

Breaking a Carcass into Pieces

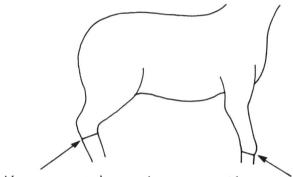

You can sever here using only a knife. Go through at the thickest part of the bulge.

You can sever here using only a knife. Go through a little below the point of the bend.

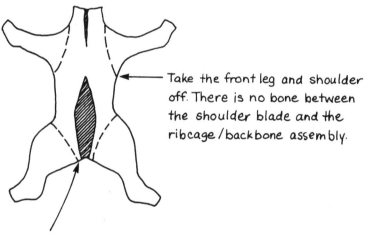

Take the front leg and shoulder off. There is no bone between the shoulder blade and the ribcage/backbone assembly.

Take the hind leg off. Cut close to the pelvic structure and push outward on the leg as you cut. The leg will give at the top where it is joined to the pelvic structure. You can separate it at the socket.

Figure 8:5

into strips for drying, to cut the meat from the bone to lighten the loads which must be carried to camp. This is sometimes necessary, but do remember that all bones should be broken up and boiled for soup while still fresh. Wild meat is often very lean, and valuable fat, which you need for health, can be extracted from the bones, particularly those with marrow content, by boiling.

PREVENTING SPOILAGE

The pieces of meat should be packed to a location close to camp where there is good shade and, if possible, exposure to wind, but your next steps are very dependent on circumstances.

The prompt dressing and skinning were necessary to prevent your meat from souring. Once the body heat is dissipated from the flesh, the danger of souring is past. Next you must protect the meat from flies and, finally, delay or prevent spoilage from bacterial action.

In the settler communuity of my boyhood, deer meat was kept in hot weather by being hung in a screened-in shed hidden away in a cool, shady place in the forest a short way out from camp or cabin. The full heat of the sun never reached the meat, and though the screen kept the flies out, it allowed full ventilation of the shed. Fresh air moved freely around the meat at all times. Even in the hottest of bush-country weather, meat could be kept in this way for most of a week.

If we were not going to be in a camp long enough to warrant construction of a shed, meat bags were made up from well-washed flour sacking, the cloth in which flour was purchased in one-hundred-pound bags. The bag would be brought up around the meat as it hung by a single rope, then tied fly-tight at the top around the rope. This bag would be removed every night at dusk and put on again every morning at daybreak. In this way the flies were kept off the meat during the day, but at night when the flies were not about, the meat was open to the cold night air.

In weather which is sunny yet cool and in which a brisk wind is blowing, freshly killed meat can be hung in the open where the drying effect of the sun and the wind will harden a thin outer layer of the meat into a tough black skin. Flies cannot penetrate this skin, and it appears to delay bacterial spoilage as well. Do not attempt this in hot weather, only in sunny yet cool weather, such as you often experience in high country in September.

If there is not enough breeze to keep away the flies near ground level, you can sometimes protect the meat by hanging it very high off the ground. Experience suggests that near tree-top height there is virtually no fly activity, and some people do use the technique for this reason. It is difficult, however, with limited gear to get any quantity of meat up high enough for this to be practical.

I believe the best course in the open seasons is to decide immediately following a kill how much meat will do the camp for five to seven days, depending on just how hot the days are running, then set about to keep this amount fresh and dry the remainder at once.

In dividing the meat at this point, keep the meat with any fat layers for the fresh supply and the straight lean for drying.

In sunny yet cool weather with a good breeze, you should hang the meat to be kept fresh in the wind but shade it from direct sunlight at the same time.

In hot weather you will need to go to the coolest place you can find, and this will be in timber which so completely blocks out the sun that it effectively excludes the wind as well.

If you have the material for it, the practice of fly-tight bagging in the daytime, with exposure of the meat to the cool air at night, will be best.

If you do not have such material, then hang your meat in the coolest place possible and maintain a light smoke fire beneath it to keep off the flies until the outer layer of the meat dries into a black, tough skin. No heat from the fire should reach the meat. A small fire using green deciduous wood to make the smoke will do the trick. Avoid any coniferous wood for this small smoke fire. Also, put up no more smoke than is needed to deter the flies.

Meat that is to be dried must be cut into thin strips. With a large animal this is a considerable task. Hundreds of pounds of meat creates an enormous number of strips, and they must be thin to ensure rapid drying. One-quarter of an inch is a good guide for thickness, though the strips can be as wide and long as is reasonably manageable.

These must be hung on a rack of light, dry poles, and if there is enough breeze to keep away the flies and a strong sun you need nothing more. Within hours the meat will have a tough leathery quality; within two or three days it will be so dry as to all but crumble when you bite on it.

If there is not enough breeze to keep the flies away, you will need to maintain your smoke fire beneath the drying rack as well. A small fire and a light, cool smoke are all that is wanted, and only until the meat is dry enough that the flies are no longer drawn to it. Now it sometimes happens that you must dry meat in damp weather. In this case you will need to maintain more fire and smoke in order that the combination of warmth, smoke, and fire-induced circulation will dry the meat in the absence of sun and wind. Do be careful not to overdo the fire. If you start to cook the meat you will not end up with palatable, long-keeping jerky. The meat should be five or six feet above ground and the fire should never be allowed to produce more heat than you can easily bear if you hold a hand over it at half the height of the racks.

Once your meat is thoroughly rid of all moisture it will keep indefinitely, provided you never allow it to become damp. The first rule for storage of dry meat is to keep it dry. Virtually any container will do, or it can be piled loosely on the platform of a covered cache. Of course, you must keep it safe from animals and birds, but once that is accomplished any arrangement will do that is certain to keep it dry.

Now, back to your fresh meat. You will have chosen whatever method seems best for keeping it safe from flies and as cool as possible. As you cook up each day's requirement you will see how well it is keeping, and with luck you will use it up just as the inevitable limit to its keeping time approaches.

Should you sense at any point that your meat is about to turn, cook the entire remaining lot at once. Someone skilled in managing fresh meat can detect a slight off-odour the day before the meat becomes unpleasant to use, and at this stage it is perfectly safe and palatable, provided it is *thoroughly* cooked without delay.

Once you cook meat thoroughly, you will to a certain extent have renewed its keeping time, provided that you reheat it thoroughly every other day or so. Obviously there is a limit to how long this will be practical, but as a way of keeping your fresh-meat supply safe for a few more days it will serve. Under no circumstances should you try to make jerky of meat that is approaching the end of its keeping time as fresh meat.

If you catch fish in quantity, you can dry these just as you did your meat. Given a good drying wind and a strong sun, you may dry your fish without a smoke fire; without a good wind or in damp weather you will need the light smoke fire to keep off flies and assist the drying process.

The best method of cooking your fresh meat is to boil it, and make sure that all the broth is consumed in addition to the meat.

Cook the meat until tender. It matters little whether you cook it a moderate while over a brisk fire or simmer it all day over a low fire, but do cook it until it is tender.

If you have a cooking pot with a bail handle, which really is a high-priority item in aircraft emergency gear, set it up as shown in the next set of sketches (Figure 8:6).

Fish also may be boiled, although when fresh it is more enjoyable if baked beside the fire or over a very low fire with a touch of smoke. Fresh meat of the tender cuts can be roasted beside the fire for a change as well. People in the bush who regularly dry meat and fish often eat much of it with no further processing, but health authorities recommend against this for fear of parasitic infection. Dried meat or fish may be soaked for a while to soften it, then boiled until it is cooked. Trial and error is the only method for discovering what you consider the most palatable result.

Whenever you cook food over or beside a fire in such a way that some smoking of the food will result, and also when using smoke to keep flies away from drying meat or fish, be sure you use deciduous wood, never coniferous wood. Use aspen, willow, birch, alder, or maple, but not pine, spruce, or fir. Start the fire with dry wood and then add green if you want more smoke.

The next set of sketches (Figures 8:7 to 8:9) will give you some ideas for cooking meat and fish.

Well, we have talked a little about general camp-management and about managing meat and fish. The subject is endless and would take a book in itself to treat exhaustively, but with this information to begin with, you can go on to build your own set of skills and techniques.

Ingenuity leads to one improvisation after another. Experienced bush people usually develop a pattern of favoured devices. Certainly this has happened in my case; yet not a season goes by that I do not see something I have never seen before which delights me in its combination of simplicity and effectiveness.

Of course, you have seen already many improvisations in the course of the subjects I have covered. To end this chapter I offer a few more suggestions (Figures 8:10 to 8:12) that have proved useful around camp.

Using a Cooking Pot

A large and heavy pot can be hung over the fire by this simple method.

Figure 8:6

Figure 8:7   Cooking Methods

If you kill a large animal but are stuck for a cooking
pot, dig a hole and line it with the hide. Put in water,
add pieces of meat, then cook by immersing hot stones,
as large as convenient to handle. It takes time and
much changing and adding of stones but it will do
the job.

Tender cuts may be
roasted beside the fire
for a pleasant change.

230

Preparing Fish for Cooking and Drying

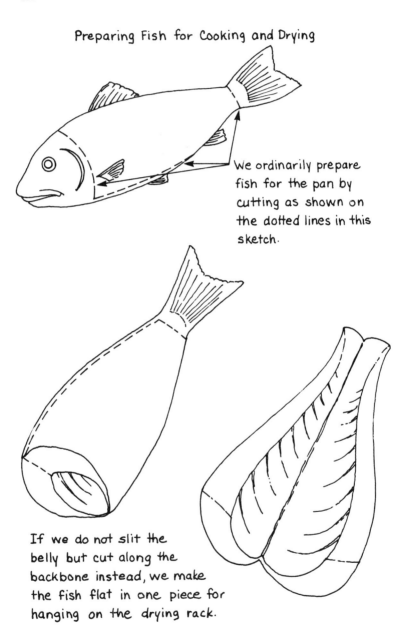

We ordinarily prepare fish for the pan by cutting as shown on the dotted lines in this sketch.

If we do not slit the belly but cut along the backbone instead, we make the fish flat in one piece for hanging on the drying rack.

Figure 8:8

Figure 8:9   More Cooking Methods

A fish or a piece of meat cut flat may be pegged to a half-round of wood for baking by the fire.

If you split the fish both back and belly, but leave the tail intact, you can lay the fish on a frame of green sticks over a <u>small</u> fire to bake it. It will be lightly smoked and tasty.

232

Figure 8:10   Improvised Ladders

A stout stem with many branch butts will make a ladder. You must secure it against turning. A wide strong fork at the top will help. Do not leave it leaning against the cache when not in use!

If you have line to spare you can make a conventional ladder, but do not cut the line. You may need it in full length later.

You can make a vise to hold
a piece of work. Start the split
with the axe. Deepen it with
wooden wedges, leaving one in
at the side. Place the work in the
split at the top then knock the
remaining wedge out.

Figure 8:11

When making a stake to be driven
into the ground, snub the top as
shown to reduce the tendency of
the stake top to split while
being driven.

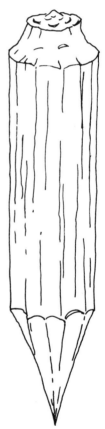

Figure 8:12

NINE

Safety and First Aid

■ **BE PREPARED**

Now let us consider safety and first aid and begin with the oft-made admonition that an ounce of prevention is worth a pound of cure. Never more than in the bush is it vastly easier to prevent an injury than to cope with its consequences. An axe-cut foot is a bad enough business when you can take it by motor transport at once to a doctor; it takes little imagination to see how much worse it will be in an isolated bush camp where you must tend it yourself and the only way of getting about is by walking.

So do think prevention, but at the same time do prepare yourself to deal with injury, either to yourself or to others. No manual by itself, and certainly not a chapter in a review such as this, will prepare you fully to manage injuries in circumstances where you may not reach professional medical help for days. Do attend a first-aid course in which a series of lessons, skilled instruction, and directed practice will equip you to do the best possible in the event of injury in the bush. Adult-education evening courses of high calibre are available in most communities, usually in the winter months, and if your community does not have a first-aid course periodically available, you could do your community a service by pressing for its provision through whatever educational facilities are at hand.

Let me stress the point: any person going into the bush for work or recreation and intending to do so competently should become skilled in first aid. One makes the bush a safer place, both for oneself and for others. This skill cannot be gained by reading only; it requires professional instruction and guided practice as well.

Much first-aid instruction is oriented mainly to the industrial workplace and, to a lesser extent, to recreation activity. In both of these situations fast evacuation to medical attention is possible. First aid in the bush does differ in that the kinds of injury that are most common will not be the same, and also that early attention by a doctor often is not possible. You should have these factors in mind when seeking training so that you get the right emphasis in your set of skills.

■ DEALING WITH INJURIES AND ILLNESS

FIRST CONSIDERATIONS

It will be useful to review the more common injuries sustained in the bush and give some summary of the practical treatment required.

In minor injuries you have, usually, only the injury itself to treat; in more serious injuries you are faced with both the injury and the concomitant shock. Both need treatment.

Shock is a general depression of body functions caused by an insufficient supply of blood to body tissue, particularly to the brain and other vital organs. The most common cause is bleeding, both external and internal. A sudden loss of a relatively small amount of blood can be more serious than a gradual loss of a larger amount.

The usual signs of shock are that the skin is pale, cold, and clammy, the pulse is fast and weak, and breathing becomes rapid and shallow. The more severe the shock, the more pronounced are these symptoms. The pupils will dilate, the pulse become difficult to feel, and the patient may become unconscious.

Fear is a common reaction to injury, and this is very understandable, particularly in someone who is threatened by the surrounding situation as well. Someone not yet fully confident in the bush but enjoying the constant discovery attending each new venture outdoors may be pushed to near panic by a relatively minor injury accompanied by vigorous initial bleeding. The bush suddenly threatens, preventing escape to help and safety. This fear adds an element of psychological shock which can worsen the physical shock.

Shock is also aggravated by pain, by tiredness, and by any discomfort from being wet and cold.

It is paramount of course to stop any bleeding, but you must not neglect to treat for shock. Follow an A B C rule: airway, make sure it is clear and keep it secure; bleeding, stop it; circulation, sustain it. See that the patient is as comfortable as you can manage and preferably resting with the head slightly lower than the rest of the body, that you keep him warm, and that you constantly reassure him that the situation is safe and under control. Try to keep the patient from looking at his injuries and emphasize the positive elements of how you are going to manage the new set of factors created by the injury.

It is of cardinal importance that no person who is less than fully at home in the bush should go into the bush alone, and it is in the event of injury accompanied by shock that the importance of this rule most vividly manifests itself. True, many an old hand has suffered injury when alone in the bush and both treated his injuries and got himself out into the bargain, hardly reckoning the experience worth telling about. Once in my life thus far, in a moment of carelessness which will embarrass me for the rest of my days, I cut my leg with an axe. Astounding volumes of blood got spread about before I arrested the flow with a field dressing and considerable back-up bandaging. It is just very fortunate for me, given how much time I spend alone in the bush, that I am not bothered by the sight of my own blood and that on this occasion I was in home camp with a vehicle at hand and could drive out to have the wound stitched up.

Do not go alone in the bush unless you are fully at home there and know with certainty that you are capable of self-treatment to the extent at least of arresting bleeding and binding a wound. Alone you must not only treat your own injury but put together an emergency shelter in which to wait for help if the injury prevents travel. With two or more people self-treatment is not necessary and the uninjured can make a secure camp, then go out for help if needed.

When an injury results in any marked degree of shock, a knowledgeable companion may well save a life with rudimentary treatment which the injured person alone could be quite unable to administer.

The common injuries in the bush, apart from those suffered in rough forced landings, are: cuts by axe or knife; sprains, most often to the ankle; fractures, most often to the leg; frozen tissue in very cold weather; and hypothermia. I will review the prevention and treatment of these, but considering the wide range of serious injuries possible in a rough forced landing I simply restate that if you wish to be competent you must get training.

CUTS

Your axe and your knife are invaluable tools in the bush. Carelessly used they can also inflict very damaging wounds. A friend in game-management administration tells me he suspects that in the hands of inexperienced users of the sort who venture to bush country at vacation season, mostly by vehicle, axes are more damaging as the cause of injury than useful in their intended purposes. That sounds a little harsh to me, but he may be right.

A basic rule for all cutting instruments is that you keep them sharp. A dull blade slips or glances from the wood or other substance it is intended to cut; a sharp blade bites in and does not slip or glance.

Good knives often come with instructions for maintaining the edge. With both axe and knife, not only must the blade be maintained at the cutting edge, but the angle of the original cutting surface must be kept up in depth at the same time. If you keep in mind that a knife blade is much thinner than an axe blade, the next set of sketches (Figure 9:1) will illustrate the sharpening principle for both tools.

When using a knife, always make the cutting stroke away from you, not toward you, and not toward your other hand, which is usually holding whatever object the knife is being used to cut.

With an axe you must always position yourself so that, if the axe misses or glances from the wood, the follow-through of the stroke cannot hit you. Take the trouble every time that you begin a task with the axe to think through your position. Will you be in the path of a stroke that misses or glances off the wood? Also, clear away from around and above you any bushes or branches which conceivably could interfere with your intended stroke.

Felling with an axe is generally safer than bucking or splitting, both of which, in the absence of a splitting block, involve axe-strikes

238

near ground level. The next set of sketches (Figure 9:2) illustrates the hazard and the simple rule for safety.

Now the rule about your end of the axe handle is simple, but do not be misled by that to suppose it is unimportant. My father gave a sharp axe each to my brother and to me when we were still children. I was less than ten years old, but I remember yet the stern admonition to keep my end of the axe handle low. We used our axes extensively. My brother never cut foot or leg, and neither did I until the stupid piece of carelessness I mentioned earlier — and that happened forty years after my father gave his stern warning.

So please do keep your end of the axe handle low.

Minor cuts can be treated with a Band-Aid or a small bandage.

The Angle for Sharpening a Blade

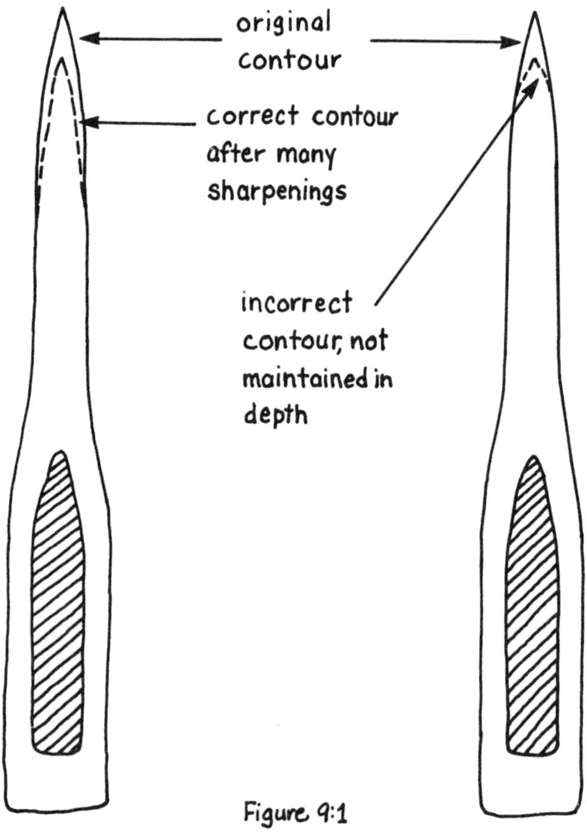

original
contour

correct contour
after many
sharpenings

incorrect
contour, not
maintained in
depth

Figure 9:1

Figure 9:2   Using an Axe Safely

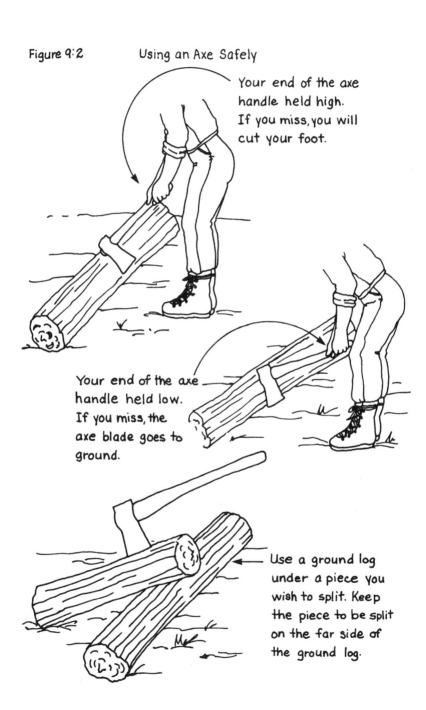

Your end of the axe handle held high. If you miss, you will cut your foot.

Your end of the axe handle held low. If you miss, the axe blade goes to ground.

Use a ground log under a piece you wish to split. Keep the piece to be split on the far side of the ground log.

The idea is to keep them clean while the healing process gets under way.

A deeper or longer cut will need immediate and careful attention. Your objective is to stop the bleeding, prevent infection, and promote healing.

An axe which is used in sound wood will carry few germs into a cut, and the same is largely true of a clean knife blade. The profuse initial bleeding of an axe or knife cut will also help to flush out of the wound any bacteria carried in with the blade.

Your primary protective measure against infection is to be sure that *what you do in treatment* does not infect the wound.

Do not touch the wound. Do not inspect it so closely that you breathe on it. Do not try to clean an already clean wound. Most attempts to clean a wound in the field only make matters worse.

Apply a pressure bandage. You can buy what is called in some quarters a compress bandage and in others a field dressing. These are individually wrapped and sterile and consist of a long strip of gauze bandage with a thick pad affixed at the centre point. An important feature is that they are packed in such a way that you can unpack them and apply them without getting your hands near the pressure pad. Even with soiled hands you can unpack and apply the bandage without contaminating that part of the dressing which will be in contact with the wound.

These dressings come in different sizes and I carry the four-inch version, on the principle that you can put a large bandage on a small cut but not the other way around.

If the bleeding persists, do not take the bandage off but reinforce it with further bandaging. Time and pressure will stop the bleeding. In cases of persistent bleeding, elevate the wound as much as possible. Put some support under a cut leg, for example, to raise it above the rest of the reclining body. You may need to place extra padding over the wound and then hold it very firmly in place with your hand for about fifteen minutes, applying considerable pressure.

Unless there are pressing and obvious reasons for doing so, do not change the dressing. If bleeding has been severe and the dressing is soaked through, you should, if you have enough clean bandage, apply more to ensure that the surface of the bandage that is exposed to the air is dry. Germs will infect through a soaked bandage more readily than through one with a dry exterior.

Once the wound has had time to begin healing — forty-eight

hours is often recommended — you can change the dressing once to ensure a dry covering during the remaining healing period.

It is clear that a serious cut will require a hefty supply of sterile dressings for its best possible management. In an aircraft survival-kit you may have this; in a hiker's kit you will likely have at most one field dressing — another good reason for leaving the initial sterile dressing as is.

If you need more material as an outer cover for the sterile dressing than you have in the kit, you can tear strips from any available material. Provided the sterile dressing is thick enough, the lack of sterility in the back-up covering won't be a great risk, but do remember that infection can penetrate a fair thickness of blood-soaked dressing. You can improve your improvised outer-dressing material by boiling the strips for forty minutes and then drying them in the air outside the camp area.

If there is any opportunity for it when the injury first occurs, wash your hands thoroughly with soap and water before applying even the field dressing, and always wash before any further attention to the dressing.

It may happen that someone suffers a wound that is obviously dirty, and you will have to do your best to clean it if the prospect of getting to a doctor quickly is poor.

Disinfectants should not be used to clean a wound. Thorough irrigation with either plain, sterile water or sterile water with salt at one teaspoon to the pint is the best course. You can produce sterile water only by boiling it in a container and setting it to cool. This takes time, during which you will still need to cover and apply pressure to the wound to stop the bleeding.

Even the shortest of delays in cleaning a thoroughly dirty wound is not desirable. Faced with a ragged wound in which soil particles and other foreign material are evident, I would if possible irrigate at once with water from a clear, fast-running stream to clear out dirt and fragments before these are glued in by wound secretion. Soap and warm water may be used in such a case to clean the wound itself and at any time to clean the skin around the wound while the wound itself is kept covered with a sterile pad.

A serious cut which gapes may have to be drawn and held to-gether. The initial dressing and pressure should be applied quickly to control bleeding and prevent infection. When bleeding has stopped, you can remove the dressing, clean and dry the skin on both sides of the cut, and then draw the two edges of the wound together with tape as shown in the next sketch (Figure 9:3). Work with your hands thoroughly scrubbed and, if possible, a sterile pad over your mouth and nose.

To do this job more easily you can buy sets of these tapes. The ones in my main kit in home camp go by the trade name of Leukoclip. I do not carry these in the field, but I do have a material which can be adapted to the same purpose. I would hope to find the ready-made ones in an aircraft kit.

Once the wound is securely closed a fresh sterile dressing should be applied.

Taping a Gaping Cut

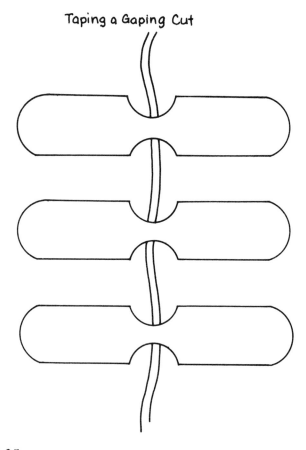

Figure 9:3

In many injuries, including some cuts, it is vital to immobilize the injured part of the body by splinting it. It is not often that splinting will be necessary with a knife or axe cut, and we will discuss splinting in more detail in relation to fractures. However, the rule is simple in relation to incised wounds: if bodily movement in the vicinity of the cut will inhibit healing by causing tissue shifting at the cut, then immobilize with a splint. A deep knife cut in a finger beside a joint, for example, will heal much more successfully if the joint is immobilized by a splint on the whole finger.

SPRAINS

A sprain, usually of the ankle, is a common and very inconvenient injury. The best way of preventing such an injury is to buy first-class footwear and to take extra care when working through terrain where the footing is poor. If it is tough going, you never lift the next foot up until the one you have just put down has found a secure grip.

When you turn an ankle the result is more often a painful but temporary disability than a partial rupture of a ligament which characterizes the true sprain. It is critically important, should you injure the ankle or any other joint, that you take the load off it at once and wait. If you have stressed but not actually damaged the ligaments, the pain will subside, and after a short rest you will be able to carry on and will not be further troubled.

On the other hand, if the pain persists and the joint swells, you must stay off it while your companions prepare a camp.

A sprain consists of the partial rupture of a ligament caused when the bones of a joint are forced beyond their normal range. There will be internal bleeding in proportion to the severity of the partial rupture. Swelling, pain, and extreme tenderness to the touch are the principal symptoms.

Management of this injury requires reduction of the swelling by elevation of the joint and the application of cold, followed by rest and support in less severe cases, immobilization in more severe cases. If the joint is used too soon after the injury it is likely to suffer further damage.

As with most injuries in the bush, the difficulty of management of both the injury and the situation it brings on will depend largely on circumstance. If you are a party of two or more and the mishap occurs near water and other things that you will need for an emergency camp, you will have little difficulty. If you are alone and high on a dry slope, your problems are a good deal stiffer.

Ideally, the injured person is made comfortable, with the injured leg elevated, while cloth soaked in cold stream-water is applied to reduce swelling. When swelling and tenderness have been controlled to a sufficient extent the joint can, if necessary, be immobilized with a splint, which must be abundantly padded. A pair of crutches should be made so that minimal movement about camp will be possible without putting weight on the healing joint.

If ideal circumstances do not exist, and this is usually the luck of it, you must still do the best job possible of managing both the injury and the new situation it brings on. No absolute rules apply; intelligent assessment followed by resolute action are the keys. No matter how difficult the situation, you do not go to ground in a funk. We will have more on that later.

FRACTURES

The next serious injury that is likely to occur in the bush is a fracture, most commonly to the leg.

Prevention is much the same as for joint sprains in the leg structure. Use first-class footwear and extreme caution in rough terrain. Do not ever hurry through this terrain. A stretch of tangled, fallen timber must be taken with patient care. Lose your balance with one leg between two windfallen tree trunks and the next sound you hear may be the sickening snap of bone.

It is imperative that weight be taken at once from any body part in which a fracture is suspected. A fracture of any complexity is a serious injury, and the slightest attempt to make further use of the injured part can result in rapid escalation of the damage.

When a bone breaks, there is damage to both the hard tissue of the bone and the soft tissue surrounding the break. The accident itself has determined the severity of injury to the bone and of the initial injury to the soft tissue; *how the injury is managed thereafter will determine to what extent the damage to soft tissue is kept to a minimum or made vastly worse.*

I can think of no injury which better illustrates the paramount importance of first-aid training as part of the preparation for outdoor pursuits than a complex bone fracture. Professional instruction, and most particularly *directed practice on simulated injuries*, is essential if you are to be competent in the application of traction and effective immobilization of a fracture together with, in open fractures, the prevention of infection and control of bleeding.

I will review the basic management of a closed fracture, but nowhere else in this book do I beg you more earnestly to pursue further training.

Think of the broken end of a bone as being as potentially dangerous to surrounding soft tissue as the broken end of a bottle. This will fix in your mind the absolute care necessary in handling the injury.

Do not move the patient unless to remove him or her from immediate danger of further injury.

Listen to the patient. He may well have heard or felt the snap of bone and can tell you of severe pain and his inability to move the limb.

Look at the limb carefully. A distorted shape indicates a break.

Feel the injury very gently. You may actually feel the break. Extreme tenderness to the touch suggests a break.

Pain, discolouration, and unnatural mobility — that is movement of a bone at other than a joint — indicate a break.

Gather to hand the material which you will need before you begin to work with the injury. If, for example, you must apply traction as well as a splint, make sure you have on hand what you will need to complete the job once you begin, since, once traction is applied, it must be maintained.

In a closed fracture with no displacement, traction is not required. You must immobilize the limb in the position of most comfort, taking care that displacement is not induced and tissue damage not increased.

In a closed fracture with displacement, the natural elasticity of the muscles will tend to shorten the limb, drawing the jagged bone ends into the tissue. Very careful traction is needed as a first step in improving the position of the limb before immobilizing it.

The following principles, taken in order, govern the application of traction:

1. It must be applied as soon as possible after the injury. There is a natural deadening of pain following injury, and the sooner you act the less additional pain will result.
2. It must be applied to the portion of the limb outward of the break.
3. It must be applied in the direct line of the limb.
4. Once begun it must be maintained.
5. It must not interfere with circulation.

In the case of the leg, the weight of the upper body lying on the ground will anchor the upper body against the gentle pull of the traction. The traction strap may be tied to a tree or stake driven in the ground *in order to maintain gentle traction* while the splint is applied. If at all possible, padding should be placed beneath the traction strap to prevent abrasion of the skin at the Achilles tendon. After the splint is applied, the traction strap can be tied to the ends of the splint sticks.

The next set of sketches (Figure 9:4) will illustrate the application of traction and splinting.

Splints must be made up from whatever is at hand. Light, straight sapling stems can be used in the round, but slightly larger stems flattened on both sides with an axe will be more effective. Sufficient padding is needed both to provide comfort and to prevent interference with circulation. One of the reasons why I favour carrying a generous piece of suitable fabric for emergency sheltering in any season is that strips of the material may be torn off for affixing a splint, with still enough left in the piece to improvise a stretcher.

The purpose of splinting is to immobilize the injured part so that there can be no movement at the point of the fracture. *The joint above and below the fracture must be included in the splint.* A break in the lower leg or the thigh will be fully splinted only if the splint stick on the outside of the leg extends up the body to a point just below the arm and inside the leg to the top of the thigh.

In a bush accident it is more likely that the lower leg will be broken than that the thigh will be broken. In anticipation of evacuating the patient on a carried stretcher or by helicopter pick-up, the full-length splint should be applied.

In the event that survival depends on some mobility on the part of the injured person, a fracture of the leg between the knee and the ankle may be splinted from the upper part of the thigh downward so that the knee joint cannot move but the thigh itself can move. This will permit limited mobility with crutches, but it is paramount that this course is only chosen where survival demands it.

There are few injuries you can imagine which more vividly raise the subject of effective self-treatment in the bush than does a broken leg. To go alone in the bush is to accept a most extensive responsibility for your own care and well-being. In the event of accident, you will have only yourself to depend on for at least as long as it will take for it to become evident that your return is overdue and for a search party to reach you.

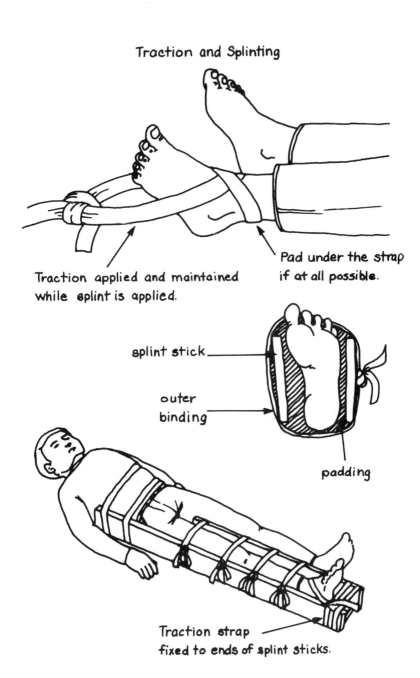

Traction and Splinting

Traction applied and maintained
while splint is applied.

Pad under the strap
if at all possible.

splint stick

outer
binding

padding

Traction strap
fixed to ends of splint sticks.

Figure 9:4

Some authorities recommend, unequivocally, that no person should go in the bush alone and that the less experienced should go in groups of three or more.

Given that, at some times in all seasons, I spend the greater part of my days in the bush alone, frequently on forays taking me many miles from my main camp and with the main camp itself often many road miles from any settlement, I cannot with comfort make sweeping rules of caution for others.

What I will say is that no person should go in the bush alone unless fully at home therein. It goes without saying, after all we have said, that such a person will be well and fully clothed, will know how to get about with map and compass, will have along some essential bits of supplies and equipment with which to fend if the unexpected happens, and will have gained experience in some emergency-sheltering methods.

To that I will add now that such a person also will have gained basic first-aid knowledge and will have thought through the actions to be taken in the event of injury while alone.

No one can foresee the circumstances surrounding all possible injuries, and I have no rules with which to govern every situation, save this: the proper management of an injury applies when you are by yourself as much as when you have companions. The only difference is that providing that treatment will likely be acutely more difficult, as will any other measures for your safety such as the preparation of an adequate shelter.

People have been known to splint up their own broken leg and then to improvise the means of getting about sufficiently to survive. If you will face up to what you require to survive, you have a good chance to manage; if you will not face up you have no chance.

HYPOTHERMIA

Now as serious as these injuries we have discussed may be, in terms of both frequency of occurrence and potentially fatal result, they fall far short of the illness we next consider, the one which takes lives in the outdoors every year, the one we call hypothermia.

Heat moves from a warmer body to a colder one. If the warmer body is yours and the colder body is the body of air surrounding you, heat moves from your body to the body of surrounding air.

Your body must maintain a minimum level of heat in order to function. If your body heat drops below this minimum level, sickness results, and if the drop is great enough, death quickly follows. The insidious nature of hypothermia lies in the fact that air temperatures of no great severity will easily produce it.

You maintain a healthy level of body heat by producing heat through metabolism and by slowing the rate of heat loss from your body to the surrounding body of air with clothing.

An increase in the rate of heat loss can come about very quickly from changes in the body of surrounding air. A drop in absolute temperature or an increase in wind speed or a combination of the two will result in an immediate increase in heat loss from your body.

Cold rain in conjunction with a drop in air temperature and an increase in wind speed can increase the rate of heat loss from your body with stunning rapidity. The cold water both draws away body heat and reduces the insulating strength of your clothing.

Hypothermia is a greater risk in wet weather at temperatures that are above freezing than in dry weather at temperatures that are below freezing.

When changes in the air surrounding your body — a drop in temperature, a rise in the wind speed, the onset of rain — increase your rate of heat loss, one or more of several things must happen. You can produce more heat to maintain a satisfactory level; you can increase the insulative strength of your clothing to maintain a satisfactory level; or you can do both of those in combination; in the absence of those choices your body will lose heat faster than it can replace it.

You can generate a quick increase in body-heat production only through an increase in the rate of physical activity. Who has not at some time gone for a short run along the trail to warm up after standing still too long on a chilly day at some less-active sport, such as trying to catch trout through a hole in the ice?

Although increasing your physical output to increase heat production is safe enough in a situation like that, it can be a dangerous choice if it must be maintained over any substantial length of time. It will deplete your energy, and when you can no longer keep it up it will leave you less able than before to maintain production of body heat.

The safe option to combat an increase in the rate of heat loss from your body is to increase the insulative strength of your clothing.

Therein, therefore, lies the first rule for the prevention of hypothermia: *wear and have with you in the day pack all the clothing you will need for the most adverse weather you could encounter in the course of your outing, including the possibility of an unexpected night out.* You will remember this advice from the chapter on clothing. Now it stands to reason that if your clothing is to be useful in conservation of body heat there has to be body heat worth conserving. You produce the energy for your day's excursion and the heat necessary for healthy body function from the food you eat.

Eat well and go well. Eat poorly and go poorly. Therein lies the second rule for the prevention of hypothermia: *eat well of food which will provide fuel for heat and energy.* Eat well before you set out and carry good food with you to eat during your travels. While it is true that you can, if necessary, survive for many days without food, it is also the case that such survival depends on good clothing and highly effective emergency sheltering for optimum conservation of the body heat that is generated from body reserves in the absence of food for intake. You cannot survive without food if you are planning on vigorous climbing and buoyant adventuring across windswept mountain slopes. For this you want good food, which we discussed in Chapter 7.

As we mentioned there, good food means a combination of proteins, fats, and carbohydrates which have not had their natural whole quality refined out of them. Bacon and eggs and whole-grain bread or cereal have their place here; not, thank you, a bowlful of corn flakes laced with sugar. Take sandwiches of whole-grain bread with a protein filling, not a chocolate-coated candy bar.

Now, even the well-dressed and well-fed people can get into trouble if they suffer an unexpected drop in vital body temperature. After many hours of steady exertion in which you've carelessly got up a big sweat in your clothing, you may feel an uncomfortable chill, even with all your layers on. Your energy level will be running down at the same time.

Perhaps you have been longer afield than you had expected, with soft snow making for unusually heavy going over several hours through the afternoon. You are determined to get out before dark, yet dark is already falling. You have struck across country in the direction of the road to save distance, and do not have the advantage of walking on your broken trail from this morning's trek in. You are not quite sure, in fact, just how far it is to the road. Your snowshoes are intolerably heavy, yet in spite of the exertion of your travel, you are feeling the chill.

Keep going in these circumstances and you could quickly find yourself in a serious stage of hypothermia, yet stop to make fire and shelter while you still have some energy for it and you will go safely in morning light.

Therein lies the third rule for prevention of hypothermia: *know your limits and do not push yourself to the point of exhaustion. Make shelter while there is time and energy for doing a proper job of it.*

In summary, prevent hypothermia by being *well clothed, well fed*, and by *avoiding exhaustion*.

The recognition of hypothermia and its treatment constitute vital knowledge for all outdoors people. Fortunately its approach and development can be read by visible symptoms. According to a brochure published by the British Columbia Department of Recreation and Conservation and the Provincial Emergency Program, the signposts along the way are these:

1. A person feels cold and has to exercise to warm up.
2. He starts to shiver and feels numb.
3. Shivering becomes more intense and uncontrollable.
4. Shivering becomes violent. There is difficulty in speaking. Thinking becomes sluggish and the mind starts to wander.
5. Shivering decreases and muscles start to stiffen. Muscle coordination becomes difficult and movements become erratic and jerky. Exposed skin may become blue or puffy. Thinking becomes fuzzy. Appreciation of the seriousness of the situation is vague or may be totally lacking. However, the victim may still be able to maintain the appearance of knowing where he is and what is going on.
6. The victim becomes irrational, loses contact with the environment, and drifts into stupor. Pulse and respiration are slowed.
7. Victim does not respond to the spoken word. Falls into unconsciousness. Most reflexes cease to function and heartbeat becomes erratic.
8. Heart and lung control centres of the brain stop functioning. The accident is complete.

It takes little imagination to realize that hypothermia is easily manageable in the early stages if a knowledgeable person will take charge of the situation. Similarly, it is going to be difficult to recover a victim from the more advanced stages, particularly in the field situation in which the illness has developed. Early recognition and prompt action are, therefore, vital.

If you are alone, you are more than ever dependent on prevention. However, a healthy and alert person can recognize the onset of symptoms in the very early stages and must muster the will and the resolution to change the course of events. Get out of the wind and get to a source of fuel immediately. Use your fire-starter to get a quick blaze going and heap it up. If you have dry clothing in your pack, change into it. Use your piece of fabric or emergency tent around your back and shoulders and over your head to help hold the heat of the fire around you. Wet clothing of any material other than wool might be better removed once you have the fire. Do not think about when you will continue your travel. Maintain your fire, warm yourself, dry your clothing, and improve your shelter.

When you are warm, dry, and rested, make a fresh assessment of your situation and plan your further travel accordingly. Do not hesitate to stay in the security of your camp until the weather improves.

The person who has advanced beyond the very early stages of hypothermia will need help if he or she is to survive. Whether you are travelling in a party of two persons or of several, it is mandatory that, when hypothermia is recognized in a party member, the entire party alters plans and turns to the aid of the victim.

If one of your party shows any of the symptoms — uncontrollable fits of shivering; vague, slow, slurred speech, with memory lapses and incoherence; immobile, fumbling hands; frequent stumbling and a lurching gait; drowsiness, apparent exhaustion, and inability to get up after a rest — he is in trouble and needs help. He may deny his difficulty. Act on the symptoms, not on what he says.

Get the victim out of the wind. Get into timber that offers shelter and fuel. Get a fire going. Remove any wet clothing from the victim and put on dry clothing gathered up among the party. Put up a quick reflecting shelter to trap the heat from the fire around the victim and to keep off further rain. Heat a billycan of water and give the victim thoroughly warm drinks. These will help to warm him from the inside, while the fire warms him from the outside.

Now those measures will recover a victim from the early stages of hypothermia. In advanced stages, the problem is much more complex.

First of all, when a person has lost body heat to a seriously low level there is no point in simply wrapping him up in dry insulating clothing or other insulative material. Conserving body heat will not save the victim when there is too little heat left to be adequate even if you conserve it all. In fact, at mid stages the victim would be better off in the lean-to shelter before the fire without clothing than with it, since the clothing at this stage is an unwanted barrier to the absorption of heat.

Second, the serious problem is the loss of heat from the *inner core* of the body. If the heating of the exterior and the limbs is too rapid, it can actually result in a further drop in the core temperature before a rise begins. This happens because the initial outer warming promotes circulation in which colder blood from the extremities and the surface reaches the core before warming in the core can begin. This is critical at more advanced stages, and research now indicates that techniques for warming the victim from the inside out, including the breathing of steam-warmed air, are the most effective and the safest. No attempt is made to warm the extremities and the body exterior until the core has been warmed.

In the field situation you are limited to providing some means of gradual rewarming from the outside, while at the same time offering as much thoroughly warm drink as the victim can take.

While the fire and the shelter will do the job safely and well in less-advanced cases, a more gradual, consistent, and safe warming can be achieved by providing heat from other persons whose bodies are functioning fully and generating normal levels of heat.

The classic method is for the healthy person to get into a sleeping bag with the hypothermic person — with neither of them clothed — so that heat from the healthy person will gradually warm the sick person.

This is fine, but a party on a day hike will seldom have a sleeping bag, so the next best thing must be done. Make the best possible bed in the shelter, paying attention to ground insulation. Then have the victim lie between two healthy persons, all three unclothed, with all possible clothing and canvas and useful material which can be mustered by the party put over and around the three in the bed.

Other members of the party can keep the fire going to make up for the clothing they have contributed to the warming bed and to heat water for hot drinks for the sick member as soon as he is able to take them.

When the patient has rewarmed to a level of obvious coherence and returning comfort, he can complete his recovery before the fire with his own clothing, now dried, put back on. Heat any food you have with you and encourage him to eat.

Once more, with recovery accomplished, the entire party can make a fresh assessment of time, weather, terrain, and distance, to decide when travel may be resumed.

FROSTBITE

In very cold weather the air is generally dry, and certainly you will not be faced with rain. Proper clothing and reasonable care not to overheat will avoid the general body-chilling which leads to hypothermia. Of greater risk is localized and rapid heat loss leading to frostbite of the face, ears, hands, or feet. The effect of wind is often critical. At −30°C (−22°F) a 16 kph (10 mph) wind will produce a rate of heat loss equivalent to still air at −44°C (−47°F). A drop in temperature of 14°C (25°F) is a significant drop, and the rate of heat-loss equivalent brought about by wind is every bit as significant. Yet we do not think of a ten-mile-an-hour wind as being much more than a light breeze.

Racing with sled dogs is a popular sport in the north these days. The Yukon Dog Mushers' Association sponsors races through the winter months, and an event is not cancelled until the temperature drops to −35°C (−31°F).

Running with dogs hitched to a light sleigh or toboggan on a well-packed trail is also a brisk and exhilarating sport. I can be carried away with the delight of it when travelling with only my three huskies and my work toboggan on a trail out on the ice of Lake Laberge; you can imagine the zest of the fast-run races with many teams competing and seven or more dogs in each team. The light racing sleighs fairly fly around the course.

You may also imagine with absolute accuracy the incidences of frozen noses, cheeks, and ears.

That is, you see, precisely how much frostbite occurs: someone is so preoccupied with the enjoyment of his or her outdoor pursuit that he does not notice the transition from a patch of flesh that is painfully cold to one that has no feeling in it at all.

Of course the first line of defence against frostbite is adequate clothing, including protection for head, hands, and feet.

The second line of defence is to pay attention to what is going on. Frostbite gives you warning, but fail to heed that warning and you do not get a second or third alarm. Instead you get the frostbite.

Pay attention and take action to avoid frostbite. If your feet are hurting with the cold, get into the timber and get a fire going; then stay by the fire until you are completely warm again. Also, determine why your footwear failed to keep you warm and take measures to improve it on the next outing. Make sure there is room in your footwear to wriggle your toes, as this is a main check for frostbite. If your toes become uncomfortably cold, perhaps because you are standing still for an extended period of time as you do while ice fishing, keep wriggling them. As long as you can wriggle your toes you have not frozen them, but *do not wait too long* before taking specific action to restore warmth.

Again, pay attention. If you must walk into the wind, be extra careful. Whenever your face feels intensely cold, keep flexing your face muscles. A surprising amount of directed movement of facial muscles is possible, and you will pick up the difference if a patch of skin is going numb.

If two or more people are together, they should constantly watch each other's face for a patch of skin that is turning distinctly white.

Do not wait to take corrective action until frostbite is under way. Take immediate steps to warm the affected part and then take further positive steps to alter the situation which produced the problem.

If your face is affected but your hands are fully warm, apply your bare palm to the affected part, at the same time turning your back to the wind. You cannot leave your hand out for long, but usually for long enough.

If your fingers are affected, put your hand inside your outer clothing and against your body. The armpit and the crotch are good places to warm a dangerously cold hand.

If your feet are affected, walk into the nearest timber in which you can find shelter and fuel and get a fire going.

Now those are the measures to take *to prevent* frostbite. If you do suffer actual frostbite, then these measures will still be appropriate *in the early stages*. One person can help another. For example, you can open and lift your clothing enough to place your companion's bare foot against your stomach to thaw out frostbitten toes.

At the same time it is absolutely vital to alter the situation that has caused the problem. If it is the wind in the open which is causing the problem, get into cover. Hold your gauntlet mitts in front of your face for increased protection as you proceed toward the timber.

The spare socks from your pack, used as an extra mitt liner, may be enough to reinforce hand protection after recovery from minor frostbite on one finger.

If dampness in the socks and felt liners in the boots is the problem, stay by the fire not only until the frost-touched toe is recovered (use your hand to warm it, not the direct heat of the fire), but also until the felt liner and the socks are fully dry as well. If this means an overnight emergency camp, then be glad you have that choice ahead of frozen feet.

You can deal effectively on the trail both with the prevention of frostbite and with recovery from the first stages of frostbite. You cannot deal effectively with advanced frostbite, and permanent damage is certain to result.

First-degree frostbite inflicts minimal damage. Following successful thawing, the skin will first appear red and later become blueish or purple. Swelling of the skin occurs some hours later. This may persist for several days. The outer layer of skin will begin to flake off after five to ten days.

In second-degree frostbite there will also be an initial reddening following rewarming, and this in turn will be followed by the formation of blisters. These eventually dry, and may form blackened areas over a period of two or three weeks. Eventually these separate from the skin, leaving the deeper layers intact. The new growth of the skin may be of poor quality.

In third-degree frostbite, damage is done to both layers of the skin and may extend into deeper tissues. Gangrene may result.

Once frostbite has occurred you must treat the affected part with great care. The white, anaesthetized part must be protected from additional injury. Do not apply ice, snow, or cold water. These procedures belong to a myth about frostbite treatment which is positively destructive.

Protect the affected part from physical damage: no rubbing, slapping, or massage, and no walking once you have reached a sheltered place where fire and an emergency camp can be made.

Too-slow warming can be harmful, and excessive heat will burn. Immersion in water at exactly 41°C (105°F) is best, but not practical on the trail.

Use your fire for general warmth to your whole body, but rewarm the frozen part by contact with other parts of your body or a companion's body. For example, if the toes on one foot are affected sit on brush before the fire and hold the affected toes in your hands.

If, after rewarming, there is considerable pain and water-filled blebs form on the skin, a soft, dry dressing will offer some protection.

If you are ever confronted with third-degree frostbite, for instance if the deep tissue in most of all of a foot or hand is frozen, the rule is not to make any attempt at thawing but to get the victim to medical help at the earliest possible moment. Some authorities say this should be done even if it means continuing to walk for some time on a frozen foot. It is only through grossly bad management of clothing and footwear selection, of travel requirements, and of response to the initial warning signals that such a disastrous degree of freezing will occur. No hard and fast rules can be given; you will have to deal with the case according to the circumstances, but do remember not to attempt thawing. Protect the injured person from further freezing. Make an emergency camp and leave him with firewood while you travel out for help if this seems best. Stay and tend the victim as best you can if you think a search will be under way quickly. If there are two of you in addition to the victim, you may manage to carry him on a stretcher.

When you have completed thawing the frozen tissue of first- or second-degree frostbite, that is to say frostbite which has not affected deep tissue, you must make a fresh assessment of your situation.

Should you stay put until the next day, investing the time left in the day to gathering firewood and improving the emergency camp?

If there are two or more of you, and the affected area was part of the foot, you should look for an alternative to having the injured person walk out. Walking with thawed toes can add seriously to the damage, unless the freezing was caught immediately and did not affect more than the surface.

The more thought you give to any of the injuries which might occur in the bush, the more committed you become to prevention. This brief review we have made of the management of common injuries illustrates in every case how much grief may be saved by effective prevention.

IMPROVISED EMERGENCY EQUIPMENT

Now in the management of injury in the bush there are three main improvisations which you must know how to construct: the splint, the crutch, and the stretcher.

A splint should be made from sound, dry wood if at all possible.

Improvised Crutches

A better crutch

A simple crutch

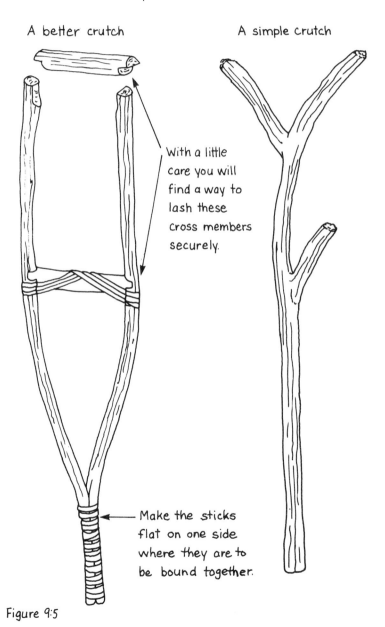

With a little care you will find a way to lash these cross members securely.

Make the sticks flat on one side where they are to be bound together.

Figure 9:5

Use green if you must, but sound, dry wood from a standing stem is the preferred choice.

Hew wood away from two sides of the stem to produce a flattened stick with enough thickness to be rigid. You want the lightest possible splint which still has the rigidity to fully immobilize the injured body part. Round off all edges.

If you have sufficient material for padding and binding, you should wrap the splint stick with light padding and place padding between the splint and the injured limb. If you are short of material, give priority to the padding between the splint and the limb. The padding must accommodate the differing widths of the injured limb so that pressure is the same along its length.

Crutches will be vital if there are imperative reasons why someone with an injured foot or leg must have mobility, however minimal.

The fastest way to make a crutch is to cut a straight, strong stem with a sound and wide fork and, one hopes, with a strong branch below the fork at the right position for a hand grip. Do not count on finding the latter feature, however. You may have to do with the rather awkward but workable method of grasping the stem itself.

Now you must pad the fork very thoroughly, as with this simple crutch the main weight will be taken at the armpit.

A much better crutch can be made with a little trouble but still quite quickly, and you should replace the forked stick with this improved crutch as soon as you can. See the sketch in Figure 9:5. This better crutch allows the injured person to take weight on the hand grip, using the armpit mainly as a control point.

If you find material which will split easily, you may make this crutch from one stem. You bind the stem about four inches from the small end and then split it from the large end all the way to the binding. The top cross-member and the hand grip are then fitted between the halves. The fitting and lashing of the cross-members are critical to the strength of the crutch.

Often you will not find material which splits readily, in which case you make the two uprights from separate stems. These may be left in the round, save for flattening at the top to fit the cross-piece and at the bottom where the two must be effectively bound together to prevent shifting in use.

How you make a stretcher depends on what material you have, and again I favour having along a fair-sized piece of tough fabric.

Improvised Stretchers

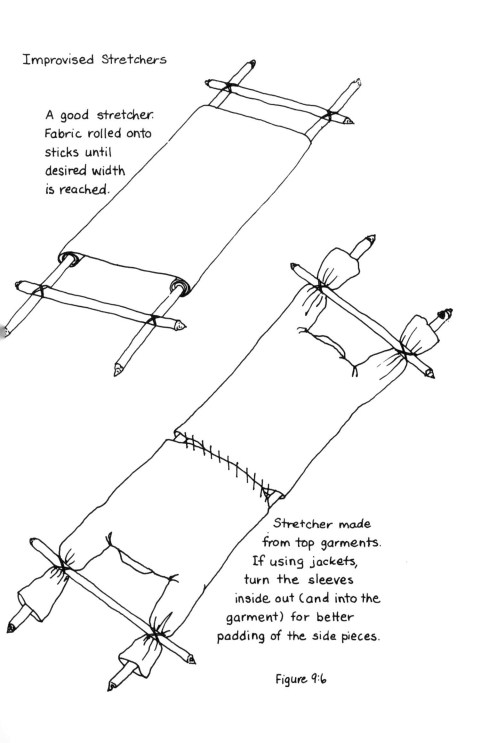

A good stretcher.
Fabric rolled onto
sticks until
desired width
is reached.

Stretcher made
from top garments.
If using jackets,
turn the sleeves
inside out (and into the
garment) for better
padding of the side pieces.

Figure 9:6

It makes a quick emergency shelter but is adaptable to so many other uses. Even after you have torn strips from it for binding a splint, you can have enough left to make a stretcher, as shown in Figure 9:6.

Use sound wood, preferably dry, for your stretcher handles and cross-members. For a short distance you can carry a person securely without the cross-members, but for any long carry you must have the cross-members for adequate control and comfort for the patient.

As with everything you do in the bush, the use of your imagination in managing injury will see you through. Use your head to prevent injury, but use it all the more should injury occur.

Even in the face of injury we have a good chance to continue to go well in the bush.

TEN

Signalling For Help

■ **WHEN TO SIGNAL**

However well you have prepared yourself and however carefully you have managed your travels, the time may come that you are in the bush and unable to come out on your own and must attract the attention of a search party.

On a day hike this will most likely be due to injury that prevents you from travelling. You, of course, know too much about using a map and compass simply to be lost. If you are on an aircraft journey this situation will occur if you are forced down in remote country.

Whatever the circumstance, there are a variety of ways to make signals, some from material at hand, some which you make with equipment from your kit. Some signals are appropriate to reach a ground party, others are suitable to reach an aircraft, and still others are useful in both respects. You will know from your circumstance what form the search will take and when it is likely to begin.

It is of cardinal importance that you do not spend energy and material in sending out signals until it has become probable or certain that a search party or passerby is within reach to see or hear the signal. However, you do expend effort in preparing signalling devices such as fuel piles for light fires and smoke fires which will be lit when the time is right.

The time of day or night, whether the landscape is covered in snow or not, whether the day is cloudy or clear, whether you are on a mountainside or in a valley bottom, and other such factors will determine which signalling devices will be most effective. Think through these factors in relation to what you can do so as to make the most use of your signalling opportunity. Light-coloured smoke won't fetch you much notice rising from a forest of snow-covered trees. Send it up in fire season and you may be absolutely embarrassed by the attention you get.

■ SIGNALLING DEVICES

So let us consider some specific devices.

FIRE AND SMOKE

Fire as light and as smoke is the most obvious device that you can create from material at hand. In conditions where the light is poor, and at night, the light of a fire can be seen for many miles. It is visible on a mountain slope from a highway in the valley below or on any terrain from the air.

Be absolutely careful. There is no point in creating a forest fire over something that can be managed so easily. Three is a universal distress number, so, in a clearing or on the exposed bar of a stream edge, prepare fuel for three fires. Space the fires enough apart to be separately distinguishable, and gather an abundance of extra fuel. Light the fires when there is a good chance of them being seen and keep them going as long as this chance persists.

If conditions are such that smoke would be more easily seen, add green grass, wet moss, mouldy leaves, green branches, and any other material that creates a thick, continuous smoke. You might decide to operate smoke fires and light fires simultaneously during particular conditions.

Now, one caution about this tradition of three fires: in some circumstances this may mean altogether too much work in gathering fuel. If this is the case, concentrate on one good fire, since the moment you are overdue and the word is out, all passing aircraft will begin to investigate every spot of light and smoke they see.

Unless you are on high ground, a ground party is going to see smoke more readily than light from a fire. If the search is from the air, both smoke and light are good, but in addition to any fire you keep alight in case of a passing aircraft, prepare an evergreen torch-tree which you will light on hearing or seeing an aircraft in the vicinity.

This tree must be off by itself, the degree of its isolation depending on the season and the weather. It must be thickly branched down to or near ground level, and around its base you place a huge pile of fuel with plenty of fast tinder. Also, in the lower branches you build another pile of high-grade tinder.

You must be absolutely certain that your torch-tree fire is going to go in a hurry when the time comes, for it must turn this tree immediately into a huge, shooting column of flame and smoke. You might have one of your signal fires near by so that burning sticks may be transferred quickly to start the tinder. If you are down in an aircraft you can, *with utmost caution,* aid the start-up with aircraft fuel. A small amount of gasoline mixed with engine oil, kept at hand in a closed container, may be sprinkled on at the right moment to assure a rapid fire. A trail of fuel should be trickled onto the ground for fifteen or twenty feet so that ignition of the enriched fuel pile can be achieved from a safe distance by putting a flame to the end of the fuel trail.

Now with all fires lit in a situation where pick-up is likely to be by helicopter, do not locate any fire near the area you have cleared for the helicopter to land. The wash from the helicopter will spread fire and ash all over the surrounding area. Keep the fires well away from the landing site.

As mentioned earlier, when the landscape is snow-covered, and particularly when the trees carry a burden of snow, the light-coloured smoke from natural materials will not show up well. If you are down in an aircraft, you can achieve a much more visible smoke by burning engine oil and rubber, but remember that your supply of these is limited. Add them to the fire to blacken the smoke at only the moments when you hear or sight search aircraft.

BRUSH

Another material at hand that is of great use in the wintertime is evergreen brush, either entire young trees of Christmas-tree size or substantial branches from the lower reaches of large trees. These, set out in a pattern on snow-covered open ground or frozen lake-surface, show up splendidly from the air. Use standard code signals to convey the necessary messages. Clear the signals of new snow as necessary.

In the open seasons a high contrast on dark ground — such as a mud flat by a stream mouth or an area of darker grass or moss — can be achieved with peeled poles of aspen, pine, spruce, or virtually any available wood. Try for poles of a good six-inch diameter and cut a number of them in lengths as long as you can find and handle. Peel these and lay them out in whatever pattern you reckon is best and they will be highly visible from the air.

FLARES

In addition to these materials from the bush you can have material and equipment with you of value.

Sporting-goods stores now sell hand-held flares which the day-hiker can have in his kit. Quality varies, and you should carry the best if you carry any. As with your torch tree, do not send up the flare until you have an indication that someone is close enough to see it. Aircraft should carry more substantial flares, again for use at the critical moment when a search aircraft is in sight, and normally the pilot will be responsible for operating these. If it falls to you as a passenger to do this, follow the directions which are packed with the flares and, again, discharge the flare at the most opportune moment for it to be seen.

CLOTH

Cloth or other material of a vivid orange colour is widely in use now in many applications because of its high visibility, for example as surveyor's flagging tape and highway traffic controllers' vests and gloves. Cloth panels of this vivid orange colour, when laid out on the ground, show up from the air with startling clarity. Regulations governing flights over sparsely settled areas require that either tents or engine and wing covers carried on the aircraft must be of, or incorporate, panels of this colour or another high-visibility colour. For other reasons I have mentioned I favour having one good-sized piece of tough fabric in your kit, and there is much to be said for having it in this vivid orange colour.

MIRRORS

A mirror, to reflect the sun in the direction from which you wish to be seen, is a highly effective signalling device. Again, aircraft flying over sparsely settled regions are required by regulation to carry these, and if you have one designed for the purpose, a sighting hole in the glass facilitates direction of the flash. Instructions should be in the kit with the glass.

On the other hand, you may be using the mirror incorporated in your compass. In this case, hold the mirror beside your eye with one hand and with the other hold a dry stick a little larger than a pencil upright at arm's length. Direct the flash to land on the stick, then play it back and forth across the stick. Have some darker trees a hundred yards in the background, and you will soon see the flash landing on the trees. In this way you will discover the relationship of the flash crossing your upright stick and the flash landing on a distant object. This established, you can now hold the stick between your eye and an aircraft and play the flash back and forth with an excellent chance of landing it on target. When the pilot of the aircraft indicates by wing dipping that he has seen your signal, stop signalling, as the flash will be a decided nuisance as he closes in on your campsite for a closer look.

RADIO

It goes without saying that the pilot of an aircraft which has been forced down will get a radio message out at the first opportunity. Also, many aircraft are now equipped with emergency locating transmitters which begin to transmit automatically on impact. There is nothing that is more certain to assure early pick-up than verified radio contact, but bear in mind that even with this accomplished you still must devise all possible ground-to-air visual signals to make certain that when aircraft arrive at your location there will be no difficulty in actually sighting the camp or the disabled craft.

SOUND SIGNALS

Signals from ground to air are all visual signals; only when the search is likely to be partly or altogether by ground party need you consider sound signals. The most effective sound signal ordinarily available to you is rifle fire, but once more do not use up valuable ammunition until you have reason to believe that a ground party is, or may be, within hearing distance.

When the time comes to signal, fire three closely spaced shots. Wait some five to ten minutes, and if there is no answering shot, repeat the signal — but again only if there is a reasonable chance of the signal being heard. If a ground party has a rifle, it is customary for your signal to be answered, and then you need fire only such additional shots as are necessary to guide the party to you. Always direct your fire in a totally safe direction.

If your activity does not require a rifle — and these days many more people venture into the bush without a firearm than with one — a shrill whistle of the sort used by referees at sporting matches can be useful, particularly in still air. Such a whistle might be a good companion to the packet of flares in your kit. While it is true that a whistle, however loud and shrill, has a limited range, it will greatly enhance the efficiency of a ground search. Your whistle can be heard over several hundred yards in favourable conditions, whereas you might be visible only from a distance of twenty or thirty yards, depending on the cover. When you leave clear advice about your planned journey you can be sure, should injury pin you down in the woods, that a search party will reach your vicinity. A frequent shrill whistle emanating from your emergency camp will assist the search party enormously.

During the times of the year when there is abundant sap between the wood and the bark of young deciduous stems, a highly audible whistle can be constructed with a pocket- or belt-knife. Figure 10:1 will show you how to proceed, but you will need some trial and error to find the combination of chamber and aperture that gives the loudest sound.

■ THE SIGNAL CODE

Many people familiar with search situations feel that anything more than the attention-fetching signals I have outlined and the basic SOS are largely redundant. Nonetheless, there is an established signal code, and I will give it here for what value you may believe it could have. These symbols, as well as the standard general distress signal SOS, are easy to lay out with brush on snow or peeled logs on a dark background, or simply to tramp into the snow for an immediate signal that you can improve on later with contrasting material.

Making a Bark Whistle

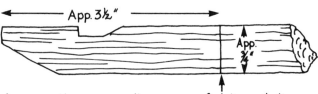

Step 1: Cut a smooth green sapling stem growing in moist ground. Shape it as shown in the first sketch.

Cut through the bark only here, all the way around.

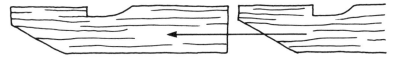

Step 2: Tap with your knife handle all over the surface of the bark to be removed, vigorously enough to help loosen it but not so as to damage it. Give it a firm twist by hand then slip it from the wood.

Step 3: Remove wood as shown in the third sketch. Do not make the wind channel at the top front very large; you can enlarge it later if necessary.

Step 4: Slip the bark back on the wood and give a stout blow. You will be delighted with your handiwork.

Figure 10:1

THE SIGNAL PATTERNS ARE AS FOLLOWS:

Require doctor, serious injuries	—
Require medical supplies	=
Unable to proceed	X
Require food and water	F
Require firearms and ammunition	⋙
Require map and compass	☐
Require signal lamp with battery and radio	▬ ▬
Indicate direction to proceed	K
Am proceeding in this direction	→
Will attempt take-off	I▷
Aircraft seriously damaged	L⌐
Probably safe to land here	△

Require fuel and oil	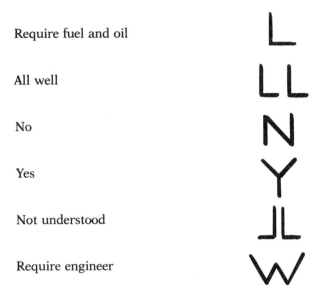
All well	
No	
Yes	
Not understood	
Require engineer	

Now you have some ideas to work with. Remember that a search is a two-way proposition: the searchers have the task of finding you; *you* have a very clear responsibility to be easily found. This responsibility begins with leaving clear instructions about your planned journey, just as a pilot will file a flight plan. In the event of emergency, your responsibility requires you to employ every possible signalling device to help bring the search to a quick and satisfactory conclusion.

With ground-to-air signalling, such devices as your fires and your mirror and your high-visibility cloth are mainly to convey the primary message that here you are, and often once this is conveyed nothing more will be needed. The next step is that you will be picked up by a craft able to land near or at your site.

ELEVEN

Walking Out

■ **MAKING THE DECISION**

For anyone who offers counsel to people forced down in aircraft in remote terrain there are few questions more difficult to answer than that of whether or not one should attempt to travel out on one's own. Many specialists fall back on the admonition to stay put whatever the circumstances, but as much, perhaps, in response to the difficulty of the question as to any universal merit in the idea.

It is a matter of historical fact that people have walked out of the bush following a forced landing in remote ground, while an air search has been in progress, and even after it has been called off. In the face of that, one can hardly fall back on the notion that whatever else you do you must stay in your initial emergency camp come hell or high water.

For the lost day-hiker the problem still exists if one has been so careless as to go out without leaving advice with anyone as to where you are venturing and for how long. You travelled to get where you are; clearly you must contrive, if at all possible, to travel back from where you are.

There is little difficulty in agreeing on the circumstances in which you should not attempt to travel. If you are down in an aircraft, and are certain that a search is being made, you clearly belong near the craft, with your attention devoted to making a secure camp and sending effective signals. If you are injured while out on a day hike, and are confident that a ground party is searching for you using the information you left with a friend, you have no business making your injury worse by trying to come out on your own.

If you want a general rule, it certainly is that in the great majority of cases in which you have lodged proper information about your intended journey before setting out, you should stay put in the event of mishap, travelling from the site — if at all — only so far as is necessary to secure adequate shelter.

It is also true that circumstances may prevent travel, however desirable it might be otherwise. Injury, inadequate gear, and unpleasant terrain and weather may well tie you down, even though you have little hope of being found and can see from your map where you need to go.

That said, we must also say that just occasionally the intelligent choice is to travel out on your own following mishap. If you have been down for some days without managing to attract attention, are in good physical condition, and are informed from your map that you are only three days' walk from a travelled roadway, you will be well advised to assemble your pack and get on with the journey.

One cannot make a checklist to cover all possible situations, and it must remain with people in the emergency to make a thorough assessment and a sound decision. Critical to that decision will be everything we have discussed and thought about through these pages: clothing, footwear, use of map and compass, shelter, food, safety, and the compact bundle of gear which will enable you to attend to all your needs.

Particularly critical is the question of food. Travel will require many more calories than does normal camp-tending, and you should not set off without both food in your pack and the means of securing more. If game is abundant in the vicinity of your camp, take as much of it as you can before setting out in order to have plenty in your pack.

■ GUIDES FOR EFFECTIVE TRAVEL

With the decision made to go, there are useful guides to effective travel, and if you will pay attention to these in all your venturing in the bush, you will benefit considerably.

Travel to your destination by the shortest route which is consistent with reasonably easy walking. The shortest route and its compass bearing are easily established from the map. However, there is no point in going over a high mountain-ridge to the next valley when, by travelling a few extra miles, you can go through a comfortable pass.

Travel with the watercourses. The gradient of the river valleys is more even than elsewhere. Do not follow every turn of the stream, however, as this will lead to many extra miles. Search out the straight route from one bend to the next.

Look for game trails. Often the best travelling along a river or smaller stream is on the trails made and used by the wildlife which also follows the watercourses.

Yet do not stick with this rule blindly. Sometimes the land in the river bottom supports a tangle of dense growth which makes for difficult going. Try the benches just above the valley floor and here you may find, once again, the game trails.

If you have reason to cut across country from one watercourse to another, try still to use the game trails, but also keep track of your bearing. Choose the trails which go mainly your way, avoid those which veer off too much from your bearing.

Avoid rough and exhausting terrain. Swampy ground, rubble-strewn slopes, and deadfallen timber will sap you of energy out of all proportion to the progress you can make travelling through them.

Do not try to complete your journey in remarkable time. Travel at an easy pace and stop to make camp with both time and energy left for doing a good job of it. A short journey every day adds up to a long journey in just a few days, and you save nothing of worth by pushing yourself. The experienced bush-traveller often pokes along, more interested in what he sees about him than in getting to where he is going, and this habit makes for safer travel.

■ TRAVELLING ON WATER

Since travel along and down the watercourses is so often the best route, the fairly obvious question is: Why not travel on the water instead of beside it?

Often this can be done, in both summer and winter, but a few important rules apply.

It is easy in the open seasons to make a raft. It can be assembled using the largest dry logs that you can find. Inverted notches with cross-pieces shaped to fit easily will seize the job together after the raft is placed in the water (see Figure 11:1). Hand-hewn, long-handled paddles can be used to direct the raft in the stream, both by sculling and by poling on the stream bed. Experience will teach you how to manage the raft. The deciding factor in whether to travel by water is the nature of the stream you plan to travel on. Fast-running water with frequent rapids and boulders in the stream bed is better avoided. A raft is not an easily manoeuvred craft, and chances are too great of breaking up against the rocks.

On the other hand, a gently flowing stream offers an excellent opportunity to go a great distance every day with virtually no effort on your part once a good raft has been made. Perhaps the most difficult problem with a gentle river is knowing that it will stay that way. Check your map to see if the gradient increases markedly downstream or if there are rapids shown on the course. Figure 11:2 shows some points to consider when travelling on a river.

■ WINTER TRAVELLING

The best walking in winter travel is often on the ice but do keep in mind that on a meandering stream you will travel many extra miles by staying on the ice. Measure the improved walking against the extra distance.

Also, there are hazards to river ice. Fast or turbulent water will keep the ice thin, and you may not recognize the difference until you have broken through it. You may also go through the snow into overflow, water which has come over the main ice to soak the first layers of the snow cover. You will be forced ashore to light a fire and dry your footwear at once, particularly in cold weather!

Unless you are very experienced, you should avoid travelling on ice during and shortly after freeze-up and again during break-up. Early and late ice offer hazards which should not be tackled by the relative novice.

Winter travel is often easier in a given terrain than summer travel provided that you have a good outfit, including skis or snowshoes. Skis cannot be improvised without exceptional skill, but workable snowshoes can be made with some persistence and ingenuity (see Figure 11:3).

Making a Raft

Log cut to length of
raft and notched to
receive cross-piece.
Do not cut all notches
at once but only as
you fit each
cross-piece.

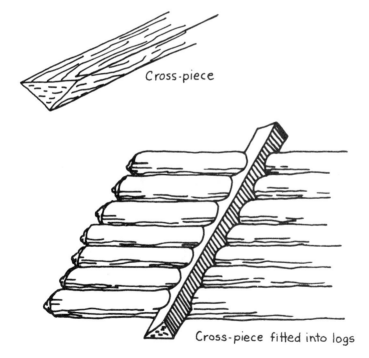

Cross-piece

Cross-piece fitted into logs

Figure 11:1

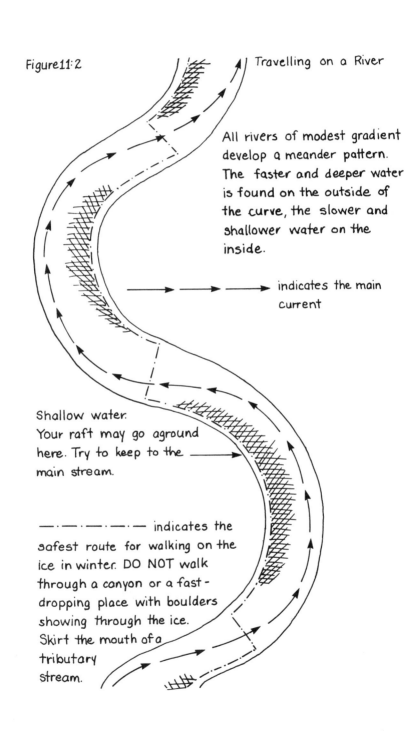

Figure 11:2

Travelling on a River

All rivers of modest gradient develop a meander pattern. The faster and deeper water is found on the outside of the curve, the slower and shallower water on the inside.

→ — → — → indicates the main current

Shallow water. Your raft may go aground here. Try to keep to the main stream.

—·—·—·—·— indicates the safest route for walking on the ice in winter. DO NOT walk through a canyon or a fast-dropping place with boulders showing through the ice. Skirt the mouth of a tributary stream.

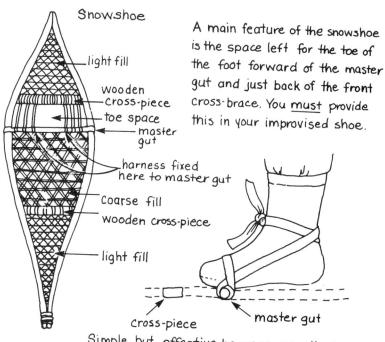

Snowshoe

light fill

wooden
cross-piece

toe space

master
gut

harness fixed
here to master gut

Coarse fill

wooden cross-piece

light fill

A main feature of the snowshoe
is the space left for the toe of
the foot forward of the master
gut and just back of the front
cross-brace. You __must__ provide
this in your improvised shoe.

cross-piece

master gut

Simple but effective harness over the toe,
around and secured to the master gut on
both sides, then back and around the ankle
to tie in front.

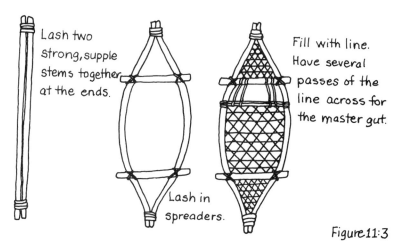

Lash two
strong, supple
stems together
at the ends.

Lash in
spreaders.

Fill with line.
Have several
passes of the
line across for
the master gut.

Figure 11:3

Even more than in summer your winter travel should be taken at an easy pace. Secure sheltering is essential and both time and energy must be saved for it. Never push yourself to or remotely near the point of exhaustion. If you come on good sign of game you may want the patience to stop travelling for a day or two to supplement your food supplies. Successful winter travel is an unhurried business.

In all seasons, good sense, unhurried and carefully directed effort, and your own wealth of previous experience, will be critical to a safe journey. Remember that to travel some distance is only to extend over a number of days the practices of safe venturing and the skills which you have already acquired for the least of your day hikes.

Conclusion

Now I have said little of a direct nature throughout these pages about maintaining a sound and confident state of mind when confronted with an unexpected time out in the bush, yet this is undoubtedly as vital to safety as is proper clothing and the wise use of the contents of one's emergency kit. It is by intent that I have left the question to these last paragraphs, and even now I propose to say little on it. I realize that if you make good use of everything said earlier you will need little advice about frame of mind; if you do not, such advice will be of little use.

Fear and consequent panic grow out of an overwhelming sense of weakness and vulnerability in the face of real or imagined danger. Fear can be prevented by developing, over time, a sense of one's own strength and competence in potentially dangerous situations. Also, when fear does occur, self-discipline can prevent panic behaviour.

Practice and training in realistic surroundings have been the methods, for centuries, of preparing people to respond usefully in the face of danger and while experiencing intense fear.

The person who has had such training and whose confidence is reinforced by the knowledge that he or she has good gear for the task at hand will not panic and will have the best chance of success however bad the odds.

If you lose your way in the bush in winter, wearing poor cloth-ing, and you have never practised any method of sheltering, it is all but a certainty that fear will grip you and panic responses might easily follow. You may lunge about blindly in the dark and may easily die when exhaustion brings you down in the snow.

It is as hazardous, in its insidious way, to do nothing when fear takes hold, to go into a sluggish inertia from which nothing results. When careful assessment followed by resolute action is needed, a numbness of mind rejects reality. No shelter is made nor fuel gathered. Disaster comes more slowly, but may arrive just as surely.

Yet, if you go well clothed, with a little of the right sort of gear in an emergency kit, and with skills acquired long since in practice camps, the prospect of an unexpected night out will be at worst an inconvenience and more likely a welcome adventure.

You can be helped much by reading, and it is for that purpose that I have written this book. You cannot, however, incorporate essential skills and constructive responses into your behaviour with-out training and practice in the field situation. So hie to the bush, my friend, to test the adequacy of your clothing and to practise the skills of the camp.

Now, however much at home you feel in the bush and however confident you are about your gear and your skills, you still may experience fear, unexpectedly, when an accident happens or when the awesome power of nature strikes you in some sudden fashion.

High on a ridge top in a developing storm, with the wind whipping your jacket and screaming in your ears, you may sud-denly be overcome with a sense of your puniness in the vast uni-verse which surrounds you.

Once, as a young man, I was returning to my cabin across a wide and open swampland. The day was late and a storm grew swiftly out of nowhere, filling the sky with black and threatening clouds. The wind picked up to lash the aspen trees at the meadow's edge, tearing some to the ground in its growing fury. A killdeer, flying across my path to cover, shrieked in high, shrill protest against the chaos.

I was in the bushland of my boyhood and not a mile from my cabin. No one could have been more surely in his own home ground, yet my scalp crawled and a scream rose up in my throat. Only by a deliberate imposition of my will on my rising fear did I keep both the fear and some irrational response at bay. Afterward I puzzled how, in such a harmless situation, I could have had such a sense of danger. How much more discipline would have been needed had I been miles from the security of my cabin, with night falling and with little means of making shelter.

So we need good clothing and gear, we need to have developed skills which will afford us confidence in ourselves, and we need discipline. Given these, we can face an emergency with rapid, yet sound, assessment, followed by prompt, yet thorough, action, and without the complications brought on by fear and undisciplined behaviour.

Our venturing into the bush will be certainly safe and probably comfortable, even in the event of the unexpected.

We want to go well. With preparation we will go well.

That is what this book has been about.

Preparation.

Appendix A

AERONAUTICS ACT (Canada)
Sparsely Settled Areas Order

ORDER RESPECTING THE CARRIAGE OF
EMERGENCY EQUIPMENT AND RADIO
COMMUNICATION SYSTEMS IN SPARSELY
SETTLED AREAS

AIR NAVIGATION ORDER, SERIES V, NO. 12

Short Title

1.   This Order may be cited as the *Sparsely Settled Areas Order.*

Interpretation

2.   (1) In this Order,

"sparsely settled area" means an area listed in Schedule I;

"multi-engine aircraft" means an aircraft having two or more engines
that is capable of maintaining flight in the event of failure of the
critical engine;

"operating base" of an aircraft means an aerodrome
   (a) that is frequently used by the aircraft,
   (b) at which shelter and means of sustaining life are available, and
   (c) at which there is a responsible person with whom the pilot-in-
   command may leave information concerning any proposed flight;

"approved" means approved by the Minister.

   (2) All other words and expressions used in this Order have the
same meaning as in the *Air Regulations.*

General

3.   Subject to sections 4 and 5, no person shall operate an aircraft
on any flight wholly or partly within a sparsely settled area unless the
aircraft is equipped with the emergency equipment described in Schedule
II and an approved, serviceable and functioning radio capable of two-
way radio communication with a ground station from any point along
the route during flight.

4.   Where a radio described in section 3 malfunctions or becomes
inoperative during the course of a planned itinerary, the aircraft may
be operated in accordance with the planned itinerary until it reaches
an aerodrome where the radio may be repaired or replaced.

Exceptions

5.   (1) An aircraft on a flight described in section 3 need not be equipped with the emergency equipment described in Schedule II if the aircraft is operated

(a) within 25 nautical miles of an airport or its operating base;

(b) by an air carrier on a commercial air service and is otherwise equipped for the operation as authorized in the air carrier's operations manual; or

(c) in the case of a multi-engine aircraft, under IFR within controlled airspace or along designated air routes and south of 66°30' north latitude.

(2) An aircraft on a flight described in section 3 need not be equipped with the radio described in that section if the aircraft is

(a) a private aircraft operated under VFR; or

(b) a commercial aircraft operated under VFR within 25 nautical miles of an airport or its operating base.

SCHEDULE I

(s. 2)

SPARSELY SETTLED AREAS

1.   The Territory of Labrador.

2.   That part of Canada lying to the North of a line commencing at a point on the boundary of Quebec and Labrador 25 miles inland from the Strait of Belle Isle; THENCE, westward along a line 25 miles inland from the North shore of the St. Lawrence River as far as the 49th parallel of latitude; THENCE, westward along the 49th parallel to the 73rd meridian; THENCE, due South to the 48th parallel of latitude; THENCE, westward along a line twenty-five miles North of the line of Canadian National Railway passing through La Tuque, Senneterre, Kapuskasing, Sioux Lookout and Minaki to the 95th meridian; THENCE, in a straight line to Winnipegosis, Manitoba; THENCE, in a straight line to 54°00' North, 101°00' West; THENCE, westward along the 54th parallel to the boundary of Alberta and Saskatchewan; THENCE, due North to 56°30' North; THENCE, due West to the Alaska Highway; THENCE, along the Alaska Highway to Dawson Creek; THENCE, South along the highway to the town of Beaverlodge; THENCE, in a straight line to the Town of Jasper; THENCE, West along the Canadian National Railway passing through Yellowhead, Tête Jaune, McBride and Prince George to the 123rd meridian; THENCE, due South to the 50th parallel and THENCE, due West to the 125th meridian.

3.   All that part of Canada lying West of the 125th meridian.

SCHEDULE II

(ss. 3 and 5)

EMERGENCY EQUIPMENT FOR FLIGHTS
IN SPARSELY SETTLED AREAS

1. Food having a calorific value of at least 10,000 calories per person carried, not subject to deterioration by heat or cold and stored in a sealed waterproof container bearing a tag or label on which the operator of the aircraft or his representative has certified the amount and satisfactory condition of the food in the container following an inspection made not more than six months prior to the flight.

2. Cooking utensils.

3. Matches in a waterproof container.

4. A stove and a supply of fuel or a self-contained means of providing heat for cooking when operating north of the tree line.

5. A portable compass.

6. An axe of at least 2½ pounds or 1 kilogram weight with a handle of not less than 28 inches or 70 centimetres in length.

7. A flexible saw blade or equivalent cutting tool.

8. Snare wire of at least 30 feet or 9 metres and instructions for its use.

9. Fishing equipment including still fishing bait and a gill net of not more than a 2 inch or 5 centimetre mesh.

10. Mosquito nets or netting and insect repellent sufficient to meet the needs of all persons carried when operating in an area where insects are likely to be hazardous.

11. Tents or engine and wing covers of suitable design, coloured or having panels coloured in international orange or other high visibility colour, sufficient to accommodate all persons carried when operating north of the tree line.

12. Winter sleeping bags sufficient in quantity to accommodate all persons carried when operating in an area where the mean daily temperature is likely to be 7°C or less.

13. Two pairs of snow shoes when operating in areas where the ground snow cover is likely to be 12 inches or 30 centimetres or more.

14. A signalling mirror.

15. At least three pyrotechnical distress signals.

16. A sharp jack-knife or hunting knife of good quality.

17. A suitable survival instruction manual.

18. Conspicuity panel.

Appendix B

Temperature and Wind Chill Charts

Celsius

COOLING POWER OF WIND EXPRESSED AS "EQUIVALENT CHILL TEMPERATURE"

EQUIVALENT CHILL TEMPERATURE

Wind Speed (Knots)	K.P.H.	TEMPERATURE (CELSIUS)																			
Calm	Calm	4	2	-1	-4	-7	-9	-12	-15	-16	-20	-23	-26	-29	-32	-34	-37	-40	-43	-46	-48	-51
3-6	8	2	-1	-4	-7	-9	-12	-15	-16	-20	-23	-26	-29	-32	-34	-37	-40	-43	-46	-48	-54	-57
7-10	16	-1	-7	-9	-12	-15	-16	-23	-26	-29	-32	-37	-40	-43	-46	-51	-54	-57	-59	-62	-68	-71
11-15	24	-4	-9	-12	-16	-20	-23	-29	-32	-34	-40	-43	-46	-51	-54	-57	-62	-65	-68	-73	-76	-79
16-19	36	-7	-12	-15	-16	-23	-26	-32	-34	-37	-43	-46	-51	-54	-59	-62	-65	-71	-73	-79	-82	-84
20-23	40	-9	-12	-16	-20	-26	-29	-34	-37	-43	-46	-51	-54	-59	-62	-68	-71	-76	-79	-84	-87	-93
24-28	48	-12	-15	-16	-23	-29	-32	-34	-40	-46	-48	-54	-57	-62	-65	-71	-73	-79	-82	-85	-90	-96
29-32	56	-12	-15	-20	-23	-29	-34	-37	-40	-46	-51	-54	-59	-62	-68	-73	-76	-82	-84	-90	-93	-98
33-36	64	-12	-16	-20	-26	-29	-34	-37	-43	-48	-51	-57	-59	-65	-71	-73	-79	-82	-85	-90	-96	-101

LITTLE DANGER
Winds above 64 K.P.H. have little additional effect

INCREASING DANGER
(Flesh may freeze within one minute)

GREAT DANGER
(Flesh may freeze within 30 seconds)

Fahrenheit

COOLING POWER OF WIND EXPRESSED AS "EQUIVALENT CHILL TEMPERATURE"

TEMPERATURE (FAHRENHEIT)

Wind Speed Knots	M.P.H.	40	35	30	25	20	15	10	5	0	-5	-10	-15	-20	-25	-30	-35	-40	-45	-50	-55	-60
										EQUIVALENT CHILL TEMPERATURE											
Calm	Calm	40	35	30	25	20	15	10	5	0	-5	-10	-15	-20	-25	-30	-35	-40	-45	-50	-55	-60
3-6	5	35	30	25	20	15	10	5	0	-5	-10	-15	-20	-25	-30	-35	-40	-45	-50	-55	-65	-70
7-10	10	30	20	15	10	5	0	-10	-15	-20	-25	-35	-40	-45	-50	-60	-65	-70	-75	-80	-90	-95
11-15	15	25	15	10	0	-5	-10	-20	-25	-30	-40	-45	-50	-60	-65	-70	-80	-85	-90	-100	-105	-110
16-19	20	20	10	5	0	-10	-15	-25	-30	-35	-45	-50	-60	-65	-75	-80	-85	-95	-100	-110	-115	-120
20-23	25	15	10	0	-5	-15	-20	-30	-35	-45	-50	-60	-65	-75	-80	-90	-95	-105	-110	-120	-125	-135
24-28	30	10	5	0	-10	-20	-25	-30	-40	-50	-55	-65	-70	-80	-85	-95	-100	-110	-115	-125	-130	-140
29-32	35	10	5	-5	-10	-20	-30	-35	-40	-50	-60	-65	-75	-80	-90	-100	-105	-115	-120	-130	-135	-145
33-36	40	10	0	-5	-15	-20	-30	-35	-45	-55	-60	-70	-75	-85	-95	-100	-110	-115	-125	-130	-140	-150

LITTLE DANGER
Winds above 40
have little additional
effect

INCREASING DANGER
(Flesh may freeze
within one minute)

GREAT DANGER
(Flesh may freeze within 30 seconds)